ILLUMINATING THE
Heart

STEPS TOWARD A
MORE SPIRITUAL MARRIAGE

Barbara G. Markway, Ph.D

Gregory P. Markway, Ph.D.

NEW HARBINGER PUBLICATIONS, INC.

Copyright © 1996 Barbara G. Markway, Ph.D., and Gregory P. Markway, Ph.D.
New Harbinger Publications, Inc.
5674 Shattuck Avenue
Oakland, CA 94609

Cover design by SHELBY DESIGNS & ILLUSTRATES.
Text design by Tracy Marie Powell.

Distributed in U.S.A. primarily by Publishers Group West; in Canada by Raincoast Books; in Great Britain by Airlift Book Company, Ltd.; in South Africa by Real Books, Ltd.; in Australia by Boobook; in New Zealand by Tandem Press.

Library of Congress Catalog Card Number: 96-67941

ISBN 1-57224-053-9 paperback

First printing, 1996, 12,000 copies.

Contents

Part II: The Essential Steps

Part III: Living the Light of Love

*This book is lovingly
dedicated to our parents,
Erika and Bill Gerth,
and
Ruby and Paul Markway,
who gave us our start.*

Acknowledgements

Illuminating the Heart is the result of the love, inspiration, and support we've received not only from each other, but from many other people. Our deepest thanks and appreciation go to:

- Our parents, to whom this book is dedicated.

- Bill and Jerri Gerth, for sharing our joys and our sorrows; and for providing needed respite along the way.

- Sue Williams and Judy Markway, for their help with childcare, and their generous giving of themselves.

- Jane Talley, secretary extradordinaire, for nurturing us and our ideas at a critical time.

- John Gray and Daphne Rose Kingma, for their books which helped and inspired us, personally and professionally.

- Brian and Sue Stahl, for proving that love triumphs over adversity.

- John Robinson and Diane Weber, for introducing us to the Association of Couples in Marriage Enrichment (ACME).

- Brian Vandenberg, for sparking our interest in existential issues. His ideas particularly helped us with Chapter 8.

- Ted Cheney, for being a marvelous "book mentor" and having a wry sense of humor that kept us laughing as we wrote and wrote and wrote.

- Everyone at New Harbinger Publications, for their excitement about this book and for encouraging our vision.

- Pamela Kane, M.D., and Barb Tallent, Ph.D., who helped us solve Jesse's health problems.

- To other friends who supported us in countless ways: Teresa Flynn, Julie McGovern, Connie O'Heron, Laura Huff, and Ann Sullivan.

- Our son, Jesse, for reminding us to notice the wonders that surround us each day.

PART I

Preparing for Spiritual Connection

Chapter 1

What Is a Spiritual Marriage?

*"Marriage is not only the expression of love between two people,
it is also the profound evocation of one of life's greatest miracles,
the weaving together of many different strands of soul."*

—Thomas Moore

When we began telling our friends and colleagues we were writing a book for married couples, most people made comments—some more politely than others—such as, "What could you possibly have to say that's new?" or "There are already so many books on relationships! What will make yours different?" We wondered about the answers to these questions ourselves. We knew there were books on how to have a "peer marriage," how not to have an "angry marriage," and how to be romantic in 1,001 ways. And yet we continually heard a note of desperation from the couples we counsel, which made us wonder whether these books were hitting the mark. Jerry and Ruth are a perfect example.

Jerry, a 39-year-old dentist, and his wife, Ruth, a 36-year-old advertising copywriter, had been married for 12 years when they first came to see us. With three bright and happy children, a beautiful Victorian house in a quiet residential neighborhood, and what they described as basically a good marriage, Jerry and Ruth should have been the epitome of a happy couple. And in many ways, they were.

"Jerry is a very caring man," Ruth told us. "I know he loves me and the children. He listens to me, he respects me, and we share the same values. I feel guilty for saying this, but I still think there's something missing. I wonder if there shouldn't be more to our marriage. Sometimes our relationship seems like it's in a vacuum—not connected to anything but making a living and raising the kids. Often I find myself thinking, on those rare moments when I'm not too exhausted to think, what's the point?"

Jerry expressed concern about Ruth's comments. He also felt there might be some problems in their marriage, but he attributed them to the time and energy he had to put into his growing dental practice. "I feel terrible that I'm not making Ruth happy," he said, "but I'm not sure what else I can do. How can I fill the void she describes? To tell you the truth, the whole thing scares me."

Jerry and Ruth had become stuck in the routine of raising and supporting a family. Although their marriage had many strengths, there was something missing—what we recognized as a spiritual component to their relationship, even though Ruth didn't articulate the problem as such. We're not talking about spiritual matters in the sense of religion per se, but rather in terms of vitality and meaning that "inspire" a relationship above and beyond the two individuals involved. Jerry was struggling to be supportive, but he was anxious about where Ruth's questions would lead them.

Jerry and Ruth are not unique in the vague sense of unease they've experienced in their marriage. We hear similar stories every day from the couples we work with; and their stories sound much like our own. Spiritual questions have plagued men and women since the dawn of history—but those questions are more difficult to ignore today, and many people feel a sense of urgency in their search for answers. In the age of information superhighways, an individual's ability to deny the cold realities of life has been severely diminished. Now you see at close range on your TV screen what happens on the front lines of war; you hear the gory details of the countless crimes committed here at home; you know the inside story of how humankind is destroying the earth with casual and careless consumption.

Too often, people feel paralyzed rather than empowered by this knowledge. They continue to live their lives and exist in their relationships, in staunch denial of their own connection to the world's ills. And yet that nagging feeling of emptiness described by Ruth continues to erode the passion, the vitality, and the joy from people's most intimate connections.

This amorphous, unnamed anxiety haunts you, and you search for ways to make it go away. You look to romance: Maybe an exotic cruise will help. You look to money: Maybe a new house is what you need. You even look to therapists: If only you can learn how to communicate, how to talk to each other, everything will work out.

And yet, hasn't everyone known couples who had beautiful children, a big fancy house, great jobs, and plenty of money, but suddenly shocked their friends and relatives by getting a divorce? We've had couples in our office who've communicated quite well, but still felt profoundly disconnected and unhappy. The reality is that romance can fail you. Money can fail you. Language can fail you. Even love can fail you. Even all of these things are sometimes not enough, because what's missing in many marriages today goes deeper.

What is the solution? We believe the answer lies in building and continually rekindling a bond of love, but not just any love. What's required is creating a love embedded deep within a spiritual framework, a framework that gives meaning to marriage. In essence, what's needed is a belief that your relationship is not only special, but sacred; a conviction that your relationship is a vehicle for healing and growth; and an acceptance that your relationship is exactly where it needs to be at any given moment. This type of love shines a light on what truly matters, bringing everything into sharper focus. When you "illuminate the heart" in this manner, you gain clarity about your emotions; your ability to love selflessly is enhanced; and your actions naturally fall in line with your values. The love that a spiritual marriage is built on creates a vision that moves couples beyond the drudgery of daily life, and provides motivation to make every moment count.

If all of this seems a bit abstract at this point, don't worry. We're going to take a very practical, step-by-step approach in this book. In this chapter, we'll examine the characteristics of a spiritual marriage. Then we'll share the story of our relationship, partly as a way for you to get to know us better, but, more importantly, to make the concepts come to life. We'll also take you through the process of remembering your own sacred love story, a crucial first step in illuminating the love that initially brought you together. In short, this chapter will show you how it's possible to create a spiritually alive marriage—a relationship that will sustain you through the darkest nights, give you meaning when nothing makes sense, and provide you with immeasurable passion and joy.

The Characteristics of a Spiritual Marriage

"Take a minute, close your eyes, and see what images come to mind when you think of a 'spiritual marriage.'" When we've asked people this question, we've gotten a variety of responses; but the most common image reported was of two people with their heads in the clouds—not in touch with reality. And yet nothing could be further from what we mean! The kind of spiritual marriage we advocate is not some pie-in-the-sky relationship with no practical relevance to life here on Earth. Rather, a spiritual marriage grounds one firmly to reality, and provides the courage needed to live life to the fullest. Below we'll discuss the characteristics of a spiritual marriage; and you'll begin to see how adopting a spiritual framework can enrich your relationship, giving it a whole new dimension of boldness and fervor.

A Spiritual Marriage Is Built on a Foundation of Care and Concern

It sounds obvious to say that you must care about your partner. Often, however, we find relationships marked not by authentic care and concern, but by clinging or controlling behavior disguised as love. Caring is an active process, one in which you continually seek to understand your partner, and to be in touch with his or her needs, both physical and emotional. It's a way of relating that asks, "How can I best help my partner grow and develop?"; not, "What's in it for me?"

We were impressed by the caring and concern shown by Ethan, part of a couple we saw briefly for marriage counseling. A 37-year-old architect, Ethan and his wife, Janine, a 35-year-old commercial artist, came to see us because Janine had been feeling depressed for several months. She had withdrawn sexually from Ethan, often lost her temper with the children, had trouble getting out of bed in the morning, and sometimes found herself sobbing for no apparent reason. Ethan had called us for the initial appointment; he was quite concerned about his wife, and wanted to find a way to help her. In the first session we learned that a significant part of Janine's depression stemmed from her job situation. She worked in a large advertising agency on a beer account. She did not feel fulfilled or creatively challenged in her current position. She worked long hours, frequently not making it home until after dinner.

Janine and Ethan discussed quite a few options in the sessions we had together. Janine's dream was to work out of their home as a freelance artist. This would allow her to be home when the children returned from school, and it would give her the flexibility to attend their school functions. In addition, she relished the idea of working on something other than beer commercials. Even though it meant an initial decrease in their income, Ethan encouraged Janine to pursue the freelance option. He knew her talents were not being fully used in her current position, and that this was a large part of her frustration. He even suggested they rearrange their house, so Janine could have her own work space. Although it involved extra time and effort for him (moving lots of heavy furniture around until Janine had things the way she liked), Ethan expressed as much excitement as she did about her new home office. As they formed a plan together, Janine's depression lifted. She remarked that even more important than solving her career crisis was realizing the extent to which Ethan truly cared about her.

We imagine that some readers may be wondering, "What if I'm the only one who ever does the giving? What if I do all this sacrificing, but *my* needs never get met?" These are important questions, and not easy ones to answer. In our experience, once the pattern of "keeping score" (who's giving more than who) is broken, remarkable changes take place. You begin to realize that although relationships may seem out of balance at any given moment, over a lifetime this shifting of the scale is insignificant. And although caring is selfless, it is not without its rewards. Offering your partner the type of authentic care and concern that we describe can transform both of you. In one of our favorite textbooks from graduate school, *Existential Psychotherapy*, Irvin Yalom writes, "To the extent one brings the other to life, one also becomes more fully alive."

A Spiritual Marriage Requires Respect and the Nurturing of Each Other's Growth

Kate and Steve, a couple who sought marriage counseling, told us the following story during one of our first meetings. They had planned a romantic evening out together to celebrate their anniversary. It wasn't always easy to find a baby-sitter to watch their six kids, but they had it all arranged. Kate had just showered and dressed in the flowered sundress she knew Steve liked when he arrived home from work. They were casually talking about their day as they finished getting ready to go out. When Kate told Steve about some sales calls she had made for her new decorating business, Steve snapped at her, "I don't know why you're even bothering. You're never going to make much money with a decorating business." Kate felt an immediate, familiar, sinking feeling in her stomach, something she always felt whenever Steve failed to show respect for Kate's ideas or abilities. Just because he was a high-powered attorney, and she had never been to college, did not give him the right to put her business ideas down.

When you think of a spiritual marriage, you may not immediately think of the word "respect," but it's part of the core foundation. To respect your partner means to think highly of them, to value who they are and what they do. This is obvious in the beginning of a relationship when you are slow to find fault with your new partner. But for a marriage to grow, you must be able to continue liking your partner, not hesitating to show that you prize his or her uniqueness, and to offer encouragement in your partner's pursuits. For Kate to feel comfortable sharing her innermost self with Steve, she needs much more than a romantic evening out: She needs to feel that he respects her talents and nurtures her growth as an individual.

A Spiritual Marriage Involves Forgiveness and the Risk of Being Vulnerable

If you're like most people, you have not escaped the agony and pain of being hurt by someone you love. It may have been a minor offense, or it may have been a major transgression. Whatever the case, you have felt betrayed. Your trust has been shaken, and you have wanted to lash out and get even. You have wanted your partner to somehow make it up to you, and you want promises that it will never happen again.

Unfortunately, none of these things guarantees absolute protection from future hurt. If you want to build a spiritual marriage with your partner, you'll eventually have to move beyond the past pain of the relationship, and risk being vulnerable again. But you don't have to do it all at once. You can, and should, begin with manageable steps that maximize your sense of safety, security, and self-esteem.

Betty and Matthew came to our office following a breach of trust in their relationship. Betty was convinced that Matthew was having an affair with a woman he worked with, although he adamantly denied it. Regardless of what was actually going on, Matthew had done enough to lead Betty to doubt him. Numerous times he had come home late from work without calling, frequently with the smell of alcohol on his breath. To make matters worse, Matthew had previously acknowledged having had a brief affair early in their marriage.

After the initial session, we met with Betty and Matthew individually. We wanted them to have a chance to air their feelings, and tell their version of the story, without having to censor what they said in front of each other. Matthew argued convincingly that he had not had an affair this time, and he felt angry that Betty doubted him. He did not feel that he deserved the treatment he was getting at home. He claimed that he still loved Betty very much, and wanted to work to improve their relationship. Betty also professed her deep love for Matthew, but questioned whether he still found her attractive or desirable. She said she was having a difficult time trusting Matthew in light of his previous confirmed affair. She felt hurt, not only by his recent actions, but by his unwillingness to listen to her talk about her feelings.

In the sessions that followed, we saw Betty and Matthew together. We first taught them communication skills, so they could begin talking about the issues without having their discussion deteriorate into a heated battle. Betty needed to be able to express her feelings of hurt and anger to Matthew without him becoming defensive. And she needed to do this repeatedly. Matthew seemed to think that if she expressed her feelings once, that ought to be enough. In addition, Betty said that several times a day Matthew asked her, "Do you trust me yet? I don't think we can have a future if you don't trust me."

We helped Betty and Matthew see that trust is not an "all-or-nothing" proposition. We asked Betty to rate on a scale of 0 to 100 percent how much she trusted Matthew, and she said 75 percent. Matthew had thought she didn't trust him at all, so this helped him realize that there was hope. As Matthew got better and better at listening to Betty's feelings, her wounds began healing, and she was able to risk being close again. She was also able to confront him with her feelings about his drinking. She thought he drank too much, and that his drinking impaired his judgment. Maybe he hadn't had an affair this time, she reasoned, but his drinking made him act in a way that jeopardized the sanctity of their marriage. By this time, they had made considerable progress; Matthew reacted undefensively to Betty's observations. He agreed to try a period of sobriety to see what effect it had on their marriage. Betty was able to let go of her feelings of hurt as she saw Matthew respond to her with understanding and concern.

A Spiritual Marriage Fosters the Expression of Feelings

It was our first session with Michael and Joyce, a professional couple who had been married for six years. Michael chose to sit in a reclining chair, while Joyce sat on the loveseat across the room from him. We glanced at each other, silently noting that the majority of the couples we see sit on the couch together.

Joyce began telling us what brought them to see us. "Our relationship has stagnated. We're lucky if we have ten minutes of decent conversation during the week. Even when we have more time to talk, I don't think Michael knows how to open up to me. We never talk about anything of substance. Sometimes I wonder if he really loves me anymore."

Before we had a chance to say anything, Michael reacted, "Of course I love you. How can you question that? I try to talk to you, but I don't know what you expect." At this point, we intervened, asking them to tell us how they met, and what initially brought them together.

We learned that they had met at a cafe in the Central West End district of St. Louis during the busy lunch hour. It was a sunny, warm day in late fall, and many people had decided to eat out to enjoy the Indian summer weather. Joyce was eating alone, reviewing some notes for a meeting later that afternoon. When Michael arrived, he couldn't find an empty table. He walked out to the patio and noticed Joyce eating alone. "I'm usually not a very outgoing person," Michael noted, "but somehow Joyce looked approachable, so I asked if I could join her."

"It turned out really nice," Joyce chimed in. "Michael wasn't at all pushy: He was very considerate and let me finish the work I had brought with me. Somehow the silence between us felt, well, kind of natural, like we had already known each other a long time."

Michael and Joyce both relaxed as they began talking during our therapy session. They seemed to enjoy reminiscing about that magical first meeting. In fact, we had to cut them off toward the end of the session, but we asked them to continue talking about the story of their relationship on the way home, as well as one other time during the week. In addition, we gave them each a questionnaire to fill out and bring to the next session.

The second session began quite differently than the first, beginning with Joyce and Michael sitting on the couch together. They reported that they had enjoyed a much better week, and had talked more than they had in the past few months. Joyce noted, however, that Michael still wasn't as "open" as she would like—that their communication seemed superficial. Again, Michael stated that he didn't know what Joyce expected: "You say we talked more this week, but it still isn't good enough."

Joyce answered, "I just feel like you're not really with me sometimes. It's like you're only partly listening, and you certainly don't share a whole lot about what's going on with you."

We switched gears and began leafing through their questionnaires to see if we could learn anything pertinent from their history. When we came to the health section, we immediately stopped. Joyce had listed that she had a rare, genetically transmitted disease that would probably cut her life short in her fifth or sixth decade. Her father also had the disease. "I knew she had it when I married her," Michael stated matter-of-factly. "I decided that I wanted to marry her regardless of her health problems. I really don't think about it that much."

Although it seemed obvious to us that this was profoundly important, Michael hadn't made the connection between his inability to be intimate with Joyce—to communicate on a deep, spiritual level—and the fact that she was likely to die at an early age. It was as if, after making his decision to marry her, he had shoved aside all his fears and feelings about her health. Although Joyce had not consciously made the connection on her own, as soon as we brought up the possibility of her health being an issue, she immediately jumped on it. "You know, you're right. Now that I look back, I think our communication began to deteriorate when my father began having active symptoms. Maybe it made it more real to Michael that this could happen to me, too. I know I've had a hard time dealing with it; and I've definitely felt like Michael didn't want to talk about it."

For Michael and Joyce, this was a turning point. In the sessions that followed, Michael began talking about Joyce's health problems. It wasn't easy at first. He often had a difficult time knowing what he felt, much less finding the words to express himself. For a while, Greg saw Michael individually to discuss his past experience with expressing his feelings and the extreme bewilderment he felt in the presence of other people's strong feelings. We worked together with Joyce and Michael on beefing up their communication skills. Their hard work paid off in the end. In discussing their feelings, they both said they felt a stronger and deeper connection than they had in a long time. In essence, they were sharing the struggle. By facing the fragility of their relationship, and of life in general, they began to appreciate more fully the time they shared together.

A Spiritual Marriage Invites Questioning and a Search for Meaning

The issue of finding meaning in one's marriage was a key point in our work with John and Susan. John, a contractor in his early 40s, sought counseling because he was contemplating having an affair. It was something he'd never imagined he could do, yet now he felt himself coming perilously close. During his first session, he said: "I'm bored with Susan, with our relationship. It's not that I hate her. In fact, I still like her a lot. I'm just not sure if I love her anymore. There's nothing new between us."

Their story was not unfamiliar: We've heard variations on the same theme from many other couples. But something made us wonder if we had the whole story. After probing a bit deeper, John revealed that he and Susan had been trying for three years to conceive a child. After working unsuccessfully with top fertility experts at a prestigious medical center, they had finally concluded that they were not to have children of their own, and neither of them was particularly interested in adoption. Toward the end of the session, we told John that we did not think their relationship was doomed. We thought there was a good chance he had mislabeled his problem as boredom when, in fact, the unexpressed feelings (grief, sadness, anger?) surrounding the fertility problem were getting in the way of him and Susan being as close as they could be. We encouraged John to bring Susan in with him for the next session, so we could begin working to rebuild the intimacy in their relationship.

John and Susan attended six sessions together, making remarkable progress in a relatively brief period of time. Our twin goals in working with them were to help them express to each other their feelings about not being able to have a child, and to help them create new meaning for their marriage.

When they actually began talking, they learned that their feelings were quite similar, even though they each expressed them in characteristically different ways. Susan tended to feel hopeless and depressed, crying often and needing a lot of reassurance from John. In contrast, John became more and more withdrawn, immersing himself in his work as a distraction from his painful feelings.

Obviously, each partner's behavior in this regard only alienated and aggravated the other: The more withdrawn John became, the more Susan felt in need of reassurance; the more Susan acted out her emotions, the more John felt an urgent need to withdraw. Once they were able to understand each other's ways of coping, it was easier to function together as a team, giving each other more of what they needed—Susan wanted more comfort, and John craved more psychological space to work through things in his own way. They also began realizing that their relationship had revolved for so long around conceiving a baby that they needed to formulate other goals. After considerable thought and discussion, they decided to explore several ideas, such as becoming foster parents or volunteering at a children's home. They felt closer than they had in years, and believed that the "magic" was returning to their marriage. It was hard to imagine that just a few short months ago John was considering having an affair because he was bored.

A Spiritual Marriage Is a Process, Not a Destination

Our view of spirituality is different from more traditional views, particularly with regard to this point. The focus of many spiritual traditions is to reach an end goal, achieving some state of idealized understanding or grace. In contrast, our view focuses on the opportunities for growth along the path, rather than on any particular destination. We believe that the day-to-day process of living and loving is more important than reaching some perfect state of being. We like the image of a "spiritual walk" described by philosopher Carol Ochs in *Women and Spirituality*, rather than the more common image of a "spiritual journey." Walking connotes taking one's time and enjoying each step for its own sake.

We also think that the image of kindling a fire works well. We're reminded how in scouting we were taught to look for the tiniest twigs to start the campfire—it was the small, delicate branches that started the biggest fires. The bigger sticks could only catch fire after the smaller pieces. If you jumped ahead too quickly, trying to add the big logs first, you'd smother the fire. And once the fire got going, if you put on the right kind of wood, it didn't take a whole lot of effort to keep it going. To take this analogy further, when you build a fire (in a fireplace), you're typically not focused only on the end product per se. You're not so much interested in the fire itself, but in the atmosphere it creates—the warmth, the glow, the sparks that fly.

A couple who came to see us recently illustrates this distinction between process and destination. Laura and Mark had moved to St. Louis over six months ago. They had been so busy settling into a new house and new jobs, they had put on hold their locating a church to attend. As a New Year's resolution, they decided they would make it a priority to join a church. After they spent a couple of Sunday mornings attending different services, Mark was ready to make a decision. Laura, on the other hand, wanted to keep "shopping around." She felt good that she and Mark were doing this together. She felt close to him and enjoyed the time they were spending together, not only attending the services, but talking about their impressions afterward. She knew that once the decision had been made, they'd fall into their old routine of attending church most Sundays, but not being truly involved together as a couple. They eventually found ways to extend this joyful sense of process to other aspects of their marriage.

Another consequence of viewing a spiritual marriage as a process rather than a destination is that you see problems differently. If your only goal is to reach a destination, then difficult times are seen as unwelcome obstacles. If you view marriage as a spiritual process, however, then problems are not obstacles, but opportunities for growth and learning. A spiritual framework that values process allows you to believe that your relationship is right where it needs to be at any given moment. Not that we expect you to jump up and down for joy whenever you and your spouse encounter difficulties. But after your initial gut reaction of getting angry about the problem, or feeling disappointed, you can step back and ask yourself, "What can I learn here? What opportunities for renewed closeness are hidden behind this obstacle?"

A Spiritual Marriage Involves Practice

It takes patience and practice to create a spiritually alive marriage. Most people don't expect to learn a foreign language without a great deal of hard work and study, yet somehow they think they can learn the language of the heart and the soul with little effort. Learning the art of a spiritual marriage can be likened to a child learning to eat with utensils. At first, when a toddler is learning to use a fork or a spoon, it's quite an awkward affair. A lot of effort is required to get just a few morsels of food into the right place. With some practice, however, the child's movements become more coordinated. Less food is dropped, although some is occasionally thrown. The whole process of getting nourishment becomes easier, more automatic, *yet still requires attention.* Such is the case with a spiritual marriage. In the beginning—or sometimes right in the middle—you might feel as if every word, every gesture, every step is flawed. That's okay. You don't have to be perfect. With practice, you'll learn what works. The effort won't seem as great, and the rewards will be plentiful.

Throughout the book, we'll provide you with structured exercises to make the practicing easy. The exercises are typically short and simple, yet highly effective. We continually find that when couples set aside as little as ten minutes a day to complete the Spiritual Sharing Exercises, they see dramatic changes in the quality of their interactions, as well as their level of satisfaction with the relationship. Keep in mind that the practice doesn't have to be drudgery. By taking the time to complete the exercises, you'll be learning fascinating things about your partner, as well as yourself. This unique knowledge bolsters not only the relationship, but spills over into other areas of your life.

The Spiritual Drama of Relationship

Now that you have an idea about what we mean by a spiritual marriage, you may be wondering, what's next? The best way to create a spiritually rich marriage is to interrupt the cycle of passivity and neglect that frequently comes about with the passing of time. One effective way we have found to begin this process is by having couples remember and reminisce about the development of their relationship—in effect, to recall their own love story. Even couples who come into our offices on the brink of divorce usually smile and remember in great detail how they met, and what attracted them to each other.

For example, Justin and Rachel described how they met on a blind date arranged by mutual acquaintances. They laughed when they talked about how relieved they were when they saw each other, because they had both had numerous bad experiences with blind dates. They also joked about how bad the food was at the restaurant they went to.

Rachel easily remembered what attracted her to Justin, as well as the qualities she found in him that allowed the relationship to blossom. "He was so gentle and easy to talk with. We talked for hours that first night. It didn't matter what the subject was—we had no problem talking. Later in the relationship, we would just go on walks, or to a park, and talk. We never had to do anything elaborate to have a good time. It was easy to feel close. We were always holding hands."

Justin had similar memories: "I had been divorced for three years. I was starting to believe that I would never have another relationship, and then Rachel came along. She was so warm and fun. And she drew me out. I've always been kind of shy. She was so outgoing, it was contagious. I liked that I never felt any pressure with her. I didn't have to impress her. Things just seemed to go well automatically."

Every couple's story is unique. Like Rachel and Justin, you may have met on a blind date. Or you may have overcome great odds to be together. Some couples may have disliked each other initially, but later something happened to change their minds. Or they may have fallen in love at first sight, and felt amazed that another human being could understand them so quickly and thoroughly. Still others may have come from backgrounds full of pain, and were surprised to be nurtured by someone. All these stories tell us about the foundations of a relationship, and depict the miracle of intimacy.

What does remembering your own love story have to do with today—right now? First of all, it can take a brick out of the wall separating you and your partner. Even one brick removed weakens the wall, allowing room for your love to return. Second, remembering can give you clues about potential strengths in your relationship, strengths you can build on. In Justin and Rachel's case, you can hear in their story that their relationship had been based on mutual regard and genuine interest in one another. Telling their story helped them remember their ability to communicate and meet each other's needs, in spite of the problems they were having now. Third, remembering can provide you with hope and motivation. Reminding yourselves that your relationship was previously fulfilling helps actualize the possibility that it can be that way—or even better—in the future.

In essence, we believe that every relationship contains its own spiritual drama, a sacred unfolding that provides a richly textured backdrop of meaning to married life. It's important to take the time to appreciate this drama. It's too easy to forget the details, the nuances, of what drew you together. You need to remember how hard you worked, and how hard you fought, to develop your relationship in the first place. It may seem now as if it just happened magically, but it didn't. You created the magic, detail by detail. You formed the sacred bond by caring, nurturing, and attending to each other's spirit, in one way or another—by paying attention to each other with the intensified focus that characterizes the process of falling in love.

We want to share the story of our relationship with you for several reasons. We want you to know us on a more personal level. We're writing this book because we're psychologists who work with couples; but, more importantly, because we *are* a couple. Thus, we feel you need to know more about us than just our professional credentials. We also want to give you a detailed example of what we mean by the "spiritual drama of relationship," and how this provides the basis for the sacred love that holds couples together for a lifetime. By sharing our story, however, we don't want to give the impression that your story has to be in any way similar to ours. Our story is just that: ours. It has meaning to us. Your story is what really matters. Our hope is that by reading our story you'll begin to see the value of taking the time to remember your story in all its exquisite detail. And in the Spiritual Sharing Exercise at the end of the chapter, we'll offer some guidelines, questions, and ideas to help structure this activity.

Our Story: Just One Example of a Spiritual Marriage

Our story began while we were in graduate school. It was a time in our lives when we had the luxury of taking seminars on existential psychology, reading everything from Scott Peck's *The Road Less Traveled* to Ernest Becker's *The Denial of Death*, and spending hours with fellow graduate students sharing thoughts and ideas (no wonder it took so long to complete our dissertations!). It was also a time when spiritual questioning became much more than an intellectual exercise for us.

Shattered Spirits

Greg: About a year before meeting Barb, I had a grand mal seizure while visiting friends out of town. I had to be taken by ambulance to a hospital and, once back in St. Louis, underwent extensive testing. The doctors mentioned numerous possibilities, including a brain tumor. After two weeks of waiting in emotional numbness, I learned I had a seizure disorder and that my medical future was uncertain. This forced me to confront my own mortality in a very real way. I was left with a multitude of questions. Could I accept myself, feeling that I was somehow diminished by my body that had a will of its own? Would others accept me? What meaning was there in all of this? What was I to learn about myself from this experience? This crisis in my life was as much spiritual as medical.

Barbara: At roughly the same time Greg was dealing with his medical problems, I suffered my own traumatic event. I was sexually assaulted by a man I had recently begun dating. Even so many years later, it's difficult to find the words to describe that horrific experience. I felt as if a part of me died, and I withdrew. As Margaret Atwood wrote in *The Handmaid's Tale,* "It's possible to go so far in, so far down and back, they could never get you out."

The spiritual questions that had once been so stimulating to discuss now tormented me. What had I done to deserve this? Where was the loving and fair God I thought I knew? How can people be so evil? What purpose is there to a life so full of pain? What was wrong with me and my judgment? How would I ever be able to trust again?

A Fateful Friendship

Greg: I had just returned to St. Louis to work on my dissertation after completing my internship at the state hospital in Norristown, Pennsylvania. I began to see Barb around school, but I knew nothing about her. I thought she was attractive, and she seemed warm, but she wasn't eccentric enough to attract my attention right away. I think I had always associated being nice with being bland. I remember the first incident that began to change my view of her. A group of us were talking, and she made a very funny, sarcastic remark about one of our professors. Everyone laughed hysterically. I realized then that she was much more three-dimensional than I had presumed.

As a part of my post-internship training, I was assigned to be a clinical supervisor for Barb. This meant that I listened to tape recordings of her therapy sessions with one of her clients at the university clinic. I clearly remember my first impression of her as a therapist—she was exceptionally talented, but she had no awareness of her ability. I felt inspired and stirred when I listened to her therapy tapes.

As time went on, I felt more and more drawn to Barb. My feelings both surprised me and scared me. I had grown accustomed to my aloneness. Barb loves to tell the story of how she asked me out for our first date. It had apparently taken a lot of courage for her to call me, and then I had the audacity to say I'd call her back. (I had planned to order pizza and watch a basketball game.) Actually, I wasn't sure I wanted to risk getting involved with someone in light of what I now knew about my health. Thankfully, though, I called her back and accepted her invitation. I remember hugging Barb at the end of our first date; I felt an electricity that can not be described. At that moment, I knew there was something strong between us.

Barbara: I was so anxious about meeting Greg for the first time. I had seen him around the hallway at the university where all the graduate students had their offices, but we had never really spoken to each other. I had created a lot of stories in my mind about what he was like. I imagined him to be an exceptionally insightful therapist who would immediately see that I didn't know what I was doing. I also pictured him as being sophisticated and worldly, yet slightly offbeat in an attractive kind of way, and as being very popular with women.

When we met, I felt an instant sense of safety and warmth, a feeling which took me completely off guard. I had always been shy and awkward with men. After being raped, I was not only still shy, but extremely fearful and suspicious. Greg had a way of putting me at ease. I'm not sure exactly what he did to make me feel so comfortable, but I felt as if I could talk with him about anything. Our relationship developed slowly, which was the perfect pace for me. At first, we talked only during our supervision sessions. Then, after a few months, he told me about a presentation he was giving to a group on campus. (I assumed that because he told me about it, he wanted me to be there.) His talk was based on Irving Polster's book, *Every Person's Life Is Worth a Novel.* I was entranced. He was funny, sincere, and he shared a lot about himself. There was something about the way he looked at me, the way his eyes lingered, that made me wonder whether there could be something more.

Soothed Souls

Greg: Although I had taken some steps toward recovery from the knowledge of my medical condition, it wasn't until Barb and I grew close that I truly began to heal on a deep spiritual level. Even before my seizure, I had always thought of myself as "pleasantly cynical." I was a nice guy in the alienated sense that help always flowed from me, but I never allowed myself to ask for anything in return. My relationships had mostly been hollow and one-sided—I never really let myself open up or feel exposed. Somehow, Barb saw through my cover to the vague feeling of emptiness I carried around. In essence, I felt broken after my seizure, but Barb's acceptance of me made me feel worthy of being loved. It was only with her that I was able to be embraced and nurtured, without feeling too threatened. I could be my authentic self. As our relationship developed, I was continually amazed at how Barb listened to me. At times, I felt that she was looking straight into my heart and soul. She responded to me in a way that stunned me: I felt more relaxed and cared for than I ever imagined myself capable of feeling. Barb also challenged me—I can so easily lapse into passivity. With her encouragement, I've been able to confront issues and feelings I had spent my life avoiding.

Barbara: As our relationship developed, I felt the pain of my past easing, not all at once, but surely and steadily. Greg's cynicism seemed to fade as he reached out his hand to mine—not letting me go "too far in" or "too far down." He listened to me, he held me, he sat in silence with me, and he cried with me. I still don't have answers to all my questions, but through our relationship, I have accessed a spiritual strength I didn't know existed. Although I continue to feel rage at the senseless violence that happened to me, I am better able to be at peace with myself—to not blame or question myself. With Greg I have a partner who not only helps me bear the weight of life, but who helps me find the joy that exists even amidst the pain.

Daily Devotion

In recent years, our life has become much more "ordinary" in some regards. Barb no longer dwells on what happened to her, and Greg's medical condition has been stabilized with medication. Now we have faced the new, perhaps more difficult challenge of how to maintain the strong spiritual bond that brought us together in the midst of changing diapers, paying the bills, and mowing the grass. We know just how easy it is to get lost in the daily routines and hassles of life, missing all the miracles and magic of marriage. Over time, however, we have learned, and continue to learn, ways to strengthen our relationship through a kind of spirituality that is both practical and relevant to our life together. Remembering our sacred love story has been one important way we continually illuminate the heart, keeping alive the meaning of our marriage. We frequently look at photo albums, read through poems and letters we've written each other (we included one of our favorite poems below), and simply talk about what drew our hearts and souls together. Recalling that what was important in creating our love was the daily tending of each other's spirit, the healing of each other's pain, and the celebration of each other's triumphs helps us clarify what we need to do in the present. Our goal in writing this book is to share our ideas with you, not as spiritual gurus who know all there is to know, but as real people who have found value in walking a spiritual path together. It's a path that has taken us through all sorts of terrain and weather, but has not once led us astray. We hope you'll find the exercise below to be as valuable, meaningful, and enjoyable as we have.

Two Winter Nights
(a study of contrast)

(one)

Rage, rage against the cold and snow

> as darkness falls
> danger calls

Rage, rage against the savage man

> who seeks control
> of body and soul

Rage, rage against the pain and sorrow
> could it be it's only borrowed

Rage, rage against this filthy death
> No. I'm gasping for breath.

> > bleeding heart
> > healing start
> (these sad rhymes
> only partially describe)

(two)

Trusting now on this cold night
> gentle arms and tender caresses
> eyes that reassure
Brave hearts speak boldly

> (the bleeding slows)

—Barbara Markway
(written for Greg, 2/88)

Spiritual Sharing Exercise 1:
Remembering Your Sacred Love Story

The directions are simple. Below are two identical sets of questions, with spaces for answers, to help you and your partner remember your sacred love story. Many people find value in writing down their answers. For others, reading over the questions will prompt them to think about their answers during the day. If you feel like you can share your responses with your spouse, that would be great. If not, that's okay. You'll benefit even if you complete the exercises independently from your spouse. In later chapters, we'll talk about important skills that will help you find ways to involve your partner, making this much more of a process of sharing and growing together. Use extra paper if you need it. If you're more comfortable talking than writing, record your answers on tape.

Partner 1

1. How did you meet your spouse? _____

_____

_____

2. What first attracted you to your spouse? _____

_____

_____

3. What did you do on your first date? _____

_____

_____

4. When did you know this relationship could be something special? __

_____

_____

5. What made you think the relationship could be special? _____

_____

_____

6. What did your friends think of your relationship? _____

_____

_____

7. What did your family think of your relationship? _____

_____

_____

8. Did you have to overcome any obstacles to be together? _____

_____

_____

9. What made you decide to get married? _____

_____

_____

10. What did you like about how the two of you communicated? _____

_____

_____

11. What kinds of things did you most enjoy doing together? _____

_____

_____

12. How did your partner let you know you were loved and cared for?

_____

_____

13. How did you nurture each other? _____

_____

_____

14. What do you feel were the strengths of your relationship early on?

_____

_____

15. What did you most enjoy about the early stages of your physical relationship? _____

_____

_____

16. Did you feel as if any past hurts or pains began to heal by virtue of
your relationship? _____

_____

_____

17. What were the times when you felt most deeply connected? What
were you doing? What were the circumstances? _____

_____

_____

Partner 2

1. How did you meet your spouse? _____

   _____

   _____

2. What first attracted you to your spouse? _____

   _____

   _____

3. What did you do on your first date? _____

   _____

   _____

4. When did you know this relationship could be something special? ___

   _____

   _____

5. What made you think the relationship could be special? _____

   _____

   _____

6. What did your friends think of your relationship? _____

   _____

   _____

7. What did your family think of your relationship? _____

   _____

   _____

8. Did you have to overcome any obstacles to be together? _____

   _____

   _____

9. What made you decide to get married? _____

   _____

   _____

10. What did you like about how the two of you communicated? _____

_____

_____

11. What kinds of things did you most enjoy doing together? _____

_____

_____

12. How did your partner let you know you were loved and cared for?

_____

_____

13. How did you nurture each other? _____

_____

_____

14. What do you feel were the strengths of your relationship early on?

_____

_____

15. What did you most enjoy about the early stages of your physical
    relationship? _____

_____

_____

16. Did you feel as if any past hurts or pains began to heal by virtue of
    your relationship? _____

_____

_____

17. What were the times when you felt most deeply connected? What
    were you doing? What were the circumstances? _____

_____

_____

Some Final Thoughts

In this first chapter, we've described the characteristics of a spiritual marriage,
and shown you how every relationship contains its own spiritual drama. At

this point, we hope you're convinced of the value of creating a spiritually alive marriage. If you're still a bit skeptical, however, that's okay. In the next chapter, we'll go over some common obstacles couples experience on the spiritual path of love, and show how to transform these obstacles into opportunities. By way of a final summary, below are some—although certainly not all—of the advantages of building a spiritual marriage. Feel free to add your own additions to the list.

A spiritual marriage:

- provides a buffer against a world that is sometimes harsh.

- mitigates against the emptiness that can come from living only for the next raise, the next vacation, the next achievement. Even building a marriage based solely on raising children together leaves you vulnerable. After all, what happens when the children leave?

- eliminates (well, almost) boredom and apathy. How can one be bored when the soul of the other can never be known completely? There are always discoveries left to be made, new gifts to unwrap.

- calls forth your unique strengths and talents, encouraging you to reach your fullest potential. In *The Conduct of Life*, Ralph Waldo Emerson says, "Our chief want in life is somebody who shall make us do what we can."

- offers to your children and others close to you a powerful model of how vital marriage can be.

- helps you discover who you really are as your partner reflects back an image of yourself that is clearer than what you get from the rest of the world.

Spotlight on Your Sacred Love Story

- Listen to music you both previously enjoyed.

- Rent movies that were meaningful and watch them together.

- Read to each other passages of books that were important to you.

- Watch your wedding video, if you have one. Reread your vows.

- Reread letters, cards, or any poems you've written to each other.

- Reread your journal entries from the time.

- Look through photo albums and reminisce.

Chapter 2

Turning Obstacles into Opportunities

". . . but I'm not really religious . . . my spouse won't join me . . . and I don't have the time . . ."

"Watch for big problems. They disguise big opportunities."

—H. Jackson Brown

*A*fter writing the first chapter, we asked a good friend and colleague, Teresa Flynn, to review it for us. As she is an avid reader and an excellent writer, we were eager to hear her feedback. This is what she told us. "I never identified with the term 'spirituality,' because it came too close to sounding like religion to me. When I think of religion, all I think about is guilt, guilt, guilt. But after reading this chapter, I'm starting to realize that spirituality can offer something more." We hope that, like Teresa, you're starting to broaden your concept of spirituality, realizing the relevant role it can play in your marriage. And yet, we realize that some of you may still be unsure. In this chapter, we'll take you through common roadblocks people experience when they contemplate sharing a spiritual life with their spouse; and then we'll describe a strategy for turning these obstacles into opportunities.

Recognizing the Roadblocks

When you're driving down the highway and you see barricades ahead with flashing lights, you know just what it means, and just what to do. Without conscious effort or thought, the lights alert you to possible danger, and steer you in the right direction. With matters of the heart and soul, you're not always so sure of where the roadblocks are—in other words, of what holds you back from enjoying a rich and satisfying spiritual marriage. And yet, this is the first step: You must recognize the roadblocks before you can find a way around them. Below are several typical comments we hear that signal some type of block (check any that fit for you):

- ☐ I'm not really religious.
- ☐ I'm not religious enough.
- ☐ I don't know what I believe.
- ☐ My spouse and I come from different religious backgrounds—this wouldn't work for us.
- ☐ I'm not into this New Age stuff—it's too weird.
- ☐ My partner would never be interested in this.
- ☐ I would be embarrassed broaching the topic of spirituality with my spouse, much less trying any ideas from the book.
- ☐ We don't have enough time as it is. I can't add one more thing into our already jam-packed schedules.
- ☐ We're so worried about day-to-day things, such as paying the bills; how can spirituality be useful to us?
- ☐ This spirituality stuff sounds good. One day I'll get around to it.

In most cases, the roadblocks you encounter are actually forms of unhealthy self-talk—things you say to yourself that guide your feelings and your behavior, but are not always accurate or helpful. In order to transform these obstacles into opportunities, the first step is to identify exactly what you're saying to yourself. Perhaps some of the comments listed above sounded familiar. There are probably other things you're saying to yourself. We suggest that you monitor and record what goes on in your mind, at least initially, on paper. Although it can be a chore to write down what you're thinking, you won't have to do this forever. Soon you'll become more aware of the constant stream of self-talk that goes on inside your head. The most necessary ingredient is simply a willingness to focus on your thoughts. We know this can be a challenge when you're busy and caught up in the ongoing surge of events that make up a single day. Nonetheless, developing the ability to identify your hidden thoughts can provide you with a useful tool to help build a spiritually alive marriage.

It's not so productive to look back days or weeks after an incident and ask yourself, "What was I thinking?" This may give you a bit of worthwhile information, but chances are good that you've forgotten many crucial details. So much more can be gleaned from keeping a written thought-record on a daily basis. On page 39 we've included a blank sample form for keeping track of your thoughts and related feelings. (An example of a partially completed form appears on page 38.) You can either make copies of the form, or simply jot down your entries in a small notebook that you carry with you. Just note the situation and whatever you were thinking and feeling at the time.

After you've tracked your thoughts, you may find that they revolve around a certain theme or a combination of themes. We've found three main areas that tend to get in people's way of creating the kind of close, spiritually alive marriage they long for: defining spirituality; dealing with a seemingly reluctant spouse; and creating time and energy for a shared spiritual life. In the sections that follow, we'll discuss these topics, providing perspectives on each. Then, we'll show you how to use the information you've gathered from tracking your thoughts and identifying certain themes.

Defining Spirituality: A Slippery Task

Although we've described a spiritual marriage, we may not yet have defined the meaning of "spirituality" to your satisfaction. This is a slippery task. The concept in many ways defies definition, confronting us with our own limits to describe things in words. It's as difficult as defining love. You know when spirituality is there, you know when it's not there, but it's difficult to say precisely what it is. People may project their own idiosyncratic meanings onto the word. For example, our friend, Teresa, balked, at the mere mention of spirituality, because she associated spirituality with religion, and religion with guilt.

We pored over the books in our library in search of a useful definition of spirituality—and yet most authors seem to talk around it without specifically defining it. In frustration, we turned to the dictionary. The American Heritage Dictionary defines spirituality as, "of, pertaining to, or consisting of spirit." Since this didn't tell us a whole lot, we looked under "spirit." This definition stated, "the life-giving principle within a human being" and "the real sense or significance of something." Finally this seemed closer to what we were looking for. Then we noticed the next line down: the word "spiritualism" is defined as, "the belief that the dead communicate with the living, usually through a medium." This sequence of definitions symbolizes a major stumbling block for us in discussing with other couples the role played by spirituality in their lives. First spirituality is defined only in reference to another word, spirit. The definition of spirit sounds pretty good, but right after that you read about mediums talking to the dead. We still needed to find a way to define spirituality as something separate from the whole circus of paranormal phenomena—to define it in a way that is personal and practical, yet not too "far out."

Scanning through our library once more, we found a book on parenting that offers a definition of spirituality we like. In *Something More: Nurturing Your Child's Spiritual Growth*, Jean Grasso Fitzpatrick writes, "... the word spiritual is used to refer to an awareness of our sacred connection with all of life. Our spirituality is our opening to one another as whole human beings, each different and precious, and our exploring how we can truly learn to love." Her point that spirituality is related to love reflects the essence of why we're writing this book. In the context of relationship, we are confronted with the fact that we are each different and yet deserving; that we are flawed and imperfect, and yet we love and are loved—not in spite of this, but because of this. Spirituality is a quest for meaning and purpose, a daring look at ourselves and our lives with an unflinching but forgiving eye. It calls us to transform what might otherwise be seen as the trivialities of everyday life into precious time together.

Below we offer some of our basic understanding about spirituality. We do not wish to imply that our views are necessarily the only right ones. Our thinking has evolved over time, and will likely continue to do so. As you progress through this book, it's important for you to know where we're coming from. If your views are similar, great. If your views are different, that's also fine. We invite each of you to doubt, to ponder, to question. Your faith in each other and in yourself can only be enriched and strengthened by such challenges.

The Experience of Spirituality May or May Not Involve Formal Religion

If you talk to many who think of themselves as spiritual, you're likely to hear them assert, "but I'm not religious." Carl Jung, the famous psychoanalyst widely considered to have been a very spiritual man, once wrote, "one of the main functions of formalized religion is to protect people against a direct experience of God." An anonymous member of Alcoholics Anonymous, a group known for its emphasis on the spiritual, made the following distinction: "Religion is for people who are afraid of going to hell; spirituality is for those who have been there." You're apt to hear something quite different if you talk to religious individuals—you might hear them argue that spirituality is reserved for those who practice a formal religion. There is a difference between spirituality and religion, but they are by no means mutually exclusive. One can be religious but not spiritual, spiritual but not religious, both, or neither. Traditionally, religion has concerned itself with organized systems of beliefs and has involved, to varying degrees, doctrines, creeds, and adherence to rules. Spirituality is less concerned with these matters, and instead deals with a "way of being" in the world. In effect, spirituality cuts across different religions, uniting all people in the search for meaning and truth in their lives.

Spirituality Involves Not Only Awareness, But Also Action

We said earlier that spirituality involves "an awareness of our sacred connection with all of life"; and yet awareness alone is not enough. In our view, spirituality is incomplete unless it transforms awareness into action. Too often we hear people engage in heady dialogue that sounds good but seems devoid of meaning in the real world. One of our professors—who has always been interested in existential issues—once described how, before taking off in an airplane, he always looks around at the passengers seated nearby and thinks to himself, "These may be the people I'll die with." We challenged him by asking whether his behavior changes at all because of this awareness. He thought for a while, and seemed to struggle for an answer. We had to prompt him a bit. "For example, would you talk more to the people near you? Would you be nicer to them?" He finally said, "Well, I might not be as rude if some-one bothered me while I was reading."

To us, it's vitally important that awareness must somehow lead to action. That's why we chose to fill *Illuminating the Heart* with stories about ourselves, our clients, and other couples we know. Stories make these concepts, which otherwise could easily remain intellectual abstractions, come alive. Our goal is to present practical suggestions for things you can *do* to make your marriage fulfilling on a deep, spiritual level.

Spirituality Is for Everyday People

When Barb was a high-school student at Kirkwood High School, a Christian youth group called Young Life was very popular with many of her friends. She attended only sporadically, because she always felt she didn't fit in. Part of this, she feels, was her general adolescent angst and perception that she didn't fit in anywhere. She also remembers feeling that she wasn't good enough for this group of spirited believers. "I felt that to be spiritual, or religious, or whatever you want to call it, you had to have it all together. You already had to know what you believed. I felt so mixed up inside—surely a sign that I didn't have enough faith. In essence, I had the mistaken idea that one had to be perfect in order to be spiritual. Now I believe just the opposite: A core part of spirituality requires us to embrace imperfections—first our own, and then others."

In a wonderful book called *The Spirituality of Imperfection*, authors Ernest Kurtz and Katherine Ketcham write, "Flawedness is the first fact about human beings. And paradoxically, in that imperfect foundation we find not despair but joy. It is only within the reality of our imperfection that we can find the peace and serenity we crave." It is our ability to be genuine, to be real, to accept ourselves as we truly are that enables us to connect fully with another person, and to love unconditionally.

Spirituality Involves Everyday Experiences

Traditionally, spirituality has involved turning away from the earthly, material world. For example, on some spiritual retreats, individuals may fast and spend their time in silence. Although there is surely value in such experiences for some, it is not the only way to become acquainted with your spiritual self or to join spiritually with others. It's possible to find the sacred in everyday experiences. These ordinary moments yield the raw and rich material for exploring what is meaningful. We'll share an example that can't get much more ordinary, and yet seems miraculous to us.

Our son, at three years old, had just begun the first stages of toilet training. Jesse had always been extremely independent (we had to work hard not to label him as oppositional!), making it difficult to get him to do what we wanted. We used all the standard lines about being a big boy and using the potty, but quickly learned what an ineffective strategy this was for our little guy. With some apprehension, we switched to an approach that went something along the lines of, "You'll learn to use the potty when you're ready." Once we "let go," he showed interest fairly quickly. Now we had a new problem: He'd stand in front of the toilet, hardly tall enough (his potty chair collecting dust, because he refused to use it); nothing would happen, and he'd become frustrated. We kept reassuring him that it would happen sometime— but as neurotic, inexperienced parents, we worried. When he actually urinated into the toilet for the first time, we were all so excited. We felt so close as a couple, as a man and a woman who had conceived this child, who was now growing and maturing in spite of all our uncertainties. In this one homely moment, our everyday struggles were surmounted, and we were reminded of our sacred connections as a family.

Spiritual Sharing Exercise 2:
Getting To Know Your Spiritual Self

Below are some questions to help you get to know your spiritual self. Think about these questions over the next several days. Keep in mind that there are no right or wrong answers. If nothing comes to mind when you read through a particular question, skip it and come back to it another time. If you feel like jotting down your ideas and reactions, great. It's often valuable to have your notes to refer to later. If you would like to share any of your responses with your partner, feel free to do so. But if you're not comfortable doing that, for whatever reason, that's also okay. There will be plenty of time for sharing your thoughts and feelings about these questions at another time.

Partner 1

1. Do you remember a time when you felt safe and secure, somehow at peace with the world? What were the circumstances? _____

_____

_____

2. Was there ever a time when religion/spirituality was important to you? What factors were involved in any changes that have occurred since that time? _____

_____

_____

3. What are your earliest memories of religion/spirituality? What images come to mind when you now think about religion? Spirituality? God? _____

_____

_____

4. Do you (did you) have a spiritual/religious role model? _____

_____

_____

5. What are the miracles in your life? What are you thankful for? _____

_____

_____

6. How do you make sense of the suffering in the world? _____

_____

_____

7. Have there been times when you felt spiritually connected with your partner? What enabled you to feel this way? _____

_____

_____

8. What about times when you felt disconnected from your partner? What was happening? How did you feel? _____

_____

_____

Partner 2

1. Do you remember a time when you felt safe and secure, somehow at peace with the world? What were the circumstances? _____

_____

_____

2. Was there ever a time when religion/spirituality was important to you? What factors were involved in any changes that have occurred since that time? _____

_____

_____

3. What are your earliest memories of religion/spirituality? What images come to mind when you now think about religion? Spirituality? God? _____

_____

_____

4. Do you (did you) have a spiritual/religious role model? _____

_____

_____

5. What are the miracles in your life? What are you thankful for? _____

_____

_____

6. How do you make sense of the suffering in the world? _____

_____

_____

7. Have there been times when you felt spiritually connected with your partner? What enabled you to feel this way? _____

_____

_____

8. What about times when you felt disconnected from your partner? What was happening? How did you feel? _____

_____

_____

Dealing With a Seemingly Reluctant Spouse

A second potential roadblock concerns what to do if one partner is enthusiastic about building a spiritual marriage while the other has reservations about the

---

Spotlight on Your Spiritual Self

- Make a time-line of the phases of your religious/spiritual journey. Share it with your partner if you wish.

- Take just five minutes a day to do nothing but breathe. Don't think about anything except for that fact that you're breathing and what a miracle that is.

- Write a letter to someone who has nurtured your spiritual development. Let that person know how important their nurturing was to you.

- If you didn't have someone who nurtured your spiritual development, write or think about what that absence meant to you. What can you do to nurture your spiritual self now?

---

whole thing. It's not too difficult to guess that since you're the one reading this book, you're probably the more interested party. That's okay. It doesn't mean that your reading will be in vain. It also doesn't mean that your spouse can't in the future become just as interested and involved as you are. We've had a lot of experience dealing with this issue: We're frequently faced with one person entering therapy with relationship problems, stating that his or her spouse will not come in for couples' counseling. Often times, we have some initial success working with just one member of the couple. Later, we help the person find ways to "invite" his or her spouse to participate in counseling.

If you sense that your spouse is less eager than you are to enrich your relationship spiritually, here are a few tips to follow.

Tip 1: Go Slowly!

We know you're probably excited (and perhaps also a bit scared) about the prospect of developing a new kind of spiritual closeness with your spouse. It may be difficult to hold back and take things slowly; but if you sense that this topic threatens your spouse, you must use some restraint in your approach. If you don't think through what you are going to say, you risk getting a defensive response and scaring your partner off. As we said in Chapter 1, developing a spiritual marriage is a process, and a lifelong one at that. You don't have to do everything at once. Read the book. Do the exercises on your own at first. This may sound contradictory, but we also need to offer a caveat: Don't presume that you know how your spouse will react. You might think that your spouse will shun the whole notion of spirituality, only to find out that you're not the only one searching for a way to make your marriage more meaningful. The best approach may be to plant seeds but be patient while the seeds take hold and sprout.

Tip 2: Notice Ways in Which Your Spouse Is Already Expressing His or Her Spiritual Nature

Remember—spirituality is not something you add to your marriage from the outside, but a process of becoming aware of and strengthening the already existing spiritual bonds between you. Instead of focusing on your partner's deficits ("My husband never talks about his feelings or what's important to him."), look for strengths. Look for times when your partner is "high on life." Or look for times when your partner is caring and tender. These are the times when your spouse will be most able to communicate about things that matter. This is how you can start connecting in a positive, affirming way.

Our sister-in-law, Jerri, recently told us a story about what she did for Barb's brother Bill that beautifully illustrates the above tip. Bill is not the most verbal of men, especially in the feelings department, but he has a huge heart. One way he connects with his spiritual side is through his love of nature. Jerri and Bill live on five acres of land in a rural town about an hour from St. Louis. One day while Bill was at work, Jerri spotted three wild turkeys by their woodpile out in the yard. She knew how excited Bill would be, and she ran to get the video camera to record them high-stepping their way through the snowy terrain. Later that night, when Bill came home, she acted like she simply had a video of some outdoor scenery to show him. When he saw the three turkeys walking by the woodpile, he was thrilled, and quite appreciative that Jerri had captured the moment for him.

Now you may be asking yourself, what do wild turkeys have to do with creating a spiritual marriage? First of all, Jerri showed an intimate knowledge of Bill and what makes him tick. Next, she took the time to transform her awareness into action. She could have just told him about it, although it wouldn't nearly have had the same impact or meaning. Seemingly small events like this one can go a surprisingly long way toward strengthening a couple's spiritual bond.

Tip 3: Respect Your Differences

You might think that what we're proposing would never work for you, because you and your spouse come from such disparate backgrounds. But forging a spiritual marriage can bridge your differences, helping you find common areas of belief and purpose. The key is to respect these differences. Don't try to sway your spouse to your way of thinking. Recognize that you can each learn truth and wisdom from many viewpoints. Later chapters will help you hone your communication skills, showing you ways to cope with your differences and even grow stronger as a couple because of them.

Spotlight on Your Spouse's Spirituality

- Collect photos and other memorabilia of your spouse from throughout his or her life. It's difficult not to see the spiritual side of your spouse when you view development in its entirety—the journey that leads to today. Ask your spouse to tell you stories about the photos you find.

- Notice what makes your partner excited about life. Look for ways to join in that excitement.

- Let your partner know about the things you see in him or her that are spiritual, even if you don't label it as such in your conversation. Show your appreciation for these qualities.

- Ask if your spouse would be willing to talk about the questions in Exercise 2. (If the answer is yes, it might be good to skip ahead to Chapter 6 and go over some of the guidelines for effective communication.)

The Reality Factor: You're Busy and Tired—Who Cares About Spirituality?

Most people live in a hurried and frantic world of rush, rush, rush. If they stopped long enough to listen, they'd probably hear a quiet inner voice asking, "What's the point?" We probably see no greater struggle in the couples we work with than that of trying to balance work and family roles. It's not an easy task. Even as we're writing this book, we have our almost-four-year-old son looking up at us saying, "Do you wanna play with me?" It's easy to feel torn in all directions; oftentimes it's our closest personal relationships that get the raw end of the deal. After giving your time and energy to your job and your children, you may have little energy left over for adult sharing, touching, loving. It's no wonder if you feel daunted about the idea of creating a spiritually vibrant marriage.

Stephen Covey's book, *First Things First*, has helped us in our own personal effort to juggle our many roles and responsibilities. He writes about the difference between what he calls the Law of the School and the Law of the Farm. When he was an undergraduate, he frequently crammed for classes, waiting until the last minute to study, and in general tried to "psyche out" his teacher to see how much work he could avoid doing. Once in graduate school, however, his shortcut methods stopped working. He found himself in a lot of trouble trying to pack what he should have learned in four years into a few short months. Many of you have probably crammed for a test, but can you imagine cramming on a farm? If no one did the long, hard work of preparing the soil and planting the seeds, would you expect to get a good harvest? It's unlikely. And yet when it comes to marriage, people think they should be able to have a great relationship without the daily cultivation a relationship requires. "Many people who marry don't want to change their lifestyle at all," writes Covey. "They're married singles. They don't take time to nurture seeds of shared vision, selflessness, caring, tenderness, and consideration, yet they're surprised at the harvest of weeds."

In *Illuminating the Heart* we hope to show you ways to tend the spirit of your marriage. Yes, some of the things we suggest take time, but it's time well spent. Having a spiritual base from which to live your life, on which to build your marriage, can actually create a surplus of energy and motivation that will spill into other areas of your life. And much of what we suggest in this book takes more of a shift in thinking than a large outlay of time. There are plenty of things you can do to tend to the spirit of your marriage that take only seconds a day, and yet will give you huge rewards and benefits. The most important thing is being receptive, being open to making your marriage a priority in your life.

Spotlight on Time

- Consider this question: "How many people on their deathbeds wish they'd spent more time at the office?" —Stephen Covey

- Keep a record for a week of how much time you devote to the various roles in your life (parent, spouse, employee, and so on). How much time does your marriage receive?

- Sometimes we assign clients to talk with each other for just ten minutes a day. They often say, "But what good is ten minutes a day?" We tell them that's more than an hour a week, about 62 hours a year. Even a little shared time each day is valuable.

Finding Your Way Around the Obstacles

At this point, you've probably noticed some constant themes running through your thoughts. You may have tried some of the suggestions in the Spotlight boxes. But in addition to your efforts thus far, there's an even more systematic way to develop healthier ways of talking with yourself—the real key to turning obstacles into opportunities. By using the information you've gathered, particularly in your Thoughts and Feelings Diary, you're now ready to examine your thoughts critically: to check the validity of what you're telling yourself, and then to create more accurate and helpful ways of thinking. This may sound a bit technical, but it's not as complicated as it might seem. Let's go through an example from Barb's Thoughts and Feelings Diary.

You can see below that the first entry has to do with this book. I had thought of a new angle, a new approach to take, but was nervous about presenting the idea to Greg. At the time, we were already working on a book for couples, but its focus was more on renewing romance than on spirituality. While I liked the renewing romance book, and it probably would have had more potential as a big seller than this book, it just wasn't ringing true with what was important in our own relationship. Sure, romance is wonderful, but I didn't feel it to be the defining element. Under the section, "What I'm telling myself," you learn that I was worried about what Greg would think; I dismissed my idea as "silly," and I presumed that he'd think I'd gone a little wacky. This resulted in my feeling discouraged, anxious, and alone.

The next step is to transfer all this useful information about the situation, your thoughts, and your feelings onto the worksheet called Turning Obstacles into Opportunities. On that page, you can see how I worked through the above example. First, I examined the chances that what I was fearing would actually happen. How likely was it, really, that Greg would react as negatively as I imagined? Maybe I was presuming that he would reject my ideas just as a way to protect myself in advance from feeling hurt. If my expectations were low, I wouldn't be disappointed. But what if I was more or less correct in my assessment of the situation—what if he did react negatively at first? So what? How bad could that be? If he doesn't like the idea, we can work it out. I can share with him the context of my thoughts for the book, and this might help him understand. His opinion of my ideas does not determine their worth, or my worth. I like it when he agrees with me, but it's not a necessity for my survival. We can learn from our disagreements and I can listen to Greg's ideas with an open mind.

Then, I end up with a coping statement—a short sentence or two that helps guide me in my actions: "I have a right and a duty to myself to present my ideas. I can tolerate it if Greg doesn't react the way I hope he will." Finally, I jot down a few thoughts about how I can learn and grow from dealing with this obstacle.

Some Final Thoughts

By working through your thoughts and feelings in the manner suggested in this chapter, you end up with a way to transform potential obstacles into opportunities. Situations may not always go exactly as you want them to; that's to be expected. Gaining clarity about your own thoughts and feelings, however, will place you in a much better position to talk with your partner about the real issues, rather than getting bogged down in tangential topics that don't really matter.

Thoughts and Feelings Diary
(excerpt from Barb's diary)

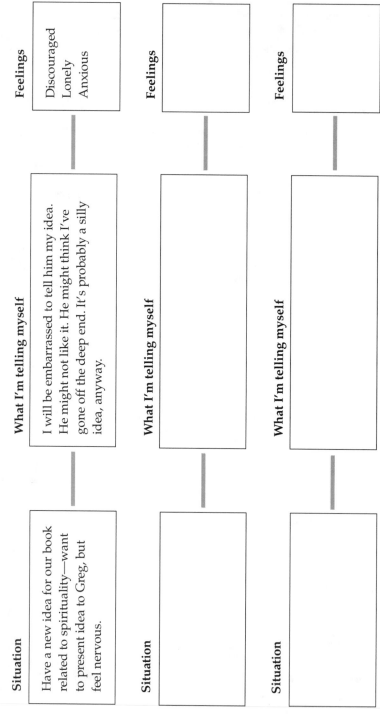

Situation

Have a new idea for our book related to spirituality—want to present idea to Greg, but feel nervous.

What I'm telling myself

I will be embarrassed to tell him my idea. He might not like it. He might think I've gone off the deep end. It's probably a silly idea, anyway.

Feelings

Discouraged
Lonely
Anxious

Situation

What I'm telling myself

Feelings

Situation

What I'm telling myself

Feelings

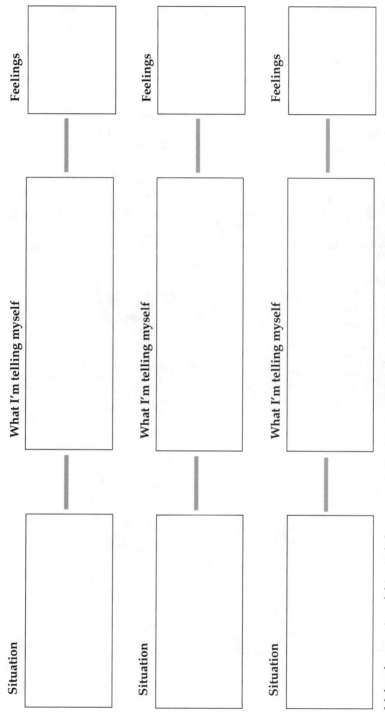

Thoughts and Feelings Diary

Situation

What I'm telling myself

Feelings

Situation

What I'm telling myself

Feelings

Situation

What I'm telling myself

Feelings

Make photocopies of this worksheet, or copy the headings into a notebook you can carry around with you.

You might be thinking, "This doesn't seem very spiritual, having to write all this stuff down on paper. Isn't that taking some of the magic and mystery away from love—after all, you can't reduce relationships to worksheets!" In many ways, you're right. Parts of this chapter are not the flowery, philosophical prose you may expect to find in a book about spirituality. We don't necessarily recommend that you fill out worksheets for the rest of your life. Some of you may never put a pen to the page, and that's fine. We do believe, though, that you need to develop an awareness of your thoughts and feelings; and we know that it's helpful to have a structure when you start out.

We ourselves have gone back and forth about the nature and form of this presentation. In many ways, our book parallels the paradox of life, and of marriage. Yes, marriage is a marvelous and graceful mystery, a divine enfolding of two people's lives—as Thomas Moore said, "a weaving together of many different strands of soul." And yes, marriage also requires hard, courageous, and conscious work. It is in light of this paradox that we offer not only our insights—which may or may not be flowery—but also our specific suggestions and concrete steps you can take to create a marriage full of sweetness, kindness, and magic.

Worksheet:
Turning Obstacles into Opportunities

Situation: Came up with idea for this book about marriage and spirituality, but have not yet presented the idea to Greg.

Thought (what I'm telling myself): I'll be too embarrassed to tell Greg my idea. It's probably silly, anyway. He probably won't like it. He might think I've gone off the deep end.

Feelings (resulting emotions): I feel nervous and somewhat embarrassed just in anticipation of sharing my idea with Greg. I feel vulnerable: I'll be taking a risk letting him know what I'm thinking about.

Probability of this occurring (How likely is it that what I'm thinking will actually happen?): Okay. So I might meet with some resistance at first. Greg's early experiences have left him less than thrilled with organized religion, and he might react negatively to the word "spirituality." He may not understand where I'm coming from. It's not likely, though, that he'll react as strongly as I'm thinking he might. Greg knows me too well to judge on the basis of one idea that I've "gone off the deep end."

Consequences if this occurs (How bad would it be?): If Greg reacts negatively at first, how bad will this be? Sure, I'd love it if he reacted with enthusiasm right away, but I can handle it if he doesn't. His reaction does not determine the validity or worth of my ideas. I also need to remember that Greg's first reaction to new ideas is sometimes cautious; later, once he has had time to think things over, he often becomes more receptive.

Coping statement (What can I say to myself that is more realistic, more encouraging?): I have a right and a duty to myself to present my ideas. I can tolerate it if Greg doesn't react the way I hope he will.

Actions I will take: To give myself the best chance of being heard and understood, I'll find a time to talk to Greg when he's not busy with other things. I'll give him time and space to think about what I've said before I press him for a response. But I'll also continue nurturing my idea on my own.

Opportunity (how I can learn or grow by dealing with this): Here I am still relating Greg like I did when he was my mentor in graduate school! This is a chance to use my intellectual wings. I need to be able to experience the excitement of my own ideas without requiring Greg's seal of approval. If he shares my excitement, fine. If not, this gives us yet another opportunity to know, respect, and admire one another.

Worksheet:
Turning Obstacles into Opportunities

Situation:

Thought (what I'm telling myself):

Feelings (resulting emotions):

Probability of this occurring (How likely is it that what I'm thinking will happen will actually happen?):

Consequences if this occurs (How bad would it be?):

Coping statement (What can I say to myself that is more realistic, more encouraging?):

Actions I will take:

Opportunity (how I can learn or grow by dealing with this):

Make photocopies of this worksheet, or copy the headings into a notebook you can carry around with you.

Chapter 3

Men, Women, and Matters of the Spirit

"At the core we are all moved by our sorrows and by the magnificence and miracles that touch us, not as men or women, but as human beings."

—Daphne Rose Kingma

*I*n the past decade, there has been an explosion of research and writing on the different ways in which men and women communicate. We are thankful for the best-selling books, *Men Are From Mars, Women Are From Venus*, by John Gray, Ph.D., *You Just Don't Understand Me*, by Deborah Tannen, *The Men We Never Knew*, by Daphne Rose Kingma, and others showing their readers the intricacies and nuances of men's and women's ways of perceiving the world and expressing themselves. Understanding these gender-based differences can help you in your quest for a spiritually rich relationship if, and only if, one condition is met: You must respect and honor those differences. Unfortunately, this condition is only rarely met. The emphasis on differences has in some ways contributed to antagonism between the sexes, blinding both men and women to the fundamental ways in which they are similar. We believe our differences to be more a matter of presentation and style than content or meaning—in other words, the difference is in *how* we communicate our innermost thoughts and feelings to one another.

In this chapter, our goals are twofold. First, we will shatter some major myths about men and women, myths that have been created and maintained by an extreme focus on differences—specifically on differences as deficits. Because these myths can kill the heart and soul of a relationship, we call them the Seven Deadly Myths. (In discussing these myths, we acknowledge that we generalize about the sexes and that for every generalization, there are many exceptions.) Second, we'll focus on how to use this knowledge to enhance the spiritual intimacy of your relationship—how to shine a light on what truly matters and gracefully let go of the rest.

The Seven Deadly Myths About Men

"I just don't understand men," Susan moaned to her best friend, Helen, over lunch. "Every time I try to talk to Jim about something the least bit emotional, I get the impression he wants to point the remote control at me and push the mute button. Sometimes I don't think he has any feelings!"

"Yeah, Joe tunes me out a lot," agreed Helen. "He really doesn't know the first thing about communicating."

Conversations like this can be heard between women every place you turn. Although this kind of dialogue may help women vent frustration, it does little to bridge the communication gap between the sexes. What women don't realize is that men do have feelings, even if they don't communicate them directly. Such myths about men are prime culprits in the erosion of trust and understanding in a relationship.

Deadly Myth 1: Men Can't Communicate

Olivia and Aaron, married for ten years, had recently moved to St. Louis from Minnesota. They were seeking marriage counseling because the stress of the move had taken a toll on their relationship. Olivia had been in public relations, but had quit her job about a year ago when they had their first child; Aaron, an engineer, had been transferred to St. Louis unexpectedly.

Olivia began the session: "Since we moved here Aaron has been completely wrapped up in his job. I try to talk to him about the baby, and he doesn't seem to care. I feel shut out and lonely. I haven't made many friends yet, so I need Aaron all the more. He's not here for me, though. I think all he cares about is his career."

For what seemed like a long time, Aaron sat silent. When we asked him what he was thinking, he said, "I know Olivia is unhappy, but I don't know what to do. I feel bad that we had to move, but we didn't have a whole lot of options. I try to suggest things she could do to make her day go faster, or ways to meet new people, but that only seems to make her more mad at me. I don't know what I'm doing wrong."

The communication pattern that Olivia and Aaron demonstrated is common. Olivia expressed her feelings to Aaron (she's lonely) and Aaron offered her solutions to her problem (get out and meet people). Here's another version we often hear: A woman comes home and tells her husband about some problems she's encountered at work. Her husband is quick to offer advice, and may even suggest she find a new job. She becomes angry and doesn't feel supported. He feels baffled, "Why is she mad? I was just trying to help."

What's going on here? Why all the confusion? In essence, men and women speak different languages, and neither is fluent in both. Most women communicate by talking, most men by doing. A man talks to solve a problem. If he doesn't have a solution already in mind, he'll remain quiet (as Aaron did in the session), figuring out the problem internally before speaking. In contrast, women speak to vent feelings, to elicit support and validation, and to build rapport.

When we were in graduate school in the 1980s, research into sex roles was a hot subject; many of us did our theses and dissertations on topics related to gender differences. The prominent sex-role researchers at the time referred to men as being more "instrumental" and women as more "expressive." Instrumental referred to being logical, rational, and analytical, while expressive referred to such traits as being nurturing and emotional. The research focused on the concept of androgyny—when someone of either sex shows a balance between instrumental and expressive traits. Results of numerous studies found that androgynous individuals fare better than sex-stereotyped individuals on a number of dimensions, including behavioral flexibility, assertiveness, and socially appropriate behavior. We remember being excited by this line of thinking: Freedom from rigid sex roles would allow men and women to express all the different aspects of their personalities, without being negatively evaluated.

Somewhere along the way, the ideal of androgyny was lost. Now the prevailing norm appears to be that, at least in the area of love, a woman's way of communicating is the most revered and the most accepted as the standard of mental health. Indeed, many popular books, women's magazines, and seminars admonish men that they'd better shape up and learn to communicate more like women—talk more, listen more, and be more expressive and intimate. When men communicate their feelings of love for their family by supporting them financially, or by fixing a leaky faucet, or by clearing ice off the driveway, it's not enough. In fact, it's often not even noticed by women as communication at all.

In reality, neither men's nor women's way of communicating is inherently superior. There is a time to talk and a time to act—either way carried to extremes has limitations.

Couples must accomplish three main tasks to bridge this communication chasm. First, each partner must acknowledge that both ways of communicating are valid—that communicating by talking and communicating by doing are both acceptable. Then they must learn to speak each other's language. Oftentimes in therapy, there is more of a focus on teaching men expressive and emotional skills; but we think it's just as important to teach women to be fluent in the language of action. Finally, it can be enormously helpful if partners don't take it personally when the other is not speaking their preferred language. Many times we hear women, in particular, assigning a negative motivation to their partner's behavior: "If he really loved me, he'd talk to me more." This is simply not so. Men don't talk as freely and easily as do women because they've been trained not to—it has nothing to do with love.

Deadly Myth 2: Men Don't Have Feelings

The myth that men are unfeeling creates perhaps the most damage of any of our misconceptions about men. It perpetuates the war between the sexes. In a personal conversation with us, author and psychotherapist Daphne Rose Kingma (*The Men We Never Knew*, 1993) said, "We've dismissed men as the feelingless gender—we've given up on them. Because of the way boys are socialized, their ability to deal with emotions has been systematically undermined. Men are taught, point-by-point, not to feel, not to cry, and not to find words to express themselves."

Just because men aren't adept at expressing their feelings, don't for a minute think they don't feel . . . and feel deeply. Many times, men express their feelings using a secret code—a code that even they can't decipher. For example, men may convert stereotypically feminine feelings, such as sadness or vulnerability, into feelings like anger or pride—feelings more socially acceptable for a man to experience. We remember a couple who came to us in distress because they had recently learned that their teenage daughter had been raped by her boyfriend. A major conflict arose because John was threatening to kill the boyfriend, upsetting his wife and daughter tremendously. They worried he might actually seek revenge and end up in jail. With a little work, we were able to help John express his true feelings: He broke down and sobbed, stating that he felt responsible for what had happened—as though he should have been able to protect his daughter. He felt terribly sad that his daughter was going through such pain, and he felt justifiably angry. After he expressed the full range of his feelings, he no longer threatened to kill the young man and was better able to support his daughter in ways that were helpful.

Men also deal with their feelings through the fine art of displacement. They quite nimbly shift feelings from one arena to another, expressing their emotions only in places where they feel safe, and where the expression of feelings is considered acceptable. To witness this phenomenon, you need only observe how men act at a sports event. It's not uncommon to see men in the audience express great exuberance and affection, giving each other hugs and high fives. Football and hockey players, probably some of the most macho men around, appear quite comfortable expressing their feelings with each other during the game. Where else would you see men slapping each other playfully on the butt? Put these same men in a boardroom and we guarantee you wouldn't see this same openness or level of comfort with affection and camaraderie.

Finally, men often experience their feelings through physical complaints, such as headaches or backaches. Probably everyone knows a man who gets headaches only on weekends, or becomes sick on vacations. Why does this happen? Because as long as men are working, they can cut themselves off from their feelings. Without the structure of work, however, their feelings and needs surface, and may be expressed through physical symptoms.

Although men may not always know what they're feeling, there's one thing many men are sure about: They're convinced they're in a major double-bind. Women tell men to express their feelings, but when they do, women are often petrified, if not horrified. Women want men to show their feelings, but only certain feelings, and only in doses they can handle. In fact, results from numerous research studies, as well as clinical experience, tell us that men may be right to be wary of women who implore them to show their true feelings. Men who deviate from the traditional masculine norm by being emotionally expressive and talking about their fears are often judged as being poorly adjusted.

Part of the problem may be that men have silenced their feelings for so long, and haven't developed resources for handling them when and if they do come forth. Such unplanned for, unexpected emotion can often prove overwhelming. Barb's brother gave us permission to share this story, which poignantly illustrates the phenomenon. Two summers ago, Bill had taken a new job located several hours away from St. Louis. Until they could sell their house and relocate, he was away much of the week. His wife, Jerri, had begged him for a dog, arguing that a dog would provide her not only with some needed company, but also make her feel more secure when alone in their home. In his logical, analytical way, Bill gave her every reason why the timing was not right for a dog. On an intellectual level Jerri knew he was right, but her heart insisted she would be happier with a dog. They went through several weekends where all they did was fight about the dog issue. Jerri thought Bill was being cold and unfeeling to deny her something that would make her more secure in his absence. Bill thought Jerri was being unreasonable. How could they show their house to potential buyers with a new puppy running around, wetting the floor?

With much coaxing, Bill agreed to accompany Jerri to the local humane society "just to look" at dogs. Jerri told us later what happened. When Bill saw all those rows and rows of dogs in cages, knowing that most of them would probably be put to death, he began sobbing uncontrollably. Jerri said she had never seen Bill cry so hard. She had been thinking to herself that he didn't have any feelings, when nothing could be further from the truth.

Our own observation has been that many men experience intense emotions; but, lacking the training and support to make sense of their feelings, they're left with few options but to bury them even deeper. It's only when men are taken off guard (such as when Bill visited the Humane Society for the first time) that their feelings are free to surface.

No, it's not that men are unfeeling. Rather, men are trapped in the confines of a socialization process that tells them it's unmanly to cry, to hurt, or to express the myriad other emotions we all experience as a result of living fully as human beings. If men do venture out of their role, either by choice or circumstance, they often face unsupportive reactions from others, reinforcing their tendency to bury their feelings.

Deadly Myth 3:   All Men Think About Is Sex

While it's true that most men think a lot about sex, it's probably not for the reasons women typically believe. For most men, sex is not about conquest, domination, or the raw physical experience itself. Rather, men have been granted very few other domains in which they can have emotional experiences—sports being one of these. One of the few other outlets in which men can feel, and feel with abandon, is sex. Physical touch is a way for men to meld their innermost selves to another person, without the sometimes heavy burden of having to use the language of words. Many women misinterpret men's sexual interest, however, as being selfish or insensitive. Such was the case for Cindy and Ted.

Ted and Cindy were having problems in their relationship. They were so busy with their careers that they had little time or energy leftover for each other. They rarely talked for more than a few minutes each day, and had stopped many of the fun activities they used to enjoy together. Despite their difficulties, Ted still loved Cindy, and missed feeling more connected with her. He especially missed cuddling with her in the morning. That was a time he cherished, feeling somehow in those few minutes that all was right with the world. Now, most mornings, Cindy was up before he was, trying to squeeze in her morning run before the hectic day began. When Ted did manage to awaken before her, he'd put his arms around her and gently stroke her hair. At such moments, Cindy often grew irritated, thinking it insensitive of him to wake her up early. Didn't he know she needed every minute of sleep she could get? She also assumed that when he cuddled up close, it was an overture to lovemaking. When Ted sensed her coldness, he felt hurt, dismayed, and confused. He only wanted to feel close to her; from his perspective, physical contact was the surest, most direct way to renew their emotional bond. Unfortunately, Cindy misinterpreted his motives, resulting in further distance between them.

With help, Ted was able to express how he simply wanted to feel close to Cindy. She was surprised to hear to what extent physical contact was a powerful emotional experience for her husband. This revelation allowed her to relax in the mornings and feel closer to him. They still had other problems to work through, but making those first few moments in the morning more pleasurable went a long way toward helping them renew their warm feelings for each other. In time, their sex life grew more satisfying as Cindy became aware of how much Ted truly cherished their closeness.

Deadly Myth 4: Men Don't Want Intimacy

Many women think it's pretty much of a given that they have the corner market on intimacy. After all, it's men who can't commit. Right? It's not simply a matter of one sex wanting intimacy more than the other, but that men and women experience intimacy from different vantage points. Lucy and Matt's situation clearly illustrates this point.

Lucy and Matt had known each other since grade school. They were the best of friends throughout high school, although they never dated. They each went to different colleges, but kept in touch and saw each other over the holidays. After college, Lucy moved to St. Louis, and got a job working as a customer service manager at a large bank. Matt attended law school in Chicago. One weekend, Matt asked Lucy to visit him at school. It was a wonderful spring weekend, and romance was in the air. During that weekend visit, it became obvious to them that they had deeper feelings for each other than simply friendship. Thus, their courtship began.

After a few months of seeing each other nearly every weekend, Lucy began to notice a pattern that bothered her. She felt quite close to Matt on Friday night and Saturday, and Matt seemed to be open and relaxed. But by Sunday morning, she could feel Matt pulling away, becoming more distant. His behavior hurt her feelings terribly; she wondered what she was doing wrong. To make matters worse, after some of these weekends, Matt wouldn't call her until late in the week, only increasing Lucy's sense of insecurity. By the time he did call, Lucy was so upset, she made sarcastic comments such as, "How nice of you to call. I thought maybe you'd forgotten about me."

As we talked with Lucy and Matt, it became clear that they each experienced intimacy differently. Lucy's reaction could be boiled down to: "Wow. This is really great. We're really close and opening up to each other. I want more of this." Matt's experience, however, was much different: "Wow. This is really great. We've been really close. Now it will feel good to have some time away." In *Men Are From Mars, Women Are From Venus*, author John Gray, Ph.D., gets to the heart of the matter: "When a man loves a woman, sometimes he needs to pull away before he can get closer." If women understand this pattern, and realize that it's not something to take personally, it won't be such a big deal. If women can accept that many men need this time away, and do something for themselves that is satisfying and fulfilling, their partners will be ready for closeness again much more quickly.

Deadly Myth 5: Men Are Fearless

Most women think of men as strong—fearless to the core. They depend on men to kill the bugs and chase away prowlers. But men have fears just like women do. Ron Scott, Ph.D., a colleague of ours who runs men's therapy groups in St. Louis, told us, "Men are basically terrified of being revealed to be inadequate. Their fears run the gamut from worrying about whether they're rich enough or handsome enough to whether they'll be able to fix all the little things that break around the house." Ron related an incident that happened early in his marriage when he tried to install a water heater in his first home. "After I was done and turned on the water, there were at least 60 leaks. I just sat on the floor and cried. I thought, 'How can I go and ask my neighbor for help? I'm a man. I'm supposed to know how to do these things.'"

Like women, men have fears—the difference is that men aren't granted permission to acknowledge their fears. They have to hide their insecurities, which often leads to a great deal of confusion in relationships. This was the case for a couple we saw recently. Dan, an auto mechanic, had met his wife Christine when she came in to have her car repaired. Dan was impressed with Christine's obvious knowledge about cars. They struck up a conversation, liked each other immediately, and began dating. As Dan learned more about Christine's background, he began to worry. Christine was divorced, her ex-husband a corporate executive who made more money in a month than Dan did in a year. Dan knew he couldn't provide for Christine in her accustomed manner. Despite his concerns, they married, and were, for the most part, happy. The only thing they consistently argued about was money. Dan thought Christine spent too much, and he became extremely controlling with their finances. After a few sessions, it became clear to us what was going on. Christine's spending wasn't the real issue—it wasn't as if she were a compulsive shopper, giving Dan good reason to worry. Dan was upset not so much by her spending, but by his own fear that he couldn't provide for Christine the way her ex-husband had. Fear was the real issue underlying Dan's controlling behavior. Once this fear was out in the open, not camouflaged by other issues, we were better able to help Dan and Christine work out ways to acknowledge his fears, and keep them from spilling over into unpleasant or inappropriate behavior.

Deadly Myth 6: Men Are Completely Satisfied in the Male Role

Especially during the height of the women's movement, but even today, women have largely believed that men have it made—that they are completely fulfilled in the male role of protector and provider. It's easy to see why this is so. Imagine you're the one at home cooking, cleaning, and changing the children's diapers. It would seem pretty glamorous to dress in professional clothes (without worrying about spit-up getting on them), work on stimulating and challenging projects, and enjoy adult conversation with your colleagues.

While women may think that men have it all, it isn't that simple. Many men feel as trapped in their current work role as women previously did when it was mandatory for them to stay at home, regardless of their other ambitions. Men carry a huge psychological burden of always being the provider. Even if their partner works outside the home, perhaps even outearning them, men still hold the job of worrying about the financial security of the family. Patrick Fanning and Matthew McKay, Ph.D., authors of *Being a Man*, assert that, "Men feel an incredible pressure to earn money. Where women are too often considered sex objects, men are just as often considered wage objects or success objects—an equally dehumanizing experience."

This myth about men being satisfied in the male role was a key point in our work with Robert and Brenda. Robert, 48, a vascular surgeon, had worked terribly long hours to make his practice a success. Now, with the changes in the health-care market, large hospitals were quickly buying up practices, offering large lump sums of money to the doctors, as well as taking many of the time-consuming administrative burdens off their backs. Robert initially hadn't wanted to sell. He thought he'd be giving up too much of his autonomy, yet he also knew he'd save an incredible amount of time by not having to manage his own office. He could spend more time focusing on patient care—and devote more time to his family.

In the months after selling his practice, Robert did indeed have considerably more free time. He started coming home for dinner, only to find his family frequently away. His two teenage daughters had numerous extracurricular activities and many friends that kept them busy. His wife, Brenda, was involved in several charitable organizations, and was not home much at all. When his wife and daughters were around, Robert felt like a stranger in his own home, an unwelcome visitor. What finally brought Robert and Brenda to our office was when Robert overheard Brenda and the girls planning a vacation for spring break. They obviously hadn't even considered whether he might want to go. The next day he looked in the phone book and called us for an appointment. He told us he was so hurt when he heard them, he had to struggle to hold back the tears.

During the first session, Robert was quite expressive about his feelings, obviously surprising Brenda. "I've missed out on so much. I was looking through photo albums the other day, and there were hardly any scenes from the girls' childhood I could remember. I realize how little I helped raise them; I just wasn't there. Now that I have time to spend with them, they want nothing to do with me. They act like I have no place in their lives. What's even worse, Brenda, is that you act that way, too. You know, I didn't even want to be a doctor, but because both my father and grandfather were in the medical field, it was assumed—no, expected—that I would follow suit. I didn't have the guts to pursue my real dream of being an artist. And, anyway, how would I have been able to provide for you and the girls then?"

These conversations in therapy led Brenda to have increased respect for how much Robert had sacrificed for her and the children. She also began to pay more attention to him as she was reminded of what a complex and caring man he was. Ultimately, they developed a stronger relationship, and Brenda turned more and more to Robert to meet her emotional needs.

Deadly Myth 7: Men Can't Change

We wouldn't be in this field if we didn't believe that people can change. We've seen it happen, often dramatically so. Many women, however, don't believe that men can change. We frequently receive calls from women telling us they have relationship problems, but that they're certain their husbands won't come in for counseling. When we ask if they've asked their husbands, we typically hear "No" as an answer. They presume, sometimes rightly and sometimes wrongly, that their husbands won't join them. Even when we have both partners in the session, the woman is typically skeptical of her partner's willingness or ability to change.

As we've stated before, it's not only men who must change. Although this may not be a popular viewpoint, we believe it to be true. First and foremost, women need to alter the ways in which they ask men to change. To be sure, it's not very effective to scream and yell about the house being such a mess, and about how your husband doesn't ever do *anything* to help. We haven't met many men who would feel especially inclined to jump up and vacuum after such a "request." In fact, most people, regardless of their gender, would probably feel attacked and defensive, and would either lash out in anger ("All you do is nag!") or retreat into silence. Similarly, admonishing a man with, "Talk to me! Why can't you just tell me what you're feeling?" isn't going to make him feel like opening up and revealing his innermost self.

What are women to do? Do women have to live with things the way they are? We don't think so. Perhaps the most important thing women can do to help men change is to change their own attitudes. Understand the way men were raised—to not express feelings, to not communicate with words, to not show fear or vulnerability. This understanding will impel you toward greater acceptance and kindheartedness; and, ultimately, you'll find yourself in a better position to guide your partner through the unfamiliar terrain of intimacy.

Tips on Using Your New Knowledge About Men To Enhance Your Relationship

We've covered a lot of ground so far in this chapter. By way of summarizing, we'll list some tips below about what women can do to increase their understanding and compassion, improve communication, and feel closer to their husbands than ever before.

Recognize there are many valid ways to communicate other than talking. Look for other ways in which your partner may be expressing his caring for you, and communicate your appreciation.

Realize that men have not been taught to recognize their feelings, much less to express them. Imploring your partner to tell you what he's feeling may not be the best approach—in fact, it may make him feel intensely uncomfortable and inadequate. Be patient. He'll come to his own insights in his own time. The best thing you can do is to create an atmosphere in which he'll feel listened to and accepted for who he is.

When your partner does express his feelings, monitor your own reactions. If you notice yourself feeling overwhelmed, remind yourself that feelings don't last forever; he'll be able to work through his feelings, just as you do.

Remember that most men deal differently with their emotions than women do. Your partner may not want to talk right away; he may prefer to take a run or go for a drive. Don't worry. If you let him do what he needs to do, he'll be more likely to open up to you later. Try not to rush him.

If your partner "needs some space" after a period of closeness, don't take it personally. You didn't do anything wrong. Do something nice for yourself in his absence.

Keep in mind that men can be insecure when it comes to their sexuality. Men, too, need a certain amount of caring and comfort to be in the mood.

Be sensitive to the fact than men feel an enormous pressure to be a good provider and that this may have an entirely different meaning to him than it does to you. Your partner is apt to feel that his working should be a sign to you that he loves you and cares about you (regardless of how much money you make yourself). He may feel deeply hurt if you complain that he doesn't care, when he perceives that his feelings are manifested—quite obviously to him—through his actions.

Men have a right, as do women, to have fears and insecurities. Why should men always be the ones to catch the mice or kill the bugs?

Try to accept your partner as he is. We know this is a difficult thing to do. Chapter 5 will cover in more detail this matter of acceptance. Our experience is that change is a paradox. Genuine change occurs most swiftly and completely when it emerges from a basis of true caring, compassion, and acceptance.

Finally, be patient with yourself. We realize you may have some anger or other feelings that make it difficult for you to put these tips into practice right away. After all, you may be thinking, why should I have to accept him? I want him to accept me! If that's the case, try to keep an open mind. After you've worked your way through the rest of the book, you'll be more willing to try out some new things. And don't worry that we're taking sides. The next section is geared toward helping your partner recognize common myths about women, giving him suggestions about things he can do differently in deference to *your* needs.

The Seven Deadly Myths About Women

While the common thread through women's complaints about men is that they lack something—they don't talk *enough*, they don't show their feelings *enough*, and so on—men's complaints about women run in the opposite direction. From men you're apt to hear, "Women talk *too* much, they're *too* emotional, *too* needy." Much of men's frustration stems from their being clueless about how to respond to women—from feeling incompetent in their ability to meet their wives' needs. In describing the Seven Deadly Myths About Women, we'll show you how understanding the context and the underlying meaning of women's communication is the key to responding in a way that helps her, and also leaves you feeling confident.

Deadly Myth 1:   Women Talk Too Much

Ed and Laurel met for dinner at the Ecco Bar and Grill, sitting at their usual booth by the bar. Ed looked at the menu as Laurel launched into describing the details of her day. Within five minutes, she had covered nearly ten different topics, ranging from the way her boss had handled a meeting, to what she'd like to do that weekend. When Ed continued looking at the menu, Laurel said, "Are you listening to me?" Ed replied, "I was trying, but I got lost after 30 seconds. Can't I first have a minute to decide what I want to eat?" "Sure," she said, "but I haven't talked to you since this morning, and I have a lot to tell you. Besides, you *always* eat the prime rib sandwich."

Men can easily feel overwhelmed by the amount of talking women do. It's not necessarily that they don't want to listen. Instead, the problem stems from the different kinds of talking that men and women are comfortable with. In the section on myths about men, we said that men view talking as a means to an end, the end being to solve a problem or transmit some useful information. Women, on the other hand, use the world of words to create understanding and establish closeness in a relationship. The difference between men's and women's relationship with language is similar to their relationship with shoes. For women, trying on many different shoes in search of the perfect pair is a given; most women seem to need a different pair of shoes for every occasion. Men, however, are more likely to own just one or two pairs of shoes; the same pair of shoes will do for almost any occasion. (This analogy was inspired by a couple we saw several years ago. During one session, the woman described how she and her husband had spent an entire weekend shopping to find him an expensive, tailored suit to wear to a formal dinner. She was very upset when, the next day, he spent $7 at Wal-Mart for a new pair of shoes to wear with his $600 suit.)

There are so many little ways this difference between men and women gets played out. For example, one day when I came home, Barb snapped at me because I paused to look at the mail before speaking to her. I felt she was overreacting—looking at the mail or the newspaper is one of the ways I unwind after spending my entire day giving of myself to other people. Even though Barb is quite understanding of this, she told me that on days like that she usually feels a slight pang of hurt if I don't acknowledge her when I first come in. She explained that after nine hours apart, she needs to feel reconnected right away. As a result of recognizing each other's needs, I now try to greet Barb right when I return home, and she frequently gives me some time to relax at the end of the day before tackling any difficult topics.

Men may wonder, "I show my wife I love her. Why do we always have to talk so much, especially about our relationship?" A large part of the answer lies in the way women were raised. Although many parents today are attempting to raise their children in a nonsexist manner, in all likelihood you grew up in a more traditional home: Girls played with dolls while boys played with blocks; girls learned to cooperate while boys learned to compete; girls nurtured friendships while boys played with "buddies." Girls' early experiences teach them to base their self-concept and self-esteem on the quality of their relationships, a pattern that endures throughout women's adult development. Men need to accept that women's talking is the primary way in which they feel a sense of communion with other people. Even a casual discussion about the day's seemingly trivial events is an opportunity to demonstrate caring and affection and to reestablish the marital bond.

Deadly Myth 2: Women Are Too Emotional

Women are schooled early and thoroughly in the language of emotion. In fact, in the area of feelings, most have achieved their doctorate degrees. Women quickly recognize when something is bothering them. They're also quick to know that their feelings won't last forever, especially if they express them. Thus, women may vent their frustrations with little forethought to the phrasing or presentation of the message. When men are the recipients of the message, they're apt to view women as being overly emotional—not so much because they are, but because men aren't always comfortable with the intensity, delivery, or spontaneity of the emotions expressed.

Let's look at an example from Carmen and Josh's marriage. Carmen had a special dinner prepared for Josh. He had been working long hours the past few weeks, but promised he would be home on time tonight. The dinner was ready at 6:15, but Josh wasn't home. He called at 6:30 and said he'd be a little late. Carmen kept her cool, and decided to keep dinner warm in the oven. When Josh wasn't home at 8:00 she decided she'd better put the food back in the refrigerator, only to have him walk in the door at 8:10. "You call this a little late! How can you be so inconsiderate? You knew I was planning a nice dinner. We've hardly seen each other in the past few weeks. I know your work is important, but isn't your family important, too?" As Carmen was talking, Josh could feel himself withdrawing. He didn't know how to respond. Yes, he *was* sorry; but he didn't think it was fair that he got attacked the moment he walked in the door. Josh's reserve only made Carmen more angry: "Aren't you going to say anything? Aren't you going to apologize?"

We've discussed socialization—the way boys and girls are raised in our culture—as being a cause of many gender behavioral differences. In the case of emotional styles, there's also another cause. Basic biological differences between the sexes play an important role in how men and women respond to emotions. Psychologist John Gottman, Ph.D., studied married couples extensively in laboratory situations, and found sex differences in blood pressure and heart rate when a man and a woman engage in a difficult emotional discussion. The results of his experiments showed that, during these discussions, a man's heart rate and blood pressure rise quickly and stay elevated for a long time. He calls this phenomenon "flooding." Thus, a man withdraws from emotionally laden conversations not because he's being a jerk and trying to make his wife angry, but because his autonomic nervous system has become over-aroused. In attempting to deal with this unpleasant state of overarousal, a man is likely to minimize his wife's emotions and try to sidestep the issues. Unfortunately, this leads to more problems, because the woman is likely to think, "He just doesn't get it!" and escalate her complaints in a futile effort to make him understand. The vicious cycle continues. The man either withdraws further or, if he feels unduly threatened, he may retaliate in anger.

Although the roots of flooding are largely physiological, there's plenty a man can learn to do to calm himself down so that he can hear what his wife is saying and respond to her in a helpful way. Keep in mind that in the heat of the moment, women may express themselves without giving much thought to their word choice. Your partner may say, "You *never* help with the dishes," or "This house is so messy, it's completely out of control." Rather than getting into an argument, pointing out the times when you did do the dishes, or stating that you think the house looks fine, take a deep breath and look a little deeper before you respond. Then try to acknowledge what your wife has expressed without being defensive. You might say: "It sounds like you feel really overwhelmed with the housework/kids/bills," or "I know that it really bothers you when the house doesn't look neat and clean." Don't worry if, at this point in the book, you feel skeptical, or think that you wouldn't be able to carry this off. We'll go over the specifics of communication skills in later chapters.

Deadly Myth 3: Women Don't Care About Sex

A discrepancy in sexual desire is a problem for many couples we see. More often than not, it's the man who wants sex more frequently. This does not mean, however, that women don't care about sex as much as men do. Women do care about sex, especially in the context of a loving, committed relationship. Unfortunately for women, as well as for the men who love them, a variety of factors can prevent women from experiencing sexuality as a completely positive experience.

On a very basic level, physiological differences can make it more difficult for a woman to experience a desire for sex, become aroused during lovemaking, and have an orgasm. For example, researchers in the 1960s discovered that testosterone, once considered the "male" hormone, is responsible for fueling the sex drive in both sexes. They also found that men have ten to twenty times more testosterone than women, a major factor in sex-drive discrepancies. Dr. Patricia Love (she must have been destined to write relationship books) explains these and other biological differences succinctly in *Hot Monogamy*, a book we highly recommend.

In addition to physiological factors, psychological factors can contribute to a lower interest in sex. Women are much more likely than men to suffer from clinical depression, a symptom of which is decreased sex drive. Ironically, the medications most frequently used to treat depression do not usually raise sex drive and, in fact, may cause anorgasmia. Imagine your depression lifting, finally feeling in a good mood, even wanting to make love, and then not being able to have an orgasm. How frustrating! Women are also more likely to have been sexually abused sometime in their lifetime. Survivors of sexual abuse may desperately want to be good lovers, but shame, fear, and frightening memories hold them back.

Body image is another problem women struggle with more than men, and one that can greatly affect feelings about sexuality. One of our clients' husbands frequently read *Playboy* magazine and compared his wife's body to the bodies of the centerfold models. Never mind that these women exercise five hours a day; never mind that they may starve themselves; never mind that the photos are computer enhanced. He expected his wife to be his sex kitten. Despite being an extremely attractive woman, she was plagued with doubts and insecurities about her appearance, and at times suffered with symptoms of anorexia and bulimia. "I feel like when we make love, all he sees are my fat thighs," she said. Sadly, even women married to more liberated men may hate their bodies. Women are given the message from early on that their task in life is to look good, and to be thin at all costs. Combine this with the traditional socialization process that teaches girls to be wary of their own sexuality, and it becomes easier to see why it might appear that women don't care for sex.

Fatigue can also be a major factor in the discrepancy between men's and women's sex drive. Many studies have confirmed that women do a disproportionate amount of housework and childcare, even if they have full-time jobs outside the home. Dr. John Gottman illustrates this point with several studies in his book, *Why Marriages Succeed or Fail*. One study found that out of a group of 50 men who described themselves as "liberated"—who stated that their wives' careers were just as important as their own—not a single one had ever initiated a discussion with his wife about how to divide the household chores. Another study found that men who support feminist ideals do only four minutes more housework each day than men with more traditional sex-role attitudes. You may wonder how sex and housework can possibly be related, but as Gottman says, "Being the sole person in a marriage to clean the toilet is definitely not an aphrodisiac!" In his extensive research on married couples, Gottman has found that men who do more housework and childcare have better sex lives and happier marriages. How's that for incentive?

Deadly Myth 4: Women Are Needy and Dependent

Frequently, we hear men complain about their wives being too needy, or not having lives of their own. In essence, these men feel that their wives are too dependent on them for emotional support and for structuring their lives on a daily basis. When discussing these problems, it often becomes clear in our marriage counseling sessions that men misinterpret women's needs for emotional intimacy as a weakness.

Briana and Raymond, an upper-middle-class couple, came in for therapy because Briana was depressed. She saw no hope for the future of the marriage because Raymond was always either working or playing golf. During the first session, she described what precipitated her calling for an appointment. She had accidentally locked herself out of the house, and called Raymond at work, hoping he could come home and let her in. Raymond told her that he had an important meeting to attend. In a rather irritable voice, he advised her to call a locksmith. Briana felt betrayed by Raymond's refusal to help her, and stunned to learn how low she ranked on his list of priorities.

In discussing this incident in the therapy session, Briana focused on how Raymond had expressed no understanding or empathy for how she felt that day. She could understand that it was impractical for him to rush to her rescue, but couldn't he at least have offered to call the locksmith for her, since she had no phone readily available? Raymond, on the other hand, saw this situation as an example of how she relied too much on him. As the session progressed, he listed other evidence of Briana's "overdependence": every Saturday morning as he prepared to play golf, she would ask if they could do something together later in the day—perhaps go out to dinner. Raymond then described how controlled he felt by his wife's "dependency." It seemed to him that she habitually tried to force him to give up his one day of relaxation, his hard-earned day of rest after the long workweek. If only she had more friends or activities to keep her busy, he reasoned, he wouldn't have to feel guilty about wanting some time on his own.

Raymond's interpretations surprised Briana. She said, "He'd drive me crazy if he was home all day on Saturday. There's no way I'd ask him to give up golf." We learned that Briana had plenty of friends and activities to fill her time. She was involved in leading a charitable organization, and was considering starting her own business. Briana's schedule wasn't the issue. Although the situation presented by this couple was complicated, one point stands out as particularly relevant to our discussion here: Briana's desire to spend some time with Raymond was not a sign of neediness or dependency, even though Raymond had come to interpret it in this light; Briana simply enjoyed her husband's company. Rather than taking this as a compliment, Raymond told himself that if he didn't keep up his guard, he'd be engulfed by his wife's neediness. In effect, he filtered (and perhaps distorted) many of Briana's requests through his belief that she was dependent.

In the sessions that followed, we helped Raymond recognize the ways in which he contributed to Briana's apparent neediness: The more he avoided making a commitment to spend time together, the more she pursued and pressured him. When he eventually made spending time with Briana a priority, Raymond enjoyed his time alone more. He felt less guilty, and his life was more in balance. Similarly, he also enjoyed his time with Briana more, because it felt like a choice, rather than an obligation.

Deadly Myth 5: Women Are Fearful

Women are frequently portrayed in movies and television as being easily flustered and frightened by even a minor crisis. The message is: Women need men to protect them. Is this true? Are women, in fact, more fearful than men? Social scientists have studied this issue extensively. On paper-and-pencil measures of fear and anxiety, such as questionnaires, women typically score as being more fearful. When more covert, physiological measures are used, however, the results are inconclusive. After many years of conducting studies, researchers have found that women are not necessarily more fearful, but they are more likely than men to acknowledge and report their fears. This makes perfect sense when you remember the clear message men receive throughout boyhood and beyond: It's unmanly to be afraid.

Women are, in general, more open about verbalizing their fears and insecurities. It's not uncommon for a woman to talk to many different people, on many different occasions, about something she's worried about. Women do this, though, not as a plea for help, but as a way to cope with and master their fear. A man may easily fall into the trap of thinking he must rescue her, only to have her retort, "What's the matter—don't you think I can manage on my own?" Men need to accept that women often need to verbalize their fears as the first step in facing them.

Several years ago, Barb received a call from New York. A producer for *Good Morning America* wanted to discuss the possibility of Barb being on the show to discuss a book Barb had co-authored on social anxiety. Initially, all Barb could talk about was how nervous she was, and how she was unsure of whether or not she wanted to go. I assured her that I thought she would do great on television, and that she should seize the opportunity. At the same time, I would understand if she decided against going for any reason. The weeks prior to the telecast, she spent hours planning what to wear. For the first time in our marriage, she didn't trust my fashion advice, and she spent hours away from the office with Jane, our office manager, trying on various outfits. Her anxiety remained at a fever pitch until about 30 minutes before the limousine arrived to take her to the studio. At that point, a remarkable transformation took place—Barb grew very calm and self-assured—and I thought to myself, "Who is this woman?" Her calmness unnerved me, but I had enough sense to keep my mouth shut. She did very well on television that day, and I was incredibly proud of how she performed, and how she had faced her fears.

Deadly Myth 6: Women Can Have
It All—Family and Career

Magazines and advertisers tell women, "You can have it all," "You've come a long way, baby." Women have made great strides in gaining equal rights and securing more options for themselves. But many women still struggle with the choices and inevitable sacrifices they must make. Women who choose to have full-time careers worry that they're shortchanging their families. Unless they have a great deal of money to spend on hired help, they must also fight fatigue as they juggle the competing demands of a career, motherhood, and homemaking. They're more likely than their husbands to be the ones who get up at night with sick children, miss work to take the kids to the doctor, find baby-sitters, attend teacher conferences, feel aggravated if the house is a mess or the refrigerator is empty, and the list goes on. Women who choose to stay home and care for their children full time face their own array of possible losses, including thwarted ambitions, quashed dreams, and diminished self-esteem. Even if they're pleased with their choice, they will inevitably be criticized for staying at home by some of their relatives and friends. For many if not most women, economic necessity limits their choices, requiring them to work even if they would prefer to stay home.

The argument that Mandy and Richard recalled during a counseling session is typical of those we hear. Richard describes himself as a "man of the nineties." He's proud of his wife and her career, and he doesn't expect her to keep the house clean, or have gourmet meals prepared. And yet Mandy worries about the way the house looks, and that they eat out too often. "I know we both work full time, but I still feel that it's going to reflect poorly on me if someone stops by and sees the house a wreck." Richard replies, "What do you care what other people think?" Mandy may be right to think that people will judge her rather than Richard if the house is unkempt. An incident that happened a few years ago made us realize how entrenched people's expectations can be. We had Greg's parents over for brunch. Despite the fact that they saw Greg doing all the cooking, they still thanked Barb for the meal—not just once, but several times.

Deadly Myth 7: Women Change Like the Weather

While many women believe that men can never change, the parallel myth about women is that they're unpredictable, forever changing their minds. This perception can make it difficult for men to keep up, to know where things stand. We'll share an example from our own marriage to illustrate this point. Bear with us while Greg gives you some necessary background information.

During the past year, Barb and I have gone through some monumental stresses and changes. Our son, Jesse, who has had chronic health problems, was hospitalized unexpectedly last spring. Seeing our three-year-old son lying in a hospital bed hooked up to IVs and oxygen was a traumatic experience, one that made us rethink everything that was important to us. We became especially aware of the fact that we had no family in St. Louis to help us through this crisis. Not a month after that, my grandmother died, and my father was diagnosed with cancer.

These events changed us. They made us realize that we didn't like the way we were living. We worked all the time; we enjoyed seeing couples for counseling, but the business aspects of being in practice took far too much of our time and energy. We were also busy writing a proposal for this book, and trying to find an interested publisher. We didn't have enough time for ourselves, for our relationship, or for our son. After some intense soul-searching, we sold our house in St. Louis, moved to Jefferson City where my family lives, found employment, and, surprise—we ended up with a book contract.

We were so busy coping with these changes, we weren't sure whether we'd be able to complete the book within the time stipulated by our contract. For months, there was a tension between us. I downplayed the difficulties—of course, we could complete the book; while Barb thought it was impossible—in her opinion, we should forget the book and get on with our new life. Throughout this time, Barb wavered frequently. One day she would agree with me, and I'd sigh with relief, thinking the issue was settled. Then, the next day, her skepticism would return.

Even though Barb's inconsistency was nerve-wracking for me, I tried to allow her to have her doubts. I had learned throughout our marriage that she often says things emphatically to indicate how she feels about something, but that I shouldn't interpret every word literally. She needed to express her thoughts and feelings before she could "settle in" to work on the book. She was "thinking out loud," whereas I (in typical male fashion) might verbalize only the conclusion of my thought processes.

Barb was not so much "changing like the weather" as she was going through a time when she needed to share her experience of feeling overwhelmed. As I became better able to accept her feelings, she became more optimistic about our completing the book. This is a good example of how men need to learn to appreciate the *process* of communication, rather than relying only on the literal meaning of spoken words.

Tips on Using Your New Knowledge About Women To Enhance Your Relationship

Now that you understand more about women, what can you do? Here are some tips for men to help you transform your newfound awareness into practical action.

Recognize that when your partner is talking to you, she wants to feel connected. She wants to make sure the relationship is on solid ground. After a period of separation, establish that closeness as soon as you can, and everything afterward will flow more freely. This doesn't mean you have put your needs completely on hold. For example, if you come home exhausted after a long day at work and your partner wants to talk, try saying: "I'm so glad to see you. I missed you and wondered how your day was going. I want to hear all about it, but I'm tired right now. I need a few minutes to unwind and relax. Can we talk in 15 minutes?"

Don't jump into a problem-solving mode prematurely. If you're not sure what your partner needs at any given moment, it's okay to ask her. You might say, "It sounds like you're really upset. Would you like me to listen, or would you like some suggestions?"

Reconsider the "division of labor" in terms of the emotional life of your relationship. As you become more aware of your own feelings, and better able to express yourself, your partner may feel less pressure to be the emotional caretaker for the two of you, and her emotionality may decrease.

If your partner is less interested in sex than you are, try a little empathy. Instead of taking the rejection personally and pressuring her for more frequent sex, consider the possible reasons for the discrepancy in desire—reasons that may have nothing to do with you. For example, does your partner feel good about the way she looks? Do what you can to make sure she knows how much you love her body the way it is (and if you don't, find ways to change your thinking!). You don't have to lie and say she looks like a *Playboy* centerfold; but you *can* find ways to make her feel good about herself. Say, "I love cuddling with you," or "Your skin feels so soft and smells so good." See the Sexuality section in the references at the back of the book for more detailed strategies and suggestions.

Be sensitive to issues from the past as well as your partner's general frame of mind. Is your partner a survivor of sexual abuse? Were there traumas in her past that make physical intimacy frightening for her? If fear is an issue for your partner, make sure she knows she's safe with you. If depression or past traumas are contributing to any sexual problems in your marriage, consider getting couples' counseling. We'll talk more about this in Chapter 12.

Think about how much work your partner does. Is she perennially exhausted? If she works outside the home, how much responsibility do you assume for cooking, shopping, cleaning, laundry, and childcare? We remember a cartoon with the heading, "What do women want?" The drawing depicted a woman vacuuming; in the bubble above her head, there was a man vacuuming. Brainstorm with your partner to figure out how you can reduce her workload. You'll be amazed by her gratitude.

Your partner's desire to spend time with you doesn't mean that she's either needy or dependent. Don't look for hidden agendas here—take it as the compliment it is! Every couple needs time alone together.

Allow your partner to voice her fears, and support her in her efforts to face new or difficult situations. Women feel empowered by their significant relationships; your caring attitude will contribute to your partner's success in attaining her goals. She doesn't need you to talk her out of her fear, or solve her problem: She just wants you to listen and understand.

Understand that communication is a process. Look at communication problems as an invitation to keep on talking, keep on listening, and eventually work things out. You and your partner may communicate very differently, but the potential is still there to reach ever higher levels of understanding and trust.

Spiritual Sharing Exercise 3: Getting the Myths Out of Your Relationship

In this chapter, we've presented the Seven Deadly Myths About Men and the Seven Deadly Myths About Women. We've shown how these myths can mislead you to erroneous assumptions about your partner's behavior, and have pointed to some alternative explanations of the motivation behind that behavior. By simply reading through the chapter and the examples we've shared, your viewpoints may have changed. You may be interpreting your partner's words and actions in a way that brings you closer together, rather than splitting you apart. We hope so. Below are some questions to move you further along in this process. Read through the questions, answering any relevant ones that interest you. Share your responses with your partner now if you feel comfortable doing so. If not, feel free to wait until you've tackled some of the communication skills in Chapter 6.

Partner 1

1. What was the communication like in your family of origin? Did there tend to be a lot of talking, or were family members typically more on the quiet side? Were there any differences by gender in the way family members communicated? _____

_____

_____

2. What messages have you received about the role of communication? Do you see communication primarily as a vehicle to solve problems, or do you value communication for other purposes as well? _____

_____

_____

3. How were feelings expressed in your family of origin? Was it okay to express feelings directly, or did feelings get stifled? _____

_____

_____

4. Were there differences in how girls and boys in the family were treated? For example, were boys allowed to express sadness or fear? Were girls allowed to express anger? _____

_____

_____

5. Are there experiences in your background that may make it difficult for you to respond sexually? Are you able to talk about these experiences with your partner? _____

_____

_____

6. Do you create a safe and supportive environment in which your partner can talk about your sexual relationship? Or do you act defensive, hurt, or angry as soon as your partner brings up something he or she may want to change? _____

_____

_____

7. How does your partner react after a period of closeness? Does he or she need space afterward? How do you interpret this? _____

_____

_____

8. What could you do to make yourself feel better when your spouse needs some space? _____

_____

_____

9. How do you show your partner that you're feeling fearful or insecure? _____

_____

_____

10. What are your biggest fears? _____

_____

_____

11. How do you react when your partner shows you his or her vulnerable side? How do you feel? _____

_____

_____

12. How did you choose your life's work? Are you satisfied with your career? _____

_____

_____

13. How much pressure do you feel to "support the family," even if your partner also works outside the home? _____

_____

_____

14. How does your partner typically react to your requests for changes in his or her behavior? _____

_____

_____

15. How might you modify the way in which you ask for these changes?

_____

_____

16. Can you think of an example of a change on his or her part? What do you think allowed this to happen? _____

_____

_____

17. How might your socialization (the way you were raised, the effects of culture) affect how you view the role of spirituality in your relationship? _____

_____

_____

18. How might your partner's socialization affect his or her view of the role of spirituality in your relationship? _____

_____

_____

Partner 2

1. What was the communication like in your family of origin? Did there tend to be a lot of talking, or were family members typically more on the quiet side? Were there any differences by gender in the way family members communicated? _____

    _____

    _____

2. What messages have you received about the role of communication? Do you see communication primarily as a vehicle to solve problems, or do you value communication for other purposes as well? _____

    _____

    _____

3. How were feelings expressed in your family of origin? Was it okay to express feelings directly, or did feelings get stifled? _____

    _____

    _____

4. Were there differences in how girls and boys in the family were treated? For example, were boys allowed to express sadness or fear? Were girls allowed to express anger? _____

    _____

    _____

5. Are there experiences in your background that may make it difficult for you to respond sexually? Are you able to talk about these experiences with your partner? _____

    _____

    _____

6. Do you create a safe and supportive environment in which your partner can talk about your sexual relationship? Or do you act defensive, hurt, or angry as soon as your partner brings up something he or she may want to change? _____

    _____

    _____

7. How does your partner react after a period of closeness? Does he or she need space afterward? How do you interpret this? _____

_____

_____

8. What could you do to make yourself feel better when your spouse needs some space? _____

_____

_____

9. How do you show your partner that you're feeling fearful or insecure? _____

_____

_____

10. What are your biggest fears? _____

_____

_____

11. How do you react when your partner shows you his or her vulnerable side? How do you feel? _____

_____

_____

12. How did you choose your life's work? Are you satisfied with your career? _____

_____

_____

13. How much pressure do you feel to "support the family," even if your partner also works outside the home? _____

_____

_____

14. How does your partner typically react to your requests for changes in his or her behavior? _____

_____

_____

15. How might you modify the way in which you ask for these changes?

_____

_____

16. Can you think of an example of a change on his or her part? What do you think allowed this to happen? _____

_____

_____

17. How might your socialization (the way you were raised, the effects of culture) affect how you view the role of spirituality in your relationship? _____

_____

_____

18. How might your partner's socialization affect his or her view of the role of spirituality in your relationship? _____

_____

_____

Some Final Thoughts

We've taken time to review common differences between men and women, to show you how much of what we accept as fact is actually fiction. Most importantly, we've pointed out that our similarities are greater than our differences. *Even though men and women may have different ways of communicating, the longing for spiritual solidarity is genderless.* The quest for meaning and purpose is no different for men than for women, as both must ask the same basic questions: "Who am I?"; "Why am I here?"; and "How can I love more fully?" It is only when you move beyond the myths of gender differences that you'll be able to see your partner's innermost, precious identity. Within the context of a spiritual relationship, you'll come to view your differences not as a chasm between you, but as a bridge that each of you will cross many times in the course of your marriage. One of the beauties of marriage is that your very differences are what allow you to help each other toward healing and wholeness. When your vision is this crystal clear—not marred by false assumptions—you will, indeed, be married to each other heart and soul.

Spotlight on Gender Differences

- Neither men's nor women's style of communication is inherently superior. There is a time to talk, just as there is a time to act. Either style carried to an extreme has limitations. Start with the assumption that both ways of communicating are valid.

- Don't take differences in communication personally—don't think there is something wrong with you, or something wrong with your partner.

- Be patient with each other as you attempt to learn each other's language. You wouldn't expect to learn a foreign language without hard work, would you?

- Apart from gender differences, it's also important to recognize the similarities between men and women. Although you may express yourselves in different ways, both of you have the same basic needs to be loved and accepted, and to feel a sense of meaning in your lives.

Chapter 4

Taking Stock: The Spiritual Marriage Survey

"The way we see the problem is the problem."

—Stephen R. Covey

*M*any of the couples who come to see us can't articulate exactly what's wrong (or even what's right) with their relationship. They may have a vague sense of what's troubling them, but haven't progressed to a point of clarity. Typical comments we hear from these couples include

- "My marriage feels empty."

- "There's no passion left in our relationship."

- "The spark is gone."

- "We don't hate each other. Our relationship just feels flat."

These broad, global generalizations may give us an intuitive feel for the situation, but tell us little about what goals to help these couples set.

An alternative and just as common scenario involves individuals who think they know exactly what the problem is: their spouse. From this group, we hear statements such as

- "If my husband would just talk more, we'd be fine."

- "If my wife would stop nagging me all the time . . ."

Such assessments of the situation ring incomplete, if not incorrect. Relinquishing responsibility for problems in a relationship may leave people feeling justified in their anger, but it prevents them from finding any common ground with their partner.

This chapter presents the Spiritual Marriage Survey, a questionnaire we've designed to help couples see their marriage clearly. It helps identify important strengths in your relationship, as well as pinpoint areas for growth. By completing this survey, you'll evaluate not only where you are, but also where you want to be with regard to sharing a spiritually alive marriage. The survey consists of 27 questions that tap into nine different but overlapping domains:

- Accepting your marriage

- Learning a common spiritual language

- Communicating with care

- Creating meaning and purpose for your marriage

- Soothing each other's soul

- Connecting with community

- Adding spice with celebrations and rituals

- Embracing the inevitable times of drought

- Energizing your relationship with retreats and/or vacations

These areas parallel the remaining chapters in the book.

We've arranged the chapters in logical order: a series of seven steps to follow in your journey, and then two other topics that focus on sustaining your gains. Keep in mind that there are always more ways than one to reach a destination. We encourage you to change the order of the steps to suit your needs as well as those of your partner.

Taking the Spiritual Marriage Survey

Take some time to complete the survey. We've included two identical questionnaires—one for you, and one for your spouse. Fill them out independently. As you take the survey, you'll notice that many of the questions ask you to assess your *own* contributions to the marriage rather than your perceptions of your spouse's contributions. In other words, we're asking you to take a look at *yourself*. You'll also notice that this survey doesn't use any special tricks to conceal the most desirable response, so it's especially important to answer the questions as honestly as possible. After you've completed the survey, we'll discuss what you can learn from it.

Spiritual Marriage Survey

Partner 1

On a scale from 0 to 6, circle the number that you think best applies to you and your relationship. Answer the questions in terms of how your relationship has been in the past few months.

Never			**Sometimes**			**Always**
0	**1**	**2**	**3**	**4**	**5**	**6**

1. I show my partner frequent caring gestures throughout the day.

   0   1   2   3   4   5   6

2. I listen to my partner in a way that engenders openness and trust.

   0   1   2   3   4   5   6

3. I believe there is value in the rough spots of our life together.

   0   1   2   3   4   5   6

4. My partner and I take time to get away from our usual surroundings together.

   0   1   2   3   4   5   6

5. In our relationship, we explore our values and beliefs together.

   0   1   2   3   4   5   6

6. I accept my partner just as he or she is.

   0   1   2   3   4   5   6

7. I know that times of "spiritual drought" are inevitable in any relationship, but that they won't last forever.

   0   1   2   3   4   5   6

8. My partner and I feel part of a community that is meaningful to us.

   0   1   2   3   4   5   6

9. My partner and I regularly spend time together in activities we consider "sacred."

   0   1   2   3   4   5   6

10. I give my partner plenty of affection throughout the day.

    0   1   2   3   4   5   6

11. I believe that our relationship is right where it needs to be at this moment.

    0   1   2   3   4   5   6

12. My parter and I set aside extended time to nurture our relationship.

    0   1   2   3   4   5   6

13. I am comfortable praying/meditating/quietly reflecting with my partner.

    0   1   2   3   4   5   6

14. I have a vocabulary of words related to spirituality from which to draw.

    0   1   2   3   4   5   6

15. My partner and I each have meaningful friendships with others both individually and as a couple.

    0   1   2   3   4   5   6

16. I feel a sense of respect for my partner's work and life goals, and I communicate this to him or her in words and attitude.

    0   1   2   3   4   5   6

17. I believe that our relationship is filled with meaning and purpose.

    0   1   2   3   4   5   6

18. I have a vocabulary of feeling words.

    0   1   2   3   4   5   6

19. My partner and I value time away from our usual roles and routines.

    0   1   2   3   4   5   6

20. I work to resolve conflict in a way that is productive, not hurtful.

    0   1   2   3   4   5   6

21. I understand and tolerate differences between my partner and myself.

    0   1   2   3   4   5   6

22. My partner and I agree on what's important in our lives.

    0   1   2   3   4   5   6

23. I think of little ways to surprise my spouse, to make his or her day better.

    0   1   2   3   4   5   6

24. My partner and I have strong connections with extended family.

    0   1   2   3   4   5   6

25. I feel comfortable talking about spirituality with my spouse.

    0   1   2   3   4   5   6

26. My partner and I share meaningful rituals and celebrations.

    0   1   2   3   4   5   6

27. The struggles in our marriage bring us closer together.

    0   1   2   3   4   5   6

Spiritual Marriage Survey

Partner 2

On a scale from 0 to 6, circle the number that you think best applies to you and your relationship. Answer the questions in terms of how your relationship has been in the past few months.

Never			**Sometimes**			**Always**
0	**1**	**2**	**3**	**4**	**5**	**6**

1. I show my partner frequent caring gestures throughout the day.

| 0 | 1 | 2 | 3 | 4 | 5 | 6 |

2. I listen to my partner in a way that engenders openness and trust.

| 0 | 1 | 2 | 3 | 4 | 5 | 6 |

3. I believe there is value in the rough spots of our life together.

| 0 | 1 | 2 | 3 | 4 | 5 | 6 |

4. My partner and I take time to get away from our usual surroundings together.

| 0 | 1 | 2 | 3 | 4 | 5 | 6 |

5. In our relationship, we explore our values and beliefs together.

| 0 | 1 | 2 | 3 | 4 | 5 | 6 |

6. I accept my partner just as he or she is.

| 0 | 1 | 2 | 3 | 4 | 5 | 6 |

7. I know that times of "spiritual drought" are inevitable in any relationship, but that they won't last forever.

| 0 | 1 | 2 | 3 | 4 | 5 | 6 |

8. My partner and I feel part of a community that is meaningful to us.

| 0 | 1 | 2 | 3 | 4 | 5 | 6 |

9. My partner and I spend regular time together in activities we consider "sacred."

| 0 | 1 | 2 | 3 | 4 | 5 | 6 |

10. I give my partner plenty of affection throughout the day.

| 0 | 1 | 2 | 3 | 4 | 5 | 6 |

11. I believe that our relationship is right where it needs to be at this moment.

| 0 | 1 | 2 | 3 | 4 | 5 | 6 |

12. My partner and I set aside extended time to nurture our relationship.

| 0 | 1 | 2 | 3 | 4 | 5 | 6 |

13. I am comfortable praying/meditating/quietly reflecting with my partner.

    0   1   2   3   4   5   6

14. I have a vocabulary of words related to spirituality from which to draw.

    0   1   2   3   4   5   6

15. My partner and I each have meaningful friendships with others both individually and as a couple.

    0   1   2   3   4   5   6

16. I feel a sense of respect for my partner's work and life goals, and communicate this to him or her in my words and attitude.

    0   1   2   3   4   5   6

17. I believe that our relationship is filled with meaning and purpose.

    0   1   2   3   4   5   6

18. I have a vocabulary of feeling words.

    0   1   2   3   4   5   6

19. My partner and I value time away from our usual roles and routines.

    0   1   2   3   4   5   6

20. I work to resolve conflict in a way that is productive, not hurtful.

    0   1   2   3   4   5   6

21. I understand and tolerate differences between my partner and myself.

    0   1   2   3   4   5   6

22. My partner and I agree on what's important in our lives.

    0   1   2   3   4   5   6

23. I think of little ways to surprise my spouse, to make his or her day better.

    0   1   2   3   4   5   6

24. My partner and I have strong connections with extended family.

    0   1   2   3   4   5   6

25. I feel comfortable talking about spirituality with my spouse.

    0   1   2   3   4   5   6

26. My partner and I share meaningful rituals and celebrations.

    0   1   2   3   4   5   6

27. The struggles in our marriage bring us closer together.

    0   1   2   3   4   5   6

Adding Up Your Scores

Transfer your ratings for each of the questions into the corresponding boxes below. Add up your scores for the three questions to determine your total score for that domain. Then use these scores to fill out the graph on the next page.

Partner 1

Accepting your marriage ☐ Q06 ☐ Q11 ☐ Q21 ☐ Total

Communicating with care ☐ Q02 ☐ Q16 ☐ Q20 ☐ Total

Learning a spiritual language ☐ Q14 ☐ Q18 ☐ Q25 ☐ Total

Meaning and purpose ☐ Q05 ☐ Q17 ☐ Q22 ☐ Total

Soothing each other's soul ☐ Q01 ☐ Q10 ☐ Q23 ☐ Total

Connecting with community ☐ Q08 ☐ Q15 ☐ Q24 ☐ Total

Adding spice with rituals ☐ Q09 ☐ Q13 ☐ Q26 ☐ Total

Embracing times of drought ☐ Q03 ☐ Q07 ☐ Q27 ☐ Total

Energizing with retreats ☐ Q04 ☐ Q12 ☐ Q19 ☐ Total

Partner 2

Accepting your marriage ☐ Q06 ☐ Q11 ☐ Q21 ☐ Total

Communicating with care ☐ Q02 ☐ Q16 ☐ Q20 ☐ Total

Learning a spiritual language ☐ Q14 ☐ Q18 ☐ Q25 ☐ Total

Meaning and purpose ☐ Q05 ☐ Q17 ☐ Q22 ☐ Total

Soothing each other's soul ☐ Q01 ☐ Q10 ☐ Q23 ☐ Total

Connecting with community ☐ Q08 ☐ Q15 ☐ Q24 ☐ Total

Adding spice with rituals ☐ Q09 ☐ Q13 ☐ Q26 ☐ Total

Embracing times of drought ☐ Q03 ☐ Q07 ☐ Q27 ☐ Total

Energizing with retreats ☐ Q04 ☐ Q12 ☐ Q19 ☐ Total

Spiritual Marriage Survey
Pattern of Results, Partner 1

Put a dot in the center of each box in which your score occurs, then connect the dots.

	0	1	2	3	4	5	6	7	8	9	10	11	12	13	14	15	16	17	18
Acceptance																			
Communicating with care																			
Spiritual language																			
Meaning and purpose																			
Soothing each other's soul																			
Connecting with community																			
Celebrations and rituals																			
Embracing times of drought																			
Spiritual retreats																			

Spiritual Marriage Survey
Pattern of Results, Partner 2

Put a dot in the center of each box in which your score occurs, then connect the dots.

	0	1	2	3	4	5	6	7	8	9	10	11	12	13	14	15	16	17	18
Acceptance																			
Communicating with care																			
Spiritual language																			
Meaning and purpose																			
Soothing each other's soul																			
Connecting with community																			
Celebrations and rituals																			
Embracing times of drought																			
Spiritual retreats																			

What Can You Learn from the Survey?

By plotting your scores on the graphs, you've created a visual image of your spiritual relationship as it is today: You can see what areas you and your partner share as strengths; you can see where you might benefit from growth and development. Let's briefly describe the dimensions you've just assessed. Keep in mind that the remaining chapters of the book address each of these topics more fully.

Accept your marriage. This step requires you to see your relationship exactly as it is, without demanding or expecting anything different. Acceptance is an attitude that shows appreciation and tolerance for your partner's uniqueness.

Communicate with care. Communicating with care means learning to listen and truly understand, expressing yourself in a way that respects your partner's feelings, and resolving conflict constructively. Care-bolstered communication engenders an openness, trust, and respect that can unite people in profound ways.

Learn a common spiritual language. This step involves listening to the "spirit within" to hear what your heart and soul are saying: It requires having a vocabulary of words—particularly "feeling words"—to describe your experience.

Create meaning for your marriage. Exploring core beliefs and values with your partner will help create a shared mission for you and your partner in your marriage.

Soothe each other's soul. Strengthening the spiritual bond of your marriage requires regular attention to your partner's spirit or soul. You must nurture your partner's growth, offer encouragement in his or her pursuits, and show affection and caring throughout each day.

Connect with community. A spiritual marriage doesn't thrive in a vacuum. Connection with community sustains the vitality of a marriage. Couples benefit greatly from close relationships with family, friends, and a community of people who share their interests, concerns, and beliefs.

Add spice with celebrations and rituals. This step shows how couples can create meaningful rituals and celebrations to crystallize the meaning of their marriage. It also emphasizes the need for "sacred time" together to sustain the spirit of the marriage.

Embracing the inevitable times of drought. Individuals in a vital marriage expect spiritual setbacks—times when the marriage feels lifeless and dull—and use these times as opportunities for growth and learning.

Energizing your relationship with retreats and/or vacations. Every couple needs extended time to rejuvenate the relationship and rekindle the spark that brought the members of the couple together in the first place.

By completing the survey, you've shone a light on your relationship, a light that will illuminate your way as you take the essential steps toward a more spiritual marriage.

Spiritual Sharing Exercise 4: Discussing the Survey Results

After you and your partner have taken the survey, set aside some time to talk over the results and answer the questions below. If possible, plan a time when you won't be disturbed, and when neither of you is apt to be tired or preoccupied. The purpose of this discussion is to gather information; you're not trying to solve problems or persuade your partner of anything. Remember—there are no right or wrong answers: The results reflect your perceptions and opinions only. Don't look for a winner here—which of you is more "spiritually adept." The idea is simply to get a snapshot of where you are now, and where you might want to go.

Some questions to help you structure your discussion follow below. Also take a look at the Spotlight box for some further suggestions.

1. What strengths do you share? (These are the places on the graphs in which both your scores in a given domain are toward the right-hand side.)

2. What growth areas do you have in common? (These are the places on the graphs in which both your scores in a given domain are toward the left-hand side.)

3. In what areas did you and your partner score quite differently? Look at the individual questions that contribute to the total score. Were you interpreting the meaning of the questions differently, or are you each at very different places here? What does this tell you about opportunities to help each other grow?

4. Do you view any of the areas as more relevant to your relationship than others? Has there been any change over time as to what areas you consider most relevant, or most important?

Some Final Thoughts

At this point, you've amply prepared yourself for a more spiritual union by

- Learning about some of the qualities of a spiritual marriage

- Being exposed to a method for transforming obstacles into opportunities

- Exploring differences between men and women as they relate to human emotions, communication, and spirituality

- Assessing the spiritual qualities of your marriage

By taking the Spiritual Marriage Survey, you've created a snapshot of your relationship in nine essential areas. Cherish not only the strengths you share, but also the weaknesses. It's counterintuitive to what you may have been taught to believe about weakness or personal shortcomings, but it is these very imperfections that contain the kernels of hope and the promise of a new beginning for your marriage.

Spotlight on the Spiritual Marriage Survey

- Express appreciation to your partner for sharing his or her survey results with you, especially if your partner revealed any personal vulnerabilities.

- Adopt an attitude of "compassionate curiosity" (a phrase coined by Daphne Rose Kingma). Find out what your partner was thinking when he or she answered a question; do your best to withhold judgment.

- Take turns talking without interrupting each other. The listener may want to paraphrase what the other person said to ensure accurate understanding.

- If any tension arises, take a break. If significant conflict breaks out, postpone this discussion until you've mastered the communication skills in Chapter 6.

PART II

The Essential Steps

Chapter 5

Step 1: Accept Your Marriage

"Acceptance is the only way out of hell."

—Marsha Linehan

We'd worked with Dan and Marlena for only two sessions. A couple in their mid-thirties, they sought counseling after Marlena suffered a fourth-month miscarriage. After completing the Spiritual Marriage Survey, Marlena was eager to get started with the "real" therapy. She took the feedback we'd shared with them seriously, and had generated a list of things she wanted to do with Dan. The list went on for nearly two pages, and included such things as: "plan some sacred couple-time each week; invite Cindy and Rob over—they seem to have a strong marriage, and are interested in similar things; write a mission statement for our marriage; start a support group at the hospital for other couples who've experienced a miscarriage; plan some sort of memorial service for our baby." Although it's certainly gratifying to have a client show such enthusiasm and initiative, we had to slow Marlena down a bit, for she was rushing ahead of herself, and ahead of Dan.

In this chapter, you'll read more about Marlena and Dan, and you'll learn the importance of not rushing to "fix" everything. Although we've written this book with the idea of change in mind—how you can improve and enrich your marriage—the strategies of change must be carefully blended and balanced with the art of acceptance. To shape a spiritual marriage, you must learn how to accept seemingly unsolvable situations, and how to utilize these situations as pathways rather than barriers to intimacy.

The Art of Acceptance

Imagine for a minute that you're driving to an important meeting when you blow out a tire. You can curse your fate, kick the tire, cry and whine, but the fact remains that your tire is flat. If you don't accept that reality, you won't take the necessary steps to deal with the situation effectively (fix the tire, call to say you'll be late) and reduce your distress. In this example, it's relatively easy to see the adaptiveness of acceptance. Oftentimes, however, the notion of acceptance seems counterintuitive to everything you've been taught. Western culture, in particular, preaches that if you refuse to accept something, and put your foot down, the situation will magically change. We tell someone who's depressed to "snap out of it." We admonish someone struggling to lose weight to "use willpower." We treat ourselves and our loved ones as a dictator would: "Hurry up and change!" is the message we send. Let's look more closely at what acceptance is, what it isn't, and why it's so important.

Acceptance Is an Attitude

Acceptance is posture toward life, involving a willingness and an openness to see things as they are, without expecting anything to be different. A keen awareness of the adventuresome nature of life is crucial to this attitude: You can't predict what will happen, you can't control what will happen, you can't will things to be different than they are. Sure, change is possible, but it doesn't typically go according to the schedule you might try to set. The crux of acceptance is not to ask, "How dare this be?" but rather, "What can I learn from this?"

Let's return to Marlena and Dan's story to see how an accepting attitude was crucial to their relationship as they coped with the loss of Marlena's pregnancy. They'd consciously chosen to delay starting their family until their careers were more settled. Now that the time was right in terms of their careers, they worried that they'd waited too long. The first trimester was rough; but once she reached the second trimester, Marlena had felt much better, and started to relax about the baby. Unfortunately, she miscarried just into the sixteenth week, and had to be taken to the hospital for emergency care. The weeks following the miscarriage were understandably difficult. Marlena questioned herself about everything she'd done during the pregnancy. While she obsessed about what had gone wrong, Dan buried himself in his work, attempting to distract himself from his painful feelings. Becoming increasingly estranged, they sought counseling a short time later.

As we mentioned at the outset of this chapter, Marlena had grown more optimistic after taking the Spiritual Marriage Survey. She wanted to try many new things to bolster their marriage. While her ideas were great, we believed she was moving too fast. She had gone from the depths of depression to acting almost manic in too short a time. We felt that she was frantically trying to bind or limit her anxiety and pain. She was also moving much too fast for Dan's comfort. Yes, they had assessed their marriage and determined some areas that would benefit from improvement, but they didn't have to do it all at once. In fact, moving too fast bypassed the important first step of developing an attitude of acceptance.

As we reviewed the list Marlena had developed, Dan acknowledged his discomfort with many of the things she had written. He said, "How can we start a support group when we haven't even begun to deal with our own grief? I'm simply not ready for that." Marlena was angry at first. She told us privately, "Dan doesn't care about our marriage or about the baby we've lost. He just wants to go on with his life as if nothing has changed." We asked Dan and Marlena to review the list again, and pick only one thing they'd feel comfortable trying. They agreed that they needed some way to grieve the loss of the pregnancy *together*. Marlena knew about a memorial service at the hospital chapel, but Dan said he'd be uncomfortable expressing his grief in a public, group setting. He said he'd rather do something more personal, just Marlena and him. They agreed that by the next session, they'd have brainstormed for some ideas.

When we saw them again in a few weeks, they'd not only come up with some ideas, they'd already followed through with one of them. They'd decorated a shoe box with some pretty wrapping paper, and inside they placed mementos they had of the baby: cards from friends and family; an ultrasound photograph; Marlena's hospital identification bracelet; a book of baby names with their favorite names highlighted. They held hands while they shared with each other the dreams they'd had for the baby. Then, a few days later, Dan surprised Marlena: He brought home a small dogwood tree for them to plant in their backyard in memory of the baby.

These events began the couple's healing process. They shared their pain, and they gradually began accepting the fact that they didn't know all the answers. They didn't know why the miscarriage occurred; in all likelihood, they never would. Although Marlena's mother told her it must have been "God's will," Marlena wasn't convinced. She stopped questioning herself so much, though, and she stopped blaming herself. She and Dan felt proud of how they'd handled the loss and how it eventually brought them closer together.

Acceptance Does Not Mean Approval

Too often, the importance of acceptance is dismissed because it's equated with approval. It's presumed that if you accept something, you're passively giving up—not trying anymore. Psychology has focused almost exclusively on developing techniques of change, paying little attention to the value that comes from learning to accept and tolerate distress. Recently, some psychologists have reversed this trend. Neal Jacobson, Ph.D., now incorporates the idea of acceptance into his counseling work with couples. Similarly, Marsha Linehan, Ph.D., integrates Eastern practices of meditation and "mindfulness" into her therapy with suicidal and other seriously disturbed individuals.

Our work with Carrie centered around this distinction between acceptance and approval. Carrie, married for five years, came to see us stating that her husband, Bob, drank too much; but, try as she might, she couldn't make him realize how much his drinking was affecting their relationship. She wanted suggestions from us on how to make him change. We knew Carrie was in pain, and we wished we could give her an easy answer. There wasn't anything easy about her situation, however, and we knew she wasn't going to like what we had to say. We suggested that she focus on herself, not her husband. We wanted her to begin to take better care of herself. She'd been running herself ragged, chasing after Bob at all hours of the night, trying to make sure he wasn't at a bar too drunk to drive home. We also suggested she attend an Al-Anon meeting, a support group for family members and friends of alcoholics. She agreed, and attended several meetings. When she came back for her next session, she said: "I don't get it. These women just *let* their husbands drink. They don't even try to stop them anymore. What good does giving them a stamp of approval do?"

Support groups like Alcoholics Anonymous and Al-Anon have long realized that acceptance doesn't mean approval. Members of such groups routinely recite the *Serenity Prayer:* "God, grant me the serenity to accept the things I cannot change, the courage to change the things I can, and the wisdom to know the difference." What Carrie hadn't yet realized was that Bob's drinking fell under the category of "things I cannot change." Bob would not—*could not*—stop drinking until *he* was ready. Over the next few months, we helped Carrie continue to decipher the difference between approval and acceptance. She didn't have to approve of Bob's drinking or the way he acted when he was drunk; she did need to accept, however, that whether or not he drank was his choice, not hers.

In adopting a more accepting attitude toward her husband, Carrie began to change her general demeanor toward him. She started to think about all the reasons why Bob drank—not in an attempt to make excuses for his behavior, but as a way to understand what prevented his changing. She grew less angry and more compassionate toward him. Bob's father had been an alcoholic, so she knew there was probably a strong genetic pull in that direction. She also knew he'd had a rough life—one of his brothers had committed suicide a few years ago, and Bob had never really recovered. She stopped criticizing him and complaining about his drinking. At the same time, she started taking better care of herself. She continued to go to Al-Anon meetings, and made some friends with whom she went to the movies occasionally. She didn't drive to the bars anymore to check up on Bob. She took a class on self-esteem at the community college. As Carrie strove to accept Bob unconditionally, his drinking actually diminished somewhat. In effect, acceptance from Carrie seemed to free Bob to begin making changes in his life.

We'd love to tell you that Bob quit drinking altogether, and that everything worked out for him and Carrie, but it didn't happen that way. Carrie had come a long way in accepting Bob, and this was an important beginning. She had also come a long way in accepting that her own needs weren't being met in the marriage, and that they weren't likely to be met anytime in the near future. The couple eventually divorced, which was probably the best thing for Carrie. We doubt whether she would've been able to take this step, however, had she not first given up the clenched-fist fight of trying to change her husband.

Acceptance Helps You Transcend Suffering

Perhaps the greatest value in learning the art of acceptance is that it alleviates unnecessary suffering. We're not saying you won't feel any more pain, because you will; but the kind of acceptance we're talking about can lead you to peace amidst pain, calm in the center of chaos, serenity in spite of suffering. Does this sound too good to be true? In a way, it is, because acceptance doesn't simply happen overnight.

We wrestled with this matter of acceptance in a most personal way for the first three years of our son's life. As we've mentioned before, Jesse has had a multitude of health problems. One of our major concerns was his chronic vomiting. When he was an infant, our pediatrician reassured us that his "spitting up" was normal. Since this was our first child, we had no way to compare how much (buckets) or how often (after every meal) was normal. We had an inkling that his vomiting was somewhat unusual when we saw others' horrified reactions as they witnessed the event. When we began introducing solid foods, we hoped the vomiting would stop. Unfortunately, the situation grew worse: Jesse stopped gaining weight at nine months, and started losing weight about the time of his first birthday.

Overwrought with worry after a particularly difficult weekend, we decided the time had come (perhaps we'd waited too long) to change pediatricians. Our new pediatrician took the matter seriously, completed extensive testing, and made the diagnosis of *gastroesophageal reflux*. We hoped an end was near when Jesse began taking a medicine frequently prescribed to treat reflux. To our dismay, however, the first medicine didn't work. We tried many other medicines: None of them worked. He still vomited daily—often several times a day.

This wasn't the way we'd envisioned our life with our firstborn child. In addition to our worry about his physical health, this problem greatly diminished our quality of life. It was a major challenge to get ready in the morning. Many times we'd be walking out the door when Jesse would vomit on himself and on at least one of us, sending us back to the bathtub. More than once he threw up on the dog. We didn't go out much socially—it's hard to find a baby-sitter mature enough to deal with this situation. We stayed awake all night listening for sounds of vomiting (he often did it when he was in bed). We spent hours and hours theorizing about what was wrong with him. We went to medical libraries, and read anything that might apply.

During one office visit, the doctor spent a lot of time with us (something quite rare in a busy pediatric practice) and gave us a good heart-to-heart talk. He told us that we had to accept Jesse's vomiting—we should stop fighting it.

It wasn't life-threatening at this point, he said; Jesse's weight had stabilized. The only thing to do was wait until he outgrew the problem. This wasn't what we'd hoped to hear. We wanted the problem fixed, solved, ended. How could we go on dealing with a child who vomited on a daily basis? Somehow, though, the doctor's message of acceptance sank in. We realized we weren't being fair to ourselves, or Jesse. We had restricted our life too much. The doctor was right: We had to start living, in spite of the vomiting.

What did acceptance involve for us? First, it meant grieving. We cried. We allowed ourselves to feel sad. As much as we'd tried to gain control of the problem, it was still out of our control. Next, we "let go" of trying to prevent the vomiting. If he was going to vomit, so be it. We started getting out of the house more, carrying a bucket and changes of clothes wherever we went. We praised each other when we calmly handled a tough situation (We vividly remember the rainy Halloween night when he started to vomit while trick-or-treating at the shopping mall—how we quickly dumped the candy he had already collected onto the floor so the pumpkin-shaped bucket would be "available.") We laughed about our situation a bit more. We impressed ourselves with our ability to clean up vomit one minute and eat dinner the next. We supported each other, and sought support from friends and family whenever possible.

As we accepted the situation, little by little, our suffering diminished. We handled things better, we enjoyed Jesse more, we were more relaxed. This attitude of acceptance carried with it other benefits: Our thinking gained clarity, and we trusted ourselves more. We knew it could not be healthy for anyone, much less someone so young, to vomit so much. Another year and a half had passed, and he'd still not outgrown the problem. When we asked our pediatrician for a consultation, he continued to assert that it probably wasn't a big deal, and he even suggested that we might have "conditioned" Jesse to vomit. The doctor nonetheless referred us to a pediatric gastroenterologist for another opinion. After another round of more invasive tests, the GI specialist found nothing conclusive. Next, we saw a psychologist who specialized in working with children and their parents. Was it possible that the doctor was right, that we'd subtly reinforced our son's vomiting? Was he doing this to gain attention—to manipulate us? The psychologist didn't think so, and she encouraged us to continue seeking medical answers.

Two weeks after his third birthday, Jesse was awake all night coughing and vomiting. When we took him to the doctor's office the next morning, we saw an associate of our regular pediatrician. She noticed that Jesse was having difficulty breathing, and hospitalized him. The next morning, the same doctor visited us in his room. She said, "I reviewed Jesse's chart from front to back, and I believe I know what's wrong with him: He has asthma and probably severe allergies." Looking back on it now, we're amazed that no one had mentioned this as a possibility to us before. (In fact, one of the theories we'd developed ourselves had to do with allergies, but Jesse's first pediatrician saw no validity in it.) Jesse received intensive treatment for his asthma while in the hospital, and continues to take breathing treatments three times a day. He's doing much better now, vomiting only rarely when his asthma or allergies flare up.

As you can see, acceptance doesn't come quickly or easily. It's a process, much in the way in which grieving someone's death is a process. Only after you go through the shock, the denial, the anger, and the despair can you move forward with a spirit of patience and trust. Practicing the art of acceptance taught us to seek answers, while at the same time tolerating uncertainty. We couldn't control what was happening in Jesse's body. We couldn't force the medical professionals to take us seriously. We couldn't change or control any of the events. All we could do was to take charge (somewhat) of our reactions to those events. Each new twist and turn, each new sign and symptom, presented us with an opportunity to embrace the paradox of suffering. We found a poignant quote by a twentieth-century philosopher, D. T. Suzuki: "Unless we agree to suffer, we cannot be free from suffering."

The Adversaries of Acceptance

We hope the examples we've shared so far have given you at least a glimmer of what acceptance is all about. You may still wonder what stands in the way of an accepting attitude, or how acceptance can be practiced in the real world. We'll offer some answers to these questions in the next section.

The Number One Foe: Fear

Oftentimes, you may balk at acceptance because you're afraid. You fear that if you let your guard down, and stop your endless worrying, a situation will worsen. You'll do anything to avoid your fears; and, in so doing, you give them greater power over you. But fear isn't something you need to run from: It's a great alarm system, warning you that something's not right. You must, however, use the system properly. (Don't do as we sometimes do and remove the battery from the smoke detector because you don't like the noise it makes when the kitchen gets smoky.) Typically, people either ignore fear's warning signals until it's too late to respond appropriately, or they exaggerate the danger out of proportion to reality. Neither extreme leads to acceptance.

To understand what we mean, try this: Form an image in your mind of what it is that you want to change—in other words, what you're having difficulty accepting. For example, Carrie wanted her husband to stop drinking; she wasn't accepting that drinking was his choice. We wanted Jesse to stop vomiting; we weren't accepting that we had no control over the matter. Imagine now that some freak accident of nature has released a harmless but potent gas into the atmosphere. This gas makes it impossible for the very thing you want to occur to occur. You realize that this gas has been released and that there's no way to reverse its effects. Take some time to immerse yourself in this imagery, and then play out the worst-case scenario. (Carrie's worst-case scenario was: "Bob continues to drink, he drinks himself to death, and I'm left all alone." Ours was: "Jesse will vomit every day, three times a day, for his entire life, and we'll all go crazy.") After you've imagined your worst fear in all its gloomy and graphic detail, think about these questions: Now that you know that whatever it is won't change, how will you choose to live your life? Will you continue to beat your head against the wall, demanding that things be different? Or will you find a way to change the way you handle the situation? What might you learn from having to tolerate the situation? How can you cope better? How can you take better care of yourself? If you weren't worrying so much about whatever it is how else would you expend your energy? By mustering the courage to confront in your mind your worst fears, your anxiety will subside as you grow more accustomed to the scenario. For example, in doing this exercise, Carrie realized that in many ways, she was already alone. Bob might be there physically; but, emotionally and spiritually, he wasn't there for her. This realization helped her become less fearful of aloneness, and find new ways to care for herself in Bob's absence.

Fear's usefulness as an alarm system also diminishes when you allow yourself to get caught in the vicious cycle of worrisome thoughts: "What if Bob gets into an accident after he's done playing pool at the bar?"; "What if Jesse becomes even sicker while we're out of town for the weekend?" Worry is counterproductive to an accepting attitude, and actually prevents constructive change from taking place. But anyone who's ever worried—*really worried*—knows how hard it is to shut off those thoughts. Here's something else to try: Make a date to worry. Schedule a specific time when you're going to do all your serious worrying. When an upsetting thought pops into your mind, save it for your "worry time." Pioneer worry expert Thomas Borkovec has actually done research on this technique, and found that half an hour each day yields good results. The idea is to worry *hard* during the allotted half hour. If you decide after 15 minutes that your worries are silly, or you'd rather be doing something else, don't stop! What does "worry time" do? It puts you back in the driver's seat of when, where, and for how long you worry.

Another technique we've found helpful for some people is the use of coping statements. (We first mentioned coping statements in Chapter 2.) Write out a coping statement related to what you're trying to accept, memorize it, and repeat it frequently throughout the day. For example:

> *I accept (partner's behavior) as a part of my life today. This doesn't mean I approve of (partner's behavior), but I can tolerate it, learn from it, grow from it. I can take steps to care for myself, and, in so doing, take pressure off my partner. If (partner's behavior) endangers me in any way, I will choose to remove myself from the situation.*

Make sure the coping statement you devise is realistic. Notice that in the example above, there are no promises or guarantees that everything will turn out perfectly. We occasionally find people misusing coping statements. They try to counter their fears with statments such as, "Everything's going to work out the way I want. Everything will be fine." This is not only unrealistic, it's too vague to be of much use. Although coping statements may seem simplistic to some people the technique has proven its worth to countless others. With regular and proper use, coping statements can become quite integrated into your thinking process, and can really help cut down on your fears.

Enemy Number Two: Lack of Empathy

Sometimes it can seem like a chore to manufacture an accepting attitude toward your partner. People are often so focused on themselves and their own needs that they fail to empathize with their partner's position—they fail to see that most people do the best they can with the resources they have available to them. In *Couple Skills*, authors Matthew McKay, Ph.D., Patrick Fanning, and Kim Paleg, Ph.D., write: "At any given time, you can be sure that your partner is doing his or her best to survive: seeking pleasure, avoiding pain or loss or danger, meeting needs, compensating for past painful experiences, and so on. Your partner's actions may not always be the most effective or reasonable solutions to the problem of survival, but that proves rather than denies your partner's essential humanity." We liked one of the exercises in their book, and asked their permission to include it here. In the space below, write down a behavior that your partner engages in that bothers you. Then answer the subsequent questions.

Behavior that bothers me:

1. How does this behavior help my partner seek pleasure? _____

_____

_____

2. How does this behavior help my partner avoid pain? _____

_____

_____

3. What need is my partner trying to meet? _____

_____

_____

4. How can I help my partner meet this need? _____

_____

_____

5. What past experience makes my partner likely to do this? _____

_____

_____

6. How can I minimize the effect of this behavior on me? _____

_____

_____

Let's look at how Marlena completed this exercise. Remember, she'd been upset because Dan had worked such long hours after she miscarried—she surmized that he didn't care about her, or about what had happened. Below we show you how she answered the questions.

Behavior that bothers me: *Dan buries himself in his work when I need his emotional support.*

1. How does this behavior help my partner seek pleasure?

   Dan enjoys his work and receives a lot of positive feedback from his co-workers.

2. How does this behavior help my partner avoid pain?

   When he's so busy with work, he doesn't have as much time to dwell on his feelings.

3. What need is my partner trying to meet?

   A need to control; and a need for things to make sense.

4. How can I help my partner meet this need?

   I can let him grieve in his own way, and at his own pace. I can invite him to share his feelings, but not pressure him to do so.

5. What past experience makes my partner likely to do this?

   He wasn't raised in a family that was emotionally expressive. His father tended to be a workaholic.

6. How can I minimize the effect of this behavior on me?

   I can reassure myself that Dan is not doing this to be cruel. He's doing the best that he can with what he has. I can sometimes reach out to other people when I need to talk.

By completing this exercise, Marlena was better able to see the situation from Dan's perspective. It wasn't that he didn't care about her, he was simply unable to show his caring in the precise way she needed. She removed the negative intention she'd assigned to his behavior, and quit blaming him for withdrawing. Instead, she sought to understand the underlying reasons for his behavior. By empathizing with him, she was able to accept him more completely. This acceptance, born of compassion for her husband's unexpressed pain, allowed him the freedom to be where he needed to be. The paradox of acceptance held true: Marlena's acceptance of Dan's emotional withdrawal actually led to increased sharing and closeness between them. She never would have dreamed that he'd think of a gesture so lovely as planting a tree in remembrance of their lost baby.

The Final Injury: Impatience

If you're like many people (ourselves included), you're probably in a hurry to mend what you perceive is wrong with your marriage. Why bother with acceptance, when what you really want is change? This impatience is understandable—you've suffered long enough. Bypassing the step of acceptance, however, won't end your suffering any sooner. Only when you wait quietly and patiently can you glean the knowledge you need. You can't solve a problem without first taking the time to find out what's wrong. (Imagine a doctor writing a prescription without first waiting for the patient to explain the symptoms.) Most people aren't taught to be patient. They believe that they're not doing anything constructive while they're merely waiting. The type of patience required isn't passive: It's patience with a purpose, or, as D. Patrick Miller writes, "Patience is waiting with intention." You have to learn to wait with the intention of illuminating your heart with wisdom and understanding.

Caitlin and Jim, a couple who came to see us in an effort to resolve a sexual problem, had to contend with the meaning of patience. Over the past several years, they'd argued frequently about how often they had sex. Jim wanted to make love every night, while Caitlin was content with a couple of times a week. Although they enjoyed good communication in other areas, when it came to talking about sex, tact went out the window. Prior to seeking counseling, they'd tried to resolve the problem on their own. Caitlin talked with several of her girlfriends about the problem. She'd also read numerous books on the subject of sexuality, and she read erotica in an effort to raise her desire level. As she phrased it, "I've tried to sort out all my own issues about sex, but it hasn't gotten us anywhere." Jim had also talked with his friends. He knew that having sex each and every night wasn't the norm, but he didn't care: He wanted his and Caitlin's sex life to be fantastic, mind-blowing.

After their own efforts hadn't helped, they came to see us. Although therapy helped diffuse some of the tension that had built up, Caitlin and Jim still reached an impasse on this issue. It seemed that the more they tried to fix the problem, the more their frustration mounted. For all their hard work, they only argued more. After we discussed the process taking place, we all agreed that they needed a break from therapy. Putting the issue on hold seemed to be the best thing they could do. They needed to wait patiently for some new information, some new understanding to surface. Although it was a tall order, Caitlin and Jim began to realize that there was something they still needed to learn from their difficult situation. At the time they ended therapy with us, they felt more comfortable with the fact that they didn't have all the answers.

A few months later, we received a call from Caitlin. She told us that although their differences were not completely resolved, their accepting attitude had allowed them to feel less pressure about the whole sex issue, and they were growing closer.

Caitlin and Jim demonstrated more patience than most, and we believe that their accepting attitude went a long way toward helping them find harmony as a married couple. It's human nature to grow weary of the puzzles of our lives: We want the pieces to fit together perfectly, with little or no work. Like anything of value, however, patience must be practiced. But how do you practice patience? Perhaps the best way is to recognize the signs of your impatience. Make check marks below next to any of the signals that sound familiar to you.

Thoughts such as

☐   *I can't stand this any longer!*

☐   *This isn't fair!*

☐   *If something doesn't change soon, I'm going to crack.*

Behaviors such as

☐   *Clock-watching*

☐   *Rushing around*

☐   *Acting angry or irritable*

☐   *Doing anything compulsively (eating, shopping . . .)*

Physical complaints (agitation in general), such as

☐   *Tension/muscle soreness*

☐   *Headaches/stomachaches*

☐   *Insomnia*

Once you notice your impatience, what then? The next step is to embrace your impatience. Allow yourself to be human, imperfect. It may sound like we're contradicting ourselves: Don't be impatient; embrace your impatience. It's that old paradox again. If you acknowledge your impatience, you're free to open yourself up to a more willing attitude—a willingness to be patient.

Perhaps we can best explain this notion of turning your mind toward acceptance—of allowing yourself the possibility that you can be patient toward all that is unresolved in your heart—by sharing a quote from Gerald May's book, *Will and Spirit:*

"Willingness implies a surrendering of one's self-separateness, an entering into, an immersion in the deepest processes of life itself. It is a realization that one already is a part of some ultimate cosmic process and it is a commitment to that process. In contrast, willfulness is setting oneself apart from the fundamental essence of life in an attempt to master, direct, control, or otherwise manipulate existence. More simply, willingness is saying yes to the mystery of being alive in each moment. Willfulness is saying no, or perhaps more commonly, 'yes, but . . .'"

Spiritual Sharing Exercise 5: Learning From Past Experiences of Acceptance

We've all had to accept things in our lives that weren't easy to deal with: the loss of a parent, a debilitating injury or illness, a financial crisis. In this exercise, we want you and your partner to share the wisdom you've accumulated from your past experiences with acceptance. Don't worry if you're thinking to yourself: "I've never accepted anything gracefully. I can't think of a positive example to share." No one accepts hardship gracefully at first; it's natural to cycle through periods of shock, denial, and anger. Pick an example of a time when you've had to come to terms with something difficult, even if you're not 100 percent pleased with how you handled the situation. At this point, we don't advise you to select anything related to your partner (For example, "I've had to accept my husband's sloppiness.") We want this to be a nonthreatening, positive exercise. Take turns talking with your partner about the experience you've selected, using your answers to the questions below to guide you.

Partner 1

Situation that called for acceptance: _____

_____

1. What meaning did this event or situation hold for you? _____

_____

_____

2. What stages did you go through in your acceptance process? _____

_____

_____

3. What barriers to acceptance did you encounter? _____

_____

_____

4. What helped you deal more gracefully with the situation? _____

_____

_____

5. How did your accepting attitude manifest itself? _____

_____

_____

6. Where are you now in this process of acceptance? _____

_____

_____

7. How did acceptance help you transcend your suffering? _____

_____

_____

8. In what ways has your partner assisted you in your acceptance process?

_____

_____

9. Is there anything else your partner could do to help you? _____

_____

_____

Partner 2

Situation that called for acceptance: _____

_____

1. What meaning did this event or situation hold for you? _____

_____

_____

2. What stages did you go through in your acceptance process? _____

_____

_____

3. What barriers to acceptance did you encounter? _____

_____

_____

4. What helped you deal more gracefully with the situation? _____

_____

_____

5. How did your accepting attitude manifest itself? _____

_____

_____

6. Where are you now in this process of acceptance? _____

_____

_____

7. How did acceptance help you transcend your suffering? _____

_____

_____

8. In what ways has your partner assisted you in your acceptance process?

_____

_____

9. Is there anything else your partner could do to help you? _____

_____

_____

If you're having difficulty understanding the gist of this exercise, perhaps an example will help. Let's look at how Bill answered the questions when doing this exercise with his wife, Erika. Notice that he didn't answer all the questions—some overlap, and some may or may not apply.

Situation that called for acceptance: *The almost complete loss of eyesight in one eye a year ago. From one day to the next, I noticed severe distortion in the vision of my left eye. The eye doctor determined it was a random, freak occurance of unknown origin, and that the damage was probably permanent.*

1. What meaning did this event or situation hold for you?

   Losing eyesight in one eye was traumatic for me because it meant I could no longer maintain my pilot's license. Flying had always been an important part of my life. It also meant facing the fact that I'm aging, that nothing in life is certain.

2. What stages did you go through in your acceptance process?

At first, I didn't believe the loss of sight would be permanent. Although the doctor never painted a positive picture, I still held to the hope that something could be done. Once I began to realize the damage was irreversible, I became depressed.

3. What barriers to acceptance did you encounter?

I kept saying to myself, "This isn't fair. What did I do to deserve this?" I felt impatient when the doctor couldn't determine what had happened, or whether he would be able to correct the damage. I was afraid: What did this mean?; What if something happened to my other eye?; What if I can't drive anymore and lose my independence?

4. What helped you deal more gracefully with the situation?

I fairly quickly learned I could compensate somewhat for the bad vision in one eye. In a few weeks' time, I felt confident in my driving abilities. Since I couldn't fly anymore, I joined a model airplane club. I gained a great deal of support from the other model airplane enthusiasts. Several of the more experienced pilots took extra time to help me learn to compensate for my depth-perception problems.

5. How did your accepting attitude manifest itself?

Once I began accepting the loss of eyesight, but realizing it wasn't the dire catastrophe I had originally imagined, I began to relax more. I wasn't so worried all the time. I was less irritable with Erika.

6. Where are you now in this process of acceptance?

I still feel a great loss at not being able to fly, but I no longer dwell on it for long periods of time. I've gotten involved in another activity I enjoy. I am living life again.

7. How did acceptance help you transcend suffering?

Same as noted in 5 and 6.

8. In what ways has your partner assisted you in your acceptance process?

Erika encouraged me to pursue my interest in radio-controlled model airplanes. She helped me become more involved with people in the model club by inviting several couples over for dinner. She came to watch me fly in competitions. She shared my joy when I won first place. She understood that this meant not simply winning the contest, but that I had mastered this activity despite my eyesight limitations.

9. Is there anything else your partner could do to help?

   Allow me the times I may still need to feel sad about not being able to crawl in the cockpit and fly. Recognize that I won't stay sad forever.

Some Final Thoughts

Acceptance is the first step and, it often seems to us, the hardest. It's hard to let go of our illusions of control, but let go is what we must do if we're to be free—free from our worries, our fears, our insecurities, and free to form a lasting spiritual relationship with our partner. Acceptance is not an all-or-nothing proposition, however; it's not a step you complete once and for all, and then you're done. Rather, acceptance is a process, something you must gently nudge yourself (or kick yourself) to do, over and over again. In truth, the process of acceptance involves gradually moving toward a more trusting place—a place where there's faith that all things are working together for our benefit; a place where love's highest purposes can be realized.

Spotlight on Acceptance

- Acceptance is an attitude. It's a willingness and an openness to look at what is real.

- Don't measure yourself, your partner, or your relationship against some idealized, perfectionistic standard.

- Accept where you are in the moment and realize that you can learn and grow from the experience of now.

- Acceptance doesn't mean you're being passive or giving up.

- Acceptance is a paradox. Once you accept something, change becomes possible.

- Acceptance means listening to what life is telling you.

Chapter 6

Step 2:
Communicate With Care

"The first duty of love is to listen."

—Paul Tillich

*W*hen couples come for counseling and we ask them their goals, the most typical response is, "We want to learn to communicate better." In fact, the number one complaint we hear from women is, "He doesn't listen to me; I don't feel heard." We go to school to learn the three *R*s: Reading, Riting, and Rithmetic, but what about the three *C*s: Care, Compassion, and Communication? It's incredible that people are expected to function well in relationships without learning the skills to do so.

Most adults long for practical guidance in the most personal areas of their lives. In this chapter, we'll offer step-by-step instructions for effective communication: how to listen, how to express yourself, how to resolve conflict. Anyone can learn the mechanics of communication skills, and, indeed, this is a necessary component of communicating with care. Simply learning the techniques, however, isn't enough. You must also explore what blocks you from applying the skills once you learn them—an exploration that inevitably leads you to examine the spiritual context of communication.

The Spiritual Context of Communication

"Our existence begins with a solitary, lonely cry, anxiously awaiting a response," said Irvin Yalom in *Existential Psychotherapy*. You emerge from the warmth of the womb, from total fusion with another, to the stark reality of your separateness. Utter terror and dread ensues, propelling you to test the marvelous machinery of your vocal cords. An individual's very first attempt at communication is an intentional act—an effort to connect with another. Babies yearn to know that they are not alone in this curious world into which they've emerged. Ideally, they are put to their mother's breast and they hear their parents' delight as they say, "Welcome to the world, baby. We're glad you've arrived." Thus, human beings commence their lives in dialogue.

Martin Buber, a prominent philosopher and theologian, based much of his thinking on this concept of dialogue. "In the beginning is the relation," he wrote. He distinguished between two types of relationships that he termed "I-It" and "I-Thou." In an "I-It" relationship, one relates to another person more or less as you would relate to an object. The relationship is functional, not mutual, and parts of the self—the "I"—are hidden, held back. An "I-It" relationship asks, "What can this person do for me?" In contrast, an "I-Thou" relationship concerns itself not with "What's in it for me?", but seeks to understand the other fully and completely, holding nothing back of the self in the process. The concept of "I-Thou" is similar to Rollo May's concept of Eros, which he describes in *Love and Will* as "the longing to establish full union, full relationship."

It's important to keep this spiritual context in mind as you learn and practice the skills in this chapter. When you view communication not simply as a set of techniques—a means to an end—but as the communion of two people's hearts and souls, you'll appreciate this act of communicating as the inspired, holy work that it is.

Listening: The Lost Virtue

In days gone by, listening was a revered and integral part of life. Neighbors sat on their front porches and talked for hours and extended family was typically nearby, available to lend an ear when needed. Televisions didn't exist, and people spent more time sharing stories, listening to each other's hopes and dreams. Now we live in a technological age in which the virtue of listening receives short shrift. Ours is a culture that requires objective evidence to prove something's value. What many people aren't aware of, however, is that there is concrete evidence to support the value of listening. Research from a number of different disciplines points to listening as a crucial, even curative, process.

Psychotherapy "outcome" research examines the effectiveness of different types of therapy: Results from numerous experiments point out that the major ingredient responsible for determining whether positive change occurs is the quality of the helper-client relationship. In other words, it doesn't seem to matter what type of therapist one sees—for example, a Jungian analyst or a cognitive therapist—so long as he or she is a good listener. One study even found that nonprofessional good listeners were as effective as trained therapists in helping people with many problems. Computer programs that "listen" to a patient's input have equally good results!

Similarly, medical research has found that cancer patients have better recovery rates if they perceive their oncologist as warm and understanding. Greg's father frequently comments on the fact that his oncologist never looks at his watch. There can be 30 other patients in the waiting room, but when the doctor is with him, he takes time to listen. Results from these studies indicate that patients who feel that their physician genuinely cares for them are more likely to follow their doctor's instructions. And yet part of the reason for some patients' superior recoveries remains hidden: There seems to be an almost mystical component to the patient-healer relationship. Part of this may have to do with listening.

The kind of listening we're talking about is often called *empathic* listening. Empathy involves identifying with and understanding another's situation. Empathic listening is a worthy goal. Listening on a spiritual level, however, goes even deeper. It's not just a matter of understanding your partner's situation: You must also feel your partner's feelings as if they were your own. In essence, communicating with care is the blurring of boundaries between two people's souls. Mind you, we don't mean this in a pathological way, which would make each individual less than whole, but rather as the intentional joining of souls—a union based on abundance and strength, rather than paucity or weakness. We'll expand on this notion in the sections below.

Listening Is an Act of Self-Transcendence

A lofty word, transcendence is frequently used with little understanding of its true meaning. The Latin root of transcendence means "to climb over"— and, indeed, transcendence requires effort. To truly listen, one must rise above the self-centeredness that plagues us all—not an easy task. You must set aside your own needs and desires, relinquish your stereotypes and assumptions about your partner, and respond to your partner with your whole being. You transcend yourself by becoming absorbed in the process of understanding and caring for your partner. This kind of listening, this kind of caring, is difficult to sustain—and it would be a mistake to expect yourself to be a perfect listener throughout your marriage. Still, careful and caring listening is a worthy ideal to strive for.

Madison and Tyler come to mind when we think about the transcendent quality of listening. When we first met them, they'd been married for three years, and had a four-month-old infant. During our first meeting, they shared with us the following background information. They'd planned the pregnancy, and looked forward to the baby's arrival. After the baby was born, Madison seemed to function okay for the first week or so. Her mother had come to help out, and Tyler took time off from work. Once she was home alone with the baby, however, things began to change. She started worrying about every little thing—not just normal, new-mother worry, but worry that led to full-blown panic. She'd call Tyler 20 times a day seeking reassurance; she frequently begged him to come home early. He wasn't pleased with so many interruptions, but he tried to be patient, coming home early whenever possible. He hoped that Madison would soon become accustomed to her new role and responsibilities. As time went on, though, her anxieties only worsened, and she sank into a deep depression. She rarely got dressed, and spent much of her time in bed. She always managed to take care of the baby's immediate needs, but she didn't seem to enjoy any part of it. She had withdrawn from Tyler, and they frequently argued.

After we heard this couple's story, we examined one of their typical conversations. Tyler was well intentioned, but the way he responded to Madison's cries for help actually made her situation much worse. In *The Seven Habits of Highly Effective People*, Stephen Covey describes four ways of responding that hinder empathic listening: evaluating (agreeing or disagreeing), probing (asking questions), advising (offering solutions), and interpreting (explaining motives—trying to "psyche out" the other person). Notice how in the conversation below, these four activities block both understanding and compassion, never allowing Madison and Tyler to reach the heart of their trouble together.

Madison: "I've had it! I can't take it anymore!"

Tyler: "What's the matter now?" (probing)

Madison: "I'm going crazy at home with the baby. I feel like I'm falling apart. You just don't understand how hard it is."

Tyler: "Why don't you call Mary? Maybe you could get together with her and her kids." (advising)

Madison: "Mary has a lot of friends already. She's not going to have much time for me. That's not going to solve anything, anyway."

Tyler: "Have you tried calling your mother? Maybe she could give you some advice on how to get yourself together." (advising, evaluating)

Madison: "You just don't get it, do you?"

Tyler: "I think it's fatigue. You haven't been sleeping well lately. Sleep deprivation is making you irritable. Why don't you go to bed early tonight? I'll take care of the baby." (interpreting, evaluating, advising)

Madison was trying to reach out to Tyler in this conversation. She may not have done it in the best way possible, but she was clearly at the end of her rope, hoping that Tyler would grab the other end. But he wasn't listening—not really. He heard her words, but he wasn't making an effort to understand her experience. He responded from his own frame of reference, thinking: "When is she going to snap out of this? What's wrong with her? We have a beautiful, healthy baby. This should be the happiest time in our life. I'm scared. I've never seen her like this. Maybe it means there's something wrong with me if I can't help her, if I can't make her happy." Clearly, at this point in time, Tyler was unable to transcend his own needs in such a way that would allow him to listen effectively to his wife.

Skip ahead three weeks. At this point, we've taught both Tyler and Madison basic listening skills. We've also discussed the spiritual context of communication. One issue became apparent in that discussion: Tyler feared that "transcending himself" in order to listen in a complete, caring way meant that he would lose himself in the process. This is a common fear, particularly among men, who aren't as comfortable as many women are with intense emotions. This raises yet another paradox about spiritual marriage. In *The Phenomenon of Man*, Pierre Teilhard de Chardin asks the reader, "At what moment do lovers come into the most complete possession of *themselves*, if it is not when they are *lost* in each other?" Although Tyler feared he would lose himself in the process of spiritual listening, in truth he gained an opportunity to find himself.

We still have some things to teach this couple about communication (we haven't yet discussed self-expression skills), but notice the remarkable difference in the following conversation.

Madison: "I feel like I'm at my breaking point. I don't know what to do."

Tyler: "It sounds like you feel pretty scared and overwhelmed."

Madison: "Yeah. I've never felt this bad in my whole life. Most of the time I feel like I'm going crazy."

Tyler: "This sounds like the worst you've ever felt. I wish there was something I could do to help. I hate seeing you in such pain."

Madison: "I feel like you don't understand. You just want me to snap out of it and be like I used to be."

Tyler: "You're probably right. It's hard for me to understand what you're going through, and I do miss the good times we used to have. I want to understand. Can you tell me more?"

Madison: "I don't think you really want to hear all the awful stuff that's going through my mind."

Tyler: "I know in the past I haven't been a very good listener, but I want to do better. I want to share your pain if you'll allow me to."

Madison: "I just want you to hold me."

Tyler cradled Madison in his arms, and she sobbed for what seemed like hours to him (he told us later). Although his first instinct was to find a way to make her stop crying, he resisted the urge, and tried to accept her where she was, and to join her in her pain. This wasn't an easy thing for him to do. He himself was frightened. "What if she never stops crying? What if the pain consumes us both? What if I get as depressed as Madison, and there's no one around here strong enough or levelheaded enough to take care of the baby?" These were the thoughts running through Tyler's head at the time, but he managed to transcend his fears by an effort of will: He took a risk and a leap of faith. He knew that his old way of communicating hadn't been working. Madison was still just as depressed as ever, and Tyler was just as anxious inside. It took courage and strength to refrain from offering Madison his usual reassurances and banal advice. As he patiently waited with hope that he was doing the right thing, he gave his wife the gift of himself: He listened to her.

Listening Is the Source of Tenderness

We recently worked with a couple, Audrey and Wesley, who learned how listening can smooth the rough edges of a relationship and soften one's perspective. Audrey had an eight-year-old son, Jason, from a previous marriage, who lived with them. Wesley and Jason had previously enjoyed a relatively warm and stable relationship, but the past few months had been horrible. Jason was not only getting in more trouble than usual at home, his teacher had called and said he often seemed angry for no apparent reason. Audrey and Wesley reacted by cracking down on Jason. They thought maybe they'd been too lenient with him; but the more rules they made, the more rules he broke. They tried removing privileges or sending him to his room, but nothing seemed to help. Not only were they both infuriated with Jason, but his disruptive behaviors and general irritability were starting to affect their marriage. They argued about each new incident that arose, and had difficulty agreeing on the best approach to take with him.

When they came to see us, we first gathered information about what they had already tried in an effort to solve the problem. What seemed to help? What seemed to make matters worse? Was there anything they hadn't yet tried? Although they had employed a number of behavior management strategies that can be effective in some situations, they hadn't tried the most obvious tool (it's always obvious when it's not your child)—listening, really listening. Especially with kids, but also with spouses, this listening business can be tricky. Sometimes you have to maneuver around the content to find the truth. Jason wasn't using words so much as his behavior to tell his mom and stepdad that something was troubling him. We suggested to Audrey and Wesley that they lie low for a while, and listen for some kind of clue to help solve the mystery of Jason's sudden change in behavior. They were skeptical, but agreed to give it a try.

When they returned the next week, Audrey and Wesley had good news to report. They were no longer lecturing or punishing, but instead had begun to observe and listen. Audrey had noticed that Jason's mood changed after he finished one of his weekly telephone conversations with his father. After he hung up the phone, he came into the kitchen and snapped, "We never have any good food around here." At first, Audrey snapped back, and they went a few rounds about the contents of the cupboards. Then she regained her composure and said, "I'm sorry I'm arguing with you about this. I have a funny feeling we're not fighting about what there is to eat. It seems like you got upset after talking with your dad. Do you want to talk about it?" This opening was all Jason needed to tell his mom what was bothering him. His father had apparently been dating a new woman, someone Jason did not care for. He felt that his father was neglecting him, as he had cut short several of their weekend visits over the past few months. As Audrey and Wesley learned what had been going on, their anger over Jason's behavior turned to tenderness. Likewise, once Jason began sharing his feelings with his mother and stepfather, his behavior improved.

Listening Is Transformative

Earlier in this chapter, we explained Martin Buber's theory of "I-It" and "I-Thou" relationships—whether one relates to the other as serviceable object or sensitive soul. In his analysis of Buber, Irvin Yalom notes an even more fundamental distinction. He asserts that the "I" in each type of relationship is also different. He explains: "The 'I' appears and is shaped in the context of some relationship. Thus the 'I' is profoundly influenced by the relationship with the 'Thou.' With each moment of relationship, the 'I' is created anew." Our analysis goes one step further: We believe that not only is the "I" transformed, but also the "Thou." In a spiritual relationship, this highest form of listening calls forth both the speaker and the listener to move beyond routine and repetition—to open up to fresh perspectives and possibilities.

Let's return to Madison and Tyler's story to witness their transformation. When Tyler held Madison, she finally felt safe enough to share her deepest, darkest thoughts: She had been considering killing herself. She knew that suicide wasn't a rational answer to her problems, but she felt powerless over the intense cycle of negativity and hopelessness she found herself in. She'd been afraid to tell Tyler how bad it had gotten: She thought he would judge her, much as she was judging herself ("How can I be so selfish, thinking about killing myself when I have a husband and baby who need me?"). At this moment, Tyler could see the excruciating pain in Madison's eyes, and he felt flooded with compassion.

The next morning, Madison's mood seemed somewhat brighter, but Tyler was still understandably concerned. He called us to see whether they could come in for a session that day. When we met with them, they told us about their experience—how Tyler had truly listened, and that he finally understood the seriousness of her situation. In our first session with this couple, we had suggested that Madison might be experiencing a postpartum depression; we thought she should consult a physician about the option of taking an antidepressant medication. Although Madison hadn't said too much about it at the time, Tyler voiced a strong opposition to the idea. Only after Tyler had really experienced the depth of Madison's pain did he become more open to the idea of medication, realizing that she needed it. He also realized now how vitally important his support was to her. For the first time in his life, he experienced the power of listening—how by meeting his wife in the murkiness of her feelings, he was actively *doing* something to help her. For Madison, having Tyler's support enabled her to follow through with the treatment she needed. The listening, talking, and holding had transformed them both.

Spiritual Sharing Exercise 6: Learning To Listen (and Truly Understand)

As you try this exercise, it's important to remember the stories you've just read. Recall the power of listening, and let that power awe you. Respect the mysterious processes of transcendence and transformation that occur when one listens with heart and soul. Although we want you to recognize listening for the labor of love that it is, we don't want you to feel overwhelmed by the challenge presented by this exercise. Don't worry if this kind of listening doesn't feel natural at first. You don't have to listen perfectly. As long as you're trying, your partner will sense your good intentions—your desire to listen and understand—and that will go a long way toward making the exercise work for you both.

Before you begin, read the Spotlight on Listening at the end of this section and the Spotlight on Expressing Yourself several pages further on. After you're familiar with the basic guidelines, follow these instructions:

1. Select one of you to take the expressing role and one to take the listening role.

2. The "expresser" begins talking about a relatively neutral topic of mutual concern—one that presents only minor problems. Don't pick something potentially explosive or likely to make your partner feel defensive. It's important to begin slowly and master these skills before working up to discussions of major issues.

3. Set a time limit. In our work with couples, we frequently set limits of ten minutes or less for this entire exercise. We want couples to minimize any chance of the exercise deteriorating into old negative communication patterns.

4. After the expresser has finished talking, the listener attempts to paraphrase what was said, paying special attention to the feelings involved, not just the contents. Wait until the expresser has finished completely before attempting to paraphrase what was said.

5. Listeners should look for signs from their partner that they are on the right track. The listener should accept calmly any corrections about

his or her interpretation of the expresser's words. The listener must keep listening throughout the entire process, being sensitive to body language as well as words.

6. We often suggest that couples let a day pass before switching roles. This way, the listener is less likely to be preoccupied with what he or she wants to say next, and can focus exclusively on understanding what the expresser has said. If you decide not to follow this suggestion, try not to switch roles until the expresser feels fully understood by the listener.

Spotlight on Listening

- While listening, try to put yourself in your partner's shoes. Focus on what he or she is feeling, not just what is said.

- Accept your partner's right to have his or her own thoughts and feelings.

- Demonstrate your acceptance through your posture, tone of voice, and facial expressions.

- While listening, try to avoid asking questions, expressing your own opinions, offering solutions, or making judgments.

- After your partner has finished speaking, summarize and restate the most important thoughts and feelings that were expressed.

Speaking: The Sacred Trust

Although we've placed a lot of emphasis on learning to listen, the speaker must also share in the responsibility of maintaining the integrity of a conversation—of ensuring that it goes smoothly. This is especially true if you desire the rewards of a spiritually rich relationship. In marriage, you've committed yourselves not only to stay together "for better, for worse; for richer, for poorer," you've also vowed to tend the spirit of the other—to be "soulmates." Your partner has entrusted you with the care of his or her soul, the most essential, life-giving part of one's being. This means that a significant part of your mission on this earth must be to help your partner grow and develop—to reach his or her fullest potential. In light of this mission, it behooves you to speak with care and consideration. What exactly does this mean? To answer this, let's examine three spiritual laws of speaking.

Spiritual Law of Speaking 1:
Recognize That You Have a Choice

Probably one of the biggest myths perpetuated by pop psychology is the notion that it's healthy to "let all your feelings out." This idea came from Freud's "hydraulic model" of emotions: He wrote that unexpressed feelings can build up if not released, and eventually exert so much pressure on the dam that it breaks, flooding the entire system. Modern research has shown the flaws in this model, especially in regard to certain negative feelings. For example, results from numerous studies show that the cathartic expression of anger only leads to increased feelings of anger. Our clinical work also bears this out. We've observed over and over again that couples meet with disaster when they mistakenly assume that it's a good thing to share all their thoughts and feelings, whenever and however the mood strikes them.

Feelings are not simply an unintentioned push from behind, they're also a pull toward something. Our feelings pull us and connect us to the world. Rollo May said, "Our feelings not only take into consideration the other person but are in a real sense partially formed by the feelings of the other person present. We feel within a magnetic field." It's that "I-Thou" concept again: In dialogue, listener and speaker both are formed and transformed.

To put this in more practical terms, you must remember that you have a choice. Simply because you experience a feeling doesn't mean that you have to express it right then and there. Imagine, for example, that you're balancing the checkbook, and you're angry about something your partner bought—you think it's an extravagant purchase, and wish you'd been consulted. Or pick a recent situation in your own relationship. Given that you're already angry (or whatever), here's a list of some of the choices you can make:

- **Whether** you will express your feelings to your partner. (Maybe you'll decide it's not really such a big deal after all.)

- **When** to express your feelings to your partner. (Do you choose to say something at the very moment when you experience the feeling? Do you wait until you've calmed down? Do you find a time when your partner might be more receptive?)

- **How** you'll express your feelings to your partner. (Do you yell, scream, whine, or pout? Do you calmly tell your partner how you feel? Are you direct? Or do you express your angry feelings passively, perhaps by doing something to retaliate or get even?)

- **How** you'll care for yourself and your relationship. (Do you take steps to soothe yourself and calm yourself down? You don't have to tell your partner every feeling about every incident. You have other options: writing in a journal, exercising, reading something funny . . .) Or do you go over in your mind all the past times your partner has done something that made you angry, adding fuel to the fire?

It might seem as if we're asking you to be overcontrolled in your expression of feeling, but we're not. Certainly, being emotionally shutdown is not the way to create a spiritual marriage. We do believe, however, that the benefits of expressing your feelings must be balanced against the potential to do harm to the integrity of the relationship, and to your partner's self-esteem. Fortunately, guidelines exist to help you speak in a way that shows respect for yourself and your partner. The next Spiritual Sharing Exercise and Spotlight box illustrate these guidelines.

Spiritual Law of Speaking 2: Assume Responsibility for Your Thoughts and Feelings

This law is intimately related to the first law, and is actually an extension of it. In communicating with your partner, you must accept the fact that you alone are responsible for your feelings. No one can "make you mad"—you choose your reactions. Certainly, external factors can conspire to make it more likely that you'll feel one way or another. For example, if your spouse approaches you in a loud, argumentative tone, accusing you of something you didn't do, you're likely to feel somewhat self-righteous and defensive. It's up to you whether to act on these feelings or to change your thinking in such a way that other feelings can take their place. You might note that your spouse has been under a lot of pressure lately, and your empathy might allow you to react in a completely different, much more generous manner. Ultimately, we all create our own reality. Keeping this in mind, you can polish the rough edges of your statements by prefacing them with, "I think . . ." or "I feel . . ." This alerts your partner to the fact that you're owning your thoughts and feelings: You're making it perfectly clear that you realize that your perceptions are subjective, perhaps even distorted.

Spiritual Law of Speaking 3: Speak With Kindness and Clarity

It's helpful when you're talking with your partner about some negative feeling or some complaint to also include positive feelings you have. For example, if you're annoyed that your husband didn't do the dishes as he'd promised, you could begin your conversation noting how much you appreciate the time he spends with the children in the evening. You might also say, "I know you've been working hard all day, but I really need your help with the dishes tonight." Also, show your partner you're aware of the impact your statements may have. You might start out by saying, "I know it's hard for you when I say things that sound critical . . ." Remember—your partner is your spiritual companion: Your goal is to not only communicate your feelings fully, but also as graciously as possible. In addition, speak with as much clarity as you can muster. By clarity we mean: Stay in the present (don't dredge up old dirt) and stick with the salient points. No matter what the content, aim for self-expression to be an opportunity to strengthen the core feelings of love and affection that originally drew you together.

Spiritual Sharing Exercise 7: Expressing Yourself and Your Needs (Without Sounding Selfish or Self-Centered)

Keep in mind the sacred trust that your partner has bestowed upon you as you practice the following exercise. In time, you'll learn to express yourself in a manner that not only shows respect for your partner, but also helps you present your own needs and wishes in a way that makes your partner willing to help.

1. Follow the directions given in the Learning To Listen exercise, but switch roles with your partner. Whoever last played listener should now play expresser.

2. Again, when you're first learning these skills, pick relatively nonthreatening, even neutral topics to discuss. Later, you'll be able to focus on more pressing issues.

3. If you have difficulty deciding what to talk about, look through the questions in previous Spiritual Sharing Exercises for ideas.

Spotlight on Expressing Yourself

- State your views as your own thoughts and feelings, acknowledging your subjectivity. Begin your statements with "I think . . . " or "I feel . . . " rather than "You never . . ." or "You always . . . ."

- When expressing negative emotions or criticisms, also include any positive feelings you have about your partner or the situation.

- Make your statements as specific as possible.

- While expressing yourself, demonstrate your respect for your partner by showing that you are aware of the impact that your statements may have. Show that you care about your partner's feelings.

- Stick to one subject at a time whenever possible.

Resolving Conflict: The Creative Challenge

Some of the couples we see presume that problems arise only in troubled relationships. They view conflict as a "win-lose" situation, falling into predictable, ineffective patterns of dealing with their differences. They rarely resolve anything, and frustration mounts. The reality is that all couples have problems. Conflict is an inevitable fact of life when two people with uniquely different needs, habits, and personalities come together to form a couple. Problems don't have to pull people apart. In fact, the process of working through conflict—if done creatively, and with compassion—can actually strengthen a relationship. In this section, we'll look at three different ways of resolving conflict. Each of these methods has its place in a spiritual marriage; but because so much has been written in other books about compromise, we'll touch on this option only briefly.

The Way of Compromise

You want spaghetti, I want steak. We agree that we'll eat spaghetti tonight, steak tomorrow. In its simplest form, this is the way of compromise. When you and your partner have different needs, you must negotiate to find an acceptable solution. Sometimes the process can be simple and straightforward: You might decide to take turns (spaghetti tonight, steak tomorrow); do both (eat steak *and* spaghetti tonight); or do neither (order Chinese takeout). Oftentimes, however, the situation's more complicated, and you're better off applying a more sophisticated problem-solving strategy. The steps of problem-solving include

1. Define the problem.

2. Set your goals—what you want to have happen.

3. Brainstorm about possible solutions.

4. Agree on a solution to try.

5. Set a trial period for implementing the solution.

6. Evaluate your results.

Here are some tips to make this type of conflict resolution work:

Don't limit yourself with practicalities during the brainstorming phase. You can worry about practical matters later. Simply let the ideas flow quickly and effortlessly. One idea is to jot your ideas down on sticky notepaper. Then you can post your ideas on a wall, group similar ideas together, and so on. Don't judge any ideas your partner suggests.

Look for solutions that are mutually acceptable to both of you whenever possible. Don't agree to try a solution if you know deep down that you're not going to follow through. This sets you both up for failure.

Set a reasonable time period for trying out the solution you choose to implement. It shouldn't be too long, or it won't have the experimental flavor it's designed to have (Does this work or doesn't it?). Likewise, the time period shouldn't be too short—you need to try out a solution long enough to know if it'll work.

Don't forget to evaluate how things are going after the trial period. Fine-tuning is an inevitable and important part of the process.

The Higher Way

The second method of problem solving is the "win-win" method made popular by best-selling author Stephen Covey. He notes that Buddhism calls this "the middle way." But, in this case, middle doesn't mean compromise—it means higher, as in the apex of a triangle. Covey writes in *The 7 Habits of Highly Effective People*, "Win/Win is a belief in the Third Alternative. It's not your way or my way; it's a *better* way, a higher way."

How is this method of conflict resolution different from compromise? In seeking the higher way, you commit yourself to finding a solution with which both you and your partner can be happy, *no matter how long it takes*. This process requires a tremendous amount of cooperation and trust. It also demands a high level of empathic listening. In order to creatively meet both parties' needs, you must listen closely to your partner's perceptions of the problem.

Diane and Austin sought counseling because of a problem they were having difficulty solving on their own: Diane wanted to drop out of the band she and Austin had been members of since they were married, seven years ago. When they began the band, it was mostly for fun. Now that they'd gained some popularity, it'd turned into more of a business venture. Her announcement that she was going to quit took Austin completely off guard. He couldn't understand how she could do this to him, to their relationship. Music was what had brought them together—it was their life, he thought. Diane, on the other hand, found it hard to believe that Austin hadn't seen this coming. She told us, "I've been upset about things going on with the band for years. I've expressed my feelings a bunch of times before. I guess he wasn't listening."

We wanted them to talk with each other, in the session, and share their feelings and perspectives on the situation. Diane was reluctant. They'd been in counseling one other time during the course of their marriage, and she noted that much of what they'd done was simply argue in front of the therapist. The thought of going through that again didn't thrill her. She also felt vulnerable: Austin was an excellent debater, she said, and she was sure we'd agree with his position. We reassured her that we'd do our best to create a net of safety in the session—that we'd intervene if they got offtrack, lapsing into destructive communication styles. We said that they'd each have their turn to talk, and asked them each to try to listen and understand what the other was saying—not try to come up with counterarguments. Diane shared her side first:

> I love music, and I used to love being in the band, too. Music was what brought us together. But now all we do is argue. The band has changed a lot over the years. Now I'm the only woman, and I feel like what I have to say isn't taken seriously, especially about our repertoire. Austin and the

other guys are always messing around with my equipment, too, criticiz-
ing the way I have things adjusted. I've heard tape recordings of our per-
formances, and I like the way my fiddle sounds.

Next, we asked Austin to check out with Diane whether he understood her thoughts and feelings. As it was the first session, he understandably had a rough time, so we quickly intervened. Greg modeled for Austin how he might respond, and he asked Diane to see how it would feel if Austin had said something like this:

It sounds like it's hard for you being the only woman in the band. You feel
left out, like we don't include you in the day-to-day decisions. It must feel
like I don't respect your abilities as a musician when I adjust your amp
the way I like it, rather than the way you like it.

Diane nodded her head in agreement and added, "It's really demeaning to me. I don't want to be treated that way." We then asked Austin to try it again, even if he simply repeated what Greg had already said. We thought it was important for Austin to practice saying the words, as well as to have Diane hear the words coming from him. As the session proceeded, we contin-ued to draw Diane's feelings out. The more Austin was able to accurately listen and understand (sometimes with Greg's help), the more Diane opened up, and the more her feelings flowed into other, deeper feelings. For example, Diane's initial feelings were mostly of anger. But as Austin validated and em-pathized with her anger, it changed to sadness and a sense of loss. She missed the closeness she and Austin once had as a result of their music. Now it seemed too much like work, with none of the pleasure.

After Diane felt convinced that Austin completely understood her posi-tion, we had them switch roles. This time Austin expressed his thoughts and feelings:

I feel terrible that you think I don't respect your abilities. I think you're a
wonderfully talented musician. I've only been trying to protect you from
having to worry about all the technical stuff with the equipment. I didn't
realize how it came across to you. I know the band has changed so much
in its composition—it really isn't as much fun for me anymore either, but
I feel like we're stuck because the rest of the band counts on us. I don't see
how either of us could just quit at this point.

Over the next several sessions, we continued to work with Diane and Austin at finding the feelings they shared. Both of them were frustrated with the band, but they'd handled their frustrations in different ways. Austin had buddied up with the guys, which led Diane to feel left out. Although Diane had tried to be assertive with the guys in the band, telling them she didn't appreciate their fiddling with the controls on her amp, she felt she'd gotten nowhere, and had started to withdraw emotionally from the situation, eventu-ally deciding that she wanted to quit the band. During their discussions, it became clear that both Diane and Austin most missed the pure pleasure their music had once brought them. Being in this band, trying to make extra money, had turned into a rat race. They had a meeting with the other band members to clarify everyone's goals. In the end, they decided to give the band notice that they were quitting, and they were checking into becoming involved with their church's choir and music program. They'd created a third alternative, a solution that met both their needs more fully than either of them could've imagined at the outset. By asking "What meaning does this conflict have for our relationship?" they were able to find a commonality of purpose—to focus on the feelings they shared.

The Abiding Way

Sometimes, despite all the best efforts and intentions, there simply isn't a win-win solution, at least not one that can be discerned anytime in the near future. Covey allows for this, writing that if you can't generate a win-win solution, it's a "no-deal" situation. "*No Deal* basically means that if we can't find a solution that would benefit us both, we agree to disagree agreeably," he writes. Covey doesn't, however, go on to specify what people should do if they're in this type of situation.

What should a couple do when they can't find a win-win solution? Call off the whole deal of marriage? We doubt that's what Covey had in mind in the majority of situations.

Let's take a look at an example from Linda and Doug's marriage to see what we mean by the "abiding way." This couple came to see us shortly after they'd moved to the St. Louis area, the latest of five relocations during the previous seven years. Doug worked in the upper management of a large international corporation. His position required him to travel a great deal, in addition to relocating often. Linda said that this latest move had "put her over the edge." She knew that Doug loved his job, but she was getting sick and tired of uprooting herself each time he had a chance to move into a position of increased responsibility. It became clear early on in our meeting with them that this was a situation that couldn't be "solved." Doug wasn't going to quit his job, and that's not what Linda wanted, anyway. What she wanted was more understanding and support from Doug. It seemed that when she expressed her feelings about their latest move, Doug felt attacked and withdrew emotionally, leaving Linda feeling all the more alone. Our work with them involved helping them commiserate about the problem together. In other words, the problem wasn't Doug, and it wasn't Linda: It was the situation.

Prominent couples therapist and researcher Neal Jacobson, Ph.D., calls this "turning the problem into an *It*." He notes that the goal is to "shift the couple from blaming each other for problems, toward a less emotionally charged experience of problems as something that happens to both of them." You might notice that this notion of "turning the problem into an *It*" relates back to the previous step of acceptance: Sometimes you can't change something, at least in the short run; so you must accept the situation, develop a tolerance for it, and not let it come between you and your partner.

How do you know when to seek the abiding way? Here are some scenarios in which giving up on problem-solving per se is probably the best course:

1. The conflict is highly emotionally charged.

2. You and your partner are polarized in your positions—at two different extremes of opinion.

3. There's no obvious middle ground in your situation—for example, if you want to have a baby, and he doesn't, you can't have half a baby.

4. You've tried to resolve the conflict several times before and your efforts have either gotten you nowhere, or actually made the problem worse.

5. Previous attempts at change have only been made halfheartedly, even begrudgingly.

The more of these that apply to your situation, the more likely it is that seeking the path of acceptance and tolerance—the abiding way—is the alternative of choice.

Spiritual Sharing Exercise 8: Turning the Problem Into an "It"

This exercise is designed to help you and your partner gain distance and perspective from a conflict festering between you. Pick a time to do this exercise when you aren't already in a heated debate. The best time would be when you have some positive feelings toward your partner, perhaps after you've enjoyed some relaxing, leisure time together. Here are the instructions:

Agree on the problem you'd like to focus on. If there's more than one problem, you can complete the exercise several different times on different occasions. Take a piece of paper (a large piece of construction paper is ideal), and write down the problem on the paper. Both of you then take turns writing down your feelings about the problem. This isn't an English exercise, so don't worry about grammar or form. Write whatever comes to mind: "The fact that we've moved five times in seven years really sucks," or "I hate the fact that this problem has come between us." If you're artistic (or even if you aren't), feel free to draw pictures of any images that come to mind, or cut pictures out of a magazine that show how you feel. Use this opportunity to practice your listening and expressing skills. As you're going through this process, notice in particular what feelings you have in common.

Then, when you both feel ready, take the piece of paper and put it in an empty box. If there are any other objects that symbolize the problem, you can add those to the box, too. Put the box on an empty chair, on a shelf, or even outside. The problem is "out there" now—in the box—not gnawing away at the love you share. Make a vow to each other that you won't allow this problem to come between the sacred space between you.

There's another part of this exercise that you can carry out over time: Plan specific times to bring the box back out to talk about "the problem" again. Brainstorm for ideas about ways to deal with the problem—not necessarily to solve it, but to find creative ways to cope with it. Limit these discussions to a set period of time, and then put the box back on its shelf. Even though this exercise might seem a bit artificial, it can help you and your partner gain sufficient distance from a problem to lead you both a new sense of perspective, and keep it from jeopardizing the sanctity of your marriage. And if this exercise leads to a bit of chuckling between yourselves, that can only help your situation.

Some Final Thoughts

The healing power of communicating with care cannot be overestimated. Listening, speaking, and resolving conflict are commonplace, everyday experiences, but they are sacred nonetheless, for communication is the vehicle for spiritual connection. Learning to communicate with care is an ongoing process. Be patient both with yourself and your partner as you learn and practice these new skills. Don't expect perfection. If you've skipped any of the previous Spiritual Sharing Exercises, you might feel more secure in trying them now, using the general communication guidelines presented in this chapter.

Spotlight on Resolving Conflict

- Focus on how you can work together to meet current goals, rather than dwelling on past problems.

- Sometimes you may need to let your partner work through his or her anger alone. Don't force a discussion during angry times: This will only lead you to attack each other, and say things you'll later regret.

- Recognize that some conflicts can't be resolved. Do what you can to commiserate about the problem together. Stay on the same team—don't let the problem come between you.

Chapter 7

Step 3: Learn a Common Spiritual Language

"Language is every man's spiritual root."

—Ludwig Binswanger

*A*lthough many people believe that sex and money are the most taboo topics for couples to discuss, we've found that talking about spirituality can be even more foreign and awkward. In our experience, it's rare for couples to talk about the purpose of their marriage, or ways in which they could better nurture each other's souls, or how they could create more meaningful celebrations and rituals, to name just a few examples. Discussing these issues is often difficult, at least in part because couples don't have the words to express themselves. In this chapter, we'll take you through the process of getting the words right—of finding the precise language you need to convey your thoughts, images, and ideas to your partner. This learning process is critical. You may know in your own mind what you mean; but to make this meaning span the existential chasm that lies between any two people, you must communicate clearly, choosing your words with care.

The Language of the Heart

Because emotions are inextricably tied to matters of the spirit, developing a vocabulary of "feeling words" is an important part of learning a common spiritual language, and perhaps the best place to begin.

First Feelings

Human beings enter the world well equipped to respond to and communicate their urgent needs and feelings. Any parent can tell you that babies cry in a variety of ways: a sharp, piercing cry may signal pain; a whimpering, constant cry may signal fatigue; a loud and raucous cry may signal rage. Similarly, parents can distinguish their own infant's cry from that of another. People's feelings have incredible adaptive significance, ensuring not only their physical survival, but also a secure attachment to their caregivers.

As children's development progresses and their language abilities begin to unfold, words are put to these sometimes primitive feelings. Imagine a child grabbing a ball out of a toddler's hand, provoking anger, even rage in the younger child. The toddler will experience these feelings in his body, and the feelings will fuel some type of action or reaction—some toddlers will bite or hit the other child to communicate their displeasure. Now let's say the toddler's mother witnesses this sequence of events. She can help her child's progress in his emotional development by giving him a name for the feeling: "I can see you're *angry* that Tommy took your ball away." When we see Jesse smile with delight when he sees his aunt at the front door, we say, "You're *happy* when your Aunt Judy stops by to see you, aren't you?"

Ideally, this process of learning names for feelings continues in a manner such that all the child's feelings are accepted and validated. In reality, the process typically derails, and children learn that some feelings are more acceptable than others. As we discussed in Chapter 3, boys and girls receive different messages about what feelings are appropriate for their gender. For example, adults tend to find overt displays of anger more disturbing in girls than boys. Boys, however, are more likely than girls to be criticized or censored when they show feelings of fear or vulnerability. Our socialization process continues, and the scope of influence widens: We learn about the world of feelings, not only from our parents, but from our peers, the media, and the culture at large.

Fear of Feelings

Somewhere along the way, many people learn to fear their feelings, which results in a complex process of adaptation, transformation, and distortion. If Jan feels angry at Jim, but she's fearful of her own anger, she's apt to do any number of dances to avoid the full experience of her feelings. She might express a lesser feeling of annoyance; she might call a friend and complain about Jim, instead of confronting him directly; she might provoke him into becoming angry with her, in effect having him express the anger that she feels; she might express sadness instead of her anger. The situation is further complicated in that everyone processes feelings through the filters of past experience. For example, if you received harsh criticism as a child, you may be unable to allow yourself any feelings that you perceive as risky—those that might force you to experience criticism or rejection again. Similarly, you may feel extremely vulnerable to the slightest complaint from your partner. If these feeling-filters aren't clear—and they aren't to most people—the nature and intensity of your reactions can be a mystery, both to yourself and your partner. In *The Heart of the Matter*, Robert A. Pierce, Ph.D., says, ". . . the basic feelings we have always make sense—if they are understood fully—and there are good reasons, as well, for those feelings. These distorting processes and the fear of feelings that usually goes with them cause couples trouble, and an important solution to this trouble is to find, express, share, and understand each other's feelings in an atmosphere as free of blame as possible."

Focusing on Feelings

To get past the distortions, allow yourself to focus fully on your feelings. This is often more difficult than it might seem. The frenetic pace of most people's lives leaves little room for noticing or attending to their feelings. It doesn't have to be this way. Perhaps even more crucial than slowing down your hectic lifestyle is adopting the mind-set that feelings are important, giving yourself permission to notice them, and, most importantly, allowing yourself to have your feelings without judging.

What can you do if you're not already adept at noticing your feelings? One tip is to pay attention to the sensations in your body. There's a reason why people talk about "gut feelings": Feelings are experienced first as physiological events. Only after you notice the physical sensations do you attempt to explain their origin. The particular feeling-name you choose to give to the physical sensation you've perceived is, to a large degree, a product of social context. For example, if while taking an exam you notice your heart racing, you're likely to label the feeling as "nervousness." On the other hand, if you feel your heart racing and you're in the presence of someone to whom you're attracted, you might label the feeling as "passion." It's not always immediately clear why people feel the way they do, and some individuals are more adept than others at deciphering their internal codes. But paying attention to your body messages can provide plenty of clues.

Another way to jump-start your emotional engine is to take a chance and guess at what you might be feeling. Men, in particular, hate to be pinned down to anything: They don't want to venture out loud a guess at their feelings, for fear their wives will presume that it's carved in stone. Once men get past this, however, forming hypotheses about their internal states can be enormously helpful.

Whether you're a man or a woman, let yourself try on different feelings to see how they fit. You can look at the list on the next page if you need inspiration. Also remember that feelings can be quite complex. You may need more than one word to accurately describe your experience. Allow yourself the freedom to play with the words. Your internal voice might sound something like this: "I feel sort of sad, but there's also something comfortable about the sadness—and a realization that the sadness won't last forever if I accept it and flow with it. I also feel some pride that I'm strong enough to let myself feel depressed." Another thing that can help some people if they don't know what they're feeling is to just start talking: Say, "I don't know what I'm feeling, but . . . " It's sometimes also helpful to talk about what it feels like not to know what you're feeling. The Spiritual Sharing Exercise that follows presents one way of playing with words, helping you become more accustomed to focusing on your feelings.

Forms of Feeling

Affectionate	Furious	Put down
Afraid	Generous	Relaxed
Amused	Glad	Relieved
Angry	Gloomy	Resentful
Annoyed	Grateful	Resigned
Anxious	Great	Sad
Apprehensive	Guilty	Safe
Bitter	Happy	Satisfied
Bored	Hateful	Secure
Calm	Helpless	Sexy
Capable	Hopeless	Silly
Cheerful	Horrified	Strong
Comfortable	Hostile	Stubborn
Competent	Impatient	Stuck
Concerned	Inhibited	Supportive
Confident	Irritated	Sympathetic
Contemptuous	Joyful	Terrified
Controlled	Lonely	Threatened
Defeated	Loving	Touchy
Dejected	Loyal	Trapped
Delighted	Melancholy	Troubled
Depressed	Miserable	Unappreciated
Desirable	Muddled	Uncertain
Despairing	Needy	Understood
Desperate	Nervous	Uneasy
Determined	Out of control	Unfulfilled
Disappointed	Overwhelmed	Upset
Discouraged	Panicky	Uptight
Disgusted	Passionate	Used
Distrustful	Peaceful	Useless
Embarrassed	Pessimistic	Victimized
Enraged	Playful	Violated
Exasperated	Pleased	Vulnerable
Excited	Powerful	Wonderful
Fearful	Prejudiced	Worn out
Frantic	Pressured	Worried
Frustrated	Proud	Worthwhile
Fulfilled	Provoked	Yearning

(Reprinted from McKay, Fanning, and Paleg's *Couple Skills*, with the authors' permission.)

Spiritual Sharing Exercise 9:
Expanding Your Emotional Repertoire

This exercise is designed to help you and your partner become more comfortable using a wide range of feeling words. Here are the instructions:

1. Select which one of you will begin the exercise.

2. Set a timer for ten minutes.

3. Go down the list of feeling words on the previous page and say,

    "I felt affectionate when _____."

    "I felt afraid when _____."

(You can do this exercise in either the past or present tense. For some couples, talking about something they felt in the past is less threatening initially than talking about a current feeling. Later, you might want to complete the exercise again using "I feel" at the beginning of the sentence.)

4. Go through as many words as you can during the ten-minute period. The idea is to not censor yourself. Don't worry if you think your answers aren't good. That's not the point. The goal is to desensitize yourself to saying and hearing a number of different feeling words. Oftentimes, people get stuck on one or two predominant feelings. It can help to break out of that rut by using different words to express yourself. If you draw a complete blank at one word, move on to the next.

5. While one person is doing the talking, the other person should simply listen. There's no need at this point to reflect back anything your partner says. If your partner has said something that surprised you, or that you'd like to hear more about, use this as an opportunity to practice your communication skills after you've finished the exercise.

6. Switch roles.

7. Remember—avoid judging anything your partner says. This is an exercise; it's only practice. Allow your partner the opportunity to stumble and fall (it's the best way to learn to walk).

8. Express appreciation to your partner for doing the exercise with you. Recognize that this exercise, which may seem simple to some, can be a real challenge for others.

The Language of the Spirit

The language of the heart naturally flows into the language of the spirit. In sharing your feelings, you've taken that monumental first step out of your own isolation and into the land of connectedness and possibility—the true terrain of spirituality. In exploring the nature of feelings, you've claimed the search for truth and understanding as your own. Of course, there's no one, ultimate truth, no one, objective reality—you've already seen how people create their own feelings and perceptions. It's the quest—the process—to own and uncover feelings that's of greatest value to you as an individual, and as one part of a couple.

This section is designed to help you and your partner share the process of uncovering feelings, diving deep into the personal meaning of spiritual language. We've offered one or two quotes that we've found poignant under each word we'd like you and your partner to explore. These pithy quotations are from a wonderfully inspiring collection compiled by Claudia Setzer called, *The Quotable Soul*. There's space for each of you to jot down any thoughts, feelings, or images that come to mind. Be sure to communicate with care as you and your partner share your ideas about each word.

Community

"We are born in relation, we live in relation, we die in relation."

—Carter Heyward

"We have merely to assert what already exists deep within us—namely a sense of kinship."

—Norman Cousins

Partner 1: My thoughts and feelings about the meaning of "community":

_____

_____

Partner 2: My thoughts and feelings about the meaning of "community":

_____

_____

Compassion

"There can be no compassion without celebration. Compassion operates at the same level as celebration because what is of most moment in compassion is not feelings of pity but feelings of togetherness."

—Matthew Fox

"The whole idea of compassion is based on a keen awareness of the interdependence of all these living beings, which are all part of one another, and all involved in one another."

—Thomas Merton

Partner 1: My thoughts and feelings about the meaning of "compassion":

_____

_____

Partner 2: My thoughts and feelings about the meaning of "compassion":

_____

_____

Courage

"Courage is the price that Life exacts for granting peace."

—Amelia Earhart

"Life shrinks or expands in proportion to one's courage."

—Anaïs Nin

Partner 1: My thoughts and feelings about the meaning of "courage":

_____

_____

Partner 2: My thoughts and feelings about the meaning of "courage":

_____

_____

Death

"Though lovers be lost love shall not, and death shall have no dominion."

—Dylan Thomas

Partner 1: My thoughts and feelings about the meaning of "death":

_____

_____

Partner 2: My thoughts and feelings about the meaning of "death":

_____

_____

Despair

"Despair [is] the rejection of God within oneself."

—Antoine de Saint-Exupéry

Partner 1: My thoughts and feelings about the meaning of "despair":

_____

_____

Partner 2: My thoughts and feelings about the meaning of "despair":

_____

_____

Doubt

"The first key to wisdom is assiduous and frequent questioning . . . For by doubting we come to inquiry, and by inquiry we arrive at the truth."

—Peter Abelard

"Serious doubt is confirmation of faith. It indicates the seriousness of concern, its unconditional character."

—Paul Tillich

Partner 1: My thoughts and feelings about the meaning of "doubt":

_____

_____

Partner 2: My thoughts and feelings about the meaning of "doubt":

_____

_____

Enlightenment

"We stumble and fall constantly even when we are most enlightened. But when we are in true spiritual darkness, we do not even know that we have fallen."

—Thomas Merton

Partner 1: My thoughts and feelings about the meaning of "enlightenment":

_____

_____

Partner 2: My thoughts and feelings about the meaning of "enlightenment":

_____

_____

Evil

*"Evil can no more be charged upon God than the darkness
can be charged upon the Sun."*

—William Law

Partner 1: My thoughts and feelings about the meaning of "evil":

_____

_____

Partner 2: My thoughts and feelings about the meaning of "evil":

_____

_____

Faith

"Without faith man becomes sterile, hopeless and afraid to the very core of his being."

—Erich Fromm

*"Faith and doubt both are needed—not as antagonists but working
side by side—to take us around the unknown curve."*

—Lillian Smith

Partner 1: My thoughts and feelings about the meaning of "faith":

_____

_____

Partner 2: My thoughts and feelings about the meaning of "faith":

_____

_____

Forgiveness

"Forgiveness is not an occasional act; it is a permanent attitude."

—Martin Luther King, Jr.

"We pardon in the degree that we love."

—Francois de la Rochefoucauld

Partner 1: My thoughts and feelings about the meaning of "forgiveness":

_____

_____

Partner 2: My thoughts and feelings about the meaning of "forgiveness":

_____

_____

God

"The issue isn't what God is like. The issue is what kind of people
we become when we attach ourselves to God."

—Harold Kushner

Partner 1: My thoughts and feelings about the meaning of "God":

_____

_____

Partner 2: My thoughts and feelings about the meaning of "God":

_____

_____

Grace

"Grace is not a strange, magic substance which is subtly filtered
into our souls to act as a kind of spiritual penicillin. Grace is unity,
oneness within ourselves, oneness with God."

—Thomas Merton

Partner 1: My thoughts and feelings about the meaning of "grace":

_____

_____

Partner 2: My thoughts and feelings about the meaning of "grace":

_____

_____

Hope

"What oxygen is to the lungs, such is hope to the meaning of life."

—Emil Brunner

"Everything that is done in the world is done by hope."

—Martin Luther

Partner 1: My thoughts and feelings about the meaning of "hope":

_____

_____

Partner 2: My thoughts and feelings about the meaning of "hope":

_____

_____

Humility

*"The feelings of my smallness and my nothingness
have always kept me good company."*

—Pope John XXIII

Partner 1: My thoughts and feelings about the meaning of "humility":

_____

_____

Partner 2: My thoughts and feelings about the meaning of "humility":

_____

_____

Love

"Someday, after mastering the winds, the waves, the tides and gravity, we shall harness for God the energies of love, and then, for a second time in the history of the world, man will have discovered fire."

—Pierre Teilhard de Chardin

"There is a land of the living and a land of the dead and the bridge is love, the only survival, the only meaning."

—Thornton Wilder

Partner 1: My thoughts and feelings about the meaning of "love":

_____

_____

Partner 2: My thoughts and feelings about the meaning of "love":

_____

_____

Prayer

"The wish to pray is a prayer in itself."

—George Bernanos

"Prayer is our humble answer to the inconceivable surprise of living."

—Abraham Joshua Heschel

Partner 1: My thoughts and feelings about the meaning of "prayer":

_____

_____

Partner 2: My thoughts and feelings about the meaning of "prayer":

_____

_____

Soul

"The life whereby we are joined into the body is called the soul."

—St. Augustine

Partner 1: My thoughts and feelings about the meaning of "soul":

_____

_____

Partner 2: My thoughts and feelings about the meaning of "soul":

_____

_____

Spirituality

"There are four things in which every man must interest himself. Who am I? Wherefore have I come from? Whither am I going? How long shall I be here? All spiritual inquiry begins with these questions and attempts to find out the answers."

—Diana Baskin

Partner 1: My thoughts and feelings about the meaning of "spirituality":

_____

_____

Partner 2: My thoughts and feelings about the meaning of "spirituality":

_____

_____

Suffering

"I do not believe that sheer suffering teaches. If suffering alone taught, all the world would be wise, since everyone suffers. To suffering must be added mourning, understanding, patience, love, openness, and the willingness to remain vulnerable."

—Anne Morrow Lindbergh

Partner 1: My thoughts and feelings about the meaning of "suffering":

_____

_____

Partner 2: My thoughts and feelings about the meaning of "suffering":

_____

_____

Other Words Meaningful to Us:

_____

_____

_____

_____

Some Final Thoughts

In this chapter, you've learned the value of focusing on feelings, as well as how this relates to developing a common spiritual language. Keep in mind that many of the spiritual words listed in this chapter are explored in greater depth later in the book. Feel free to return to this chapter at any time, jotting down additional notes as new insights occur to you. Also remember that the goal isn't to know precisely what you think about each and every word or concept. Part of the value in this step is allowing yourself to wonder, to marvel, to be awed by the mystery of life.

Spotlight on Learning a Spiritual Language

- Feeling words are an important part of a spiritual vocabulary. When you share your feelings, you move from an objective reality to a subjective one, which is the realm of spiritual experience.

- Collect quotes that are meaningful to you, and share them with your partner. Post them on the bathroom mirror—let them seep into your soul.

- Share with your spouse books, poems, films, or musical recordings that have had an emotional impact on you.

Chapter 8

Step 4: Create Meaning for Your Marriage

"Marriage hadn't taken away all our problems. It wasn't a babbling brook of happy kids and an ever-rising standard of living. We wondered, 'What is marriage for?'"

—Kevin and Karen Miller

"What is marriage for?" is a question few of us pondered when we were falling in love. "It's probably the only time in my life when I forgot to eat," said one woman describing the early stage of her relationship with her husband-to-be. Perhaps you can remember a time when you "lived on love," seemingly needing nothing except your partner. Suddenly, swept away with the rapture of romance, you functioned on three hours of sleep for weeks on end. Conversation came easily, and you hung on your new lover's every word. You laughed at each other's jokes, and lavished high praise on each other. The simplest pleasures—a walk in the park holding hands, a warm hug, or a light kiss—were exhilarating.

It's in such moments of divine madness that people find their soulmate, the one who magically singles them out from the masses, proclaims them as special; the one person with whom they'll forge their future. This experience of romantic love is truly an epiphany, infusing your life with a sense of meaning and purpose—a thrill beyond all compare. Unfortunately, for many couples who've been married for even a brief while, romance is smothered by the dead weight of everyday life. You're too busy driving carpools and climbing the career ladder to feel the magic that once overwhelmed you.

It doesn't have to be this way. You *can* bring back the magic. This time, however, it must be rooted not in romantic fantasy, but in the reality of life's limitations. In this chapter, we'll guide you through what Irvin Yalom, Ph.D., calls in his *Existential Psychotherapy* the four "ultimate concerns": death, freedom, isolation, and meaninglessness. We'll show you how by grappling with these gnarly, complex issues, you and your partner can transcend the banality of everyday life, once again finding fervor and fulfillment in your marriage.

Facing the Fragility of Life: How It Can Shift Your Perspective

The first ultimate concern couples must face in transforming the nature of married life is the fact of each other's finiteness. You might question the therapeutic value of dwelling on something so unpleasant, but considerable clinical and scientific evidence speaks to the benefits of thoughtfully considering the inevitability of death.

In his extensive work with cancer patients and their families, Dr. Yalom has found that the monumental shock of such a diagnosis results in far-reaching changes in the patient's life. He summarizes these changes as follows:

- A rearrangement of life's priorities: What is trivial emerges as such, and can be ignored

- A sense of liberation: being able to choose not to do those things you do not wish to do

- An enhanced sense of living in the immediate present, rather than postponing life until retirement or some other point in the future

- A vivid appreciation of the elemental facts of life: the changing seasons, the wind, falling leaves, the last Christmas, and so forth

- Deeper communication with loved ones than before the crisis

- Fewer interpersonal fears, less concern about rejection, greater willingness to take risks than before the crisis

We mentioned in a previous chapter that Greg's father, Paul, was diagnosed with cancer nearly a year ago. Since his diagnosis, and our subsequent move to Jefferson City to be closer to the family, we've been privileged to witness in Paul many of the changes Dr. Yalom describes. When we first decided to move, I was a little nervous about how I'd fit into Greg's family, with not only his parents but also four of his five siblings and their families living close by. I'd always known Paul to be a good man, but he tended to intimidate people. It wasn't so much what he said, from what I could tell, but more of an aura about him. Once he proudly declared, "people either love me or they hate me."

When Paul went into the hospital for his first round of chemotherapy, I tried to take my cues from Greg's brothers and sisters about what my role should be. I learned that there were many unspoken family rules related to illness, hospitals, and what you could and couldn't talk about. When someone from my family was in the hospital, you naturally went to visit him or her. In Greg's family, this wasn't the case. Everyone told me that Paul wouldn't want anyone to know he was in the hospital, much less pay him a visit. There also seemed to be a rule that the children in the family shouldn't know about Paul's diagnosis, or even that he was in the hospital. This was all a bit foreign to me, I guess in part because when our son Jesse had been in the hospital just a few months ago, Greg and I had become accustomed to dealing with medical topics in an open and honest manner with him.

I soon realized that I wanted to forge my own way: I decided I would visit Paul in the hospital, and that I would tell Jesse that his grandfather was in the hospital, receiving some "special medicine." Jesse took this information in stride, immediately asking to draw Grandpa some pictures to decorate his hospital room. He also wanted me to take Grandpa a "special friend"—Jesse's favorite stuffed bear, Corduroy, to keep Grandpa company. Now, I wondered, would I have the courage not only to break the rules and visit Paul in the hospital, but to take this large, rather imposing man a cute, little stuffed animal? Thankfully, the incident turned out well, and Paul seemed to appreciate my visit, and especially the bear from Jesse. Corduroy claimed a special place beside Paul in his hospital bed. When the nurses commented on the bear, Paul enjoyed telling them the whole story about how it was from his youngest grandson.

From then on, I started to notice the softer side of Paul emerging more and more. He seemed more relaxed and content than I'd ever seen him—it was eerie. Previously, his wife would do all the telephoning, but now Paul telephoned family members directly. They put up more Christmas decorations than they had in years, and invited more people to their home for the holidays. It was as if Paul had rediscovered the child within himself: He got down on the floor and played cars with Jesse; he switched the television channel from the Cable News Network to the Disney Channel the moment Jesse entered the family room; he even colored pictures with Jesse in a Barney coloring book. Paul and Greg also talked on a deeper level than they'd ever done before: They discussed the medical procedures Paul was going through; they said the word "cancer," and talked about his prognosis; and they told each other "I love you." Paul's story is an excellent example of what Dr. Yalom must have meant when he wrote, "Death and life are interdependent: Though the physicality of death destroys us, the *idea* of death saves us."

It's unfortunate that for many people, it takes some kind of drastic situation, such as an accident or an illness, to make this kind of transformation occur. Unless they're facing a crisis, most people don't go around thinking about death all the time. Even if they did, would this awareness be enough to transform them in the way in which Paul was transformed? Let's look at the major hurdles you must overcome to allow an awareness of your own mortality, and then to follow through—to call on this knowledge to inform your daily conduct and actions.

The Denial of Death

It must be a cruel joke: We're thrown with no choice of our own into a world of apparent randomness; we struggle to make some sort of sense of things—to live, to learn, to love; and once we fashion a life worth having, we realize it can be snatched away in a second. This awareness, both threatening and painful, lies at the core of much human anxiety. To cope with the absurdity—that we are both mortal, and aware of our mortality—we must defend ourselves against this knowledge. Dr. Yalom asserts that we build two basic buttresses against the awareness of our approaching death: a belief in our own specialness and inviolability; and/or, a belief in the existence of a uniquely personal, ultimate rescuer.

In the first defense, one assumes that the limits imposed by life, such as aging and death, apply to other people, but certainly not to one's self. This defense begins early, in the egocentricity of childhood. Just today, we spent some time on the playground with Jesse. We overheard him and another child engaged in a deep discussion about how robins die, but children don't. As we grow up, we learn on one level that we will die, just as the robins do, but on another level, we continue to believe in our specialness. The second defense against death, that of enjoying the safety and protection of an "ultimate rescuer"—someone who shields us against the stark realities of life—also begins in childhood. As parents, we carefully watch over our children, responding to their needs often before they're even expressed. We're always close by, hovering, protecting. Don't misunderstand us: This is exactly as it should be. Both defenses are necessary, for danger lies in learning too much, too soon. The problem arises when, in adulthood, these defenses are carried to an extreme.

An all too common example of the "specialness defense" gone awry is that of the "workaholic." Compulsively striving to achieve, the workaholic is consumed with a race against time, frantically trying to get ahead. The workaholic constantly pushes and drives him or herself, typically ignoring other human needs, such as for rest, nourishment, leisure time, and relationship. In contrast, the "ultimate rescuer defense," carried to an extreme, results in a person fusing with another so completely that his or her individuality is compromised. An extreme example of this defense is the woman who so desperately fears being alone that she remains in an abusive relationship: She truly believes that she cannot exist without a man in her life. In effect, the specialness defense leads to separation and individuation, the ultimate rescuer defense to merging and dependency.

It's our impression that, in general, men more commonly use the defense of specialness as their primary mode of warding off death anxiety, whereas women are more apt to use the defense of the ultimate rescuer as their bulwark. Most people employ a combination of the two. As Yalom writes, *"Because* we have an observing, omnipotent being or force continuously concerned with our welfare, we are unique and immortal and have the courage to emerge from embeddedness. *Because* we are unique and special beings, special forces in the universe are concerned with us."* It's important to reiterate: Although these defenses pose risks, you nonetheless need them in order to function without undue fear and anxiety. The question is, with what degree of illusion do you choose to live your life? How can you live most fully in the here and now, without lapsing into utter terror or complete despair? Let's examine another crucial factor in this equation.

The Problem of Ego

If you succeed in dealing with your denial of death (which is, again, a process and not a destination), you have yet another problem to face: that of your own ego. Oftentimes, even when people allow themselves to be aware of their limited time together, they don't follow through with this awareness—they don't act any differently because of it. Greg and I faced this situation just last night. Immersed in this chapter, I'd been thinking about death all day. When Greg came home, I wasn't in the best of moods. Despite the fact that throughout the time I'd been writing, my mind had frequently wandered to how much I love him, and to wondering how I could possibly survive without him, when he walked through the door, my positive feelings all but vanished. I asked him to look over what I'd written, and when he didn't immediately love what he'd read, I turned into a vicious monster. I said things I knew hurt him, and, at the time, I didn't care. The more submissive he looked, the angrier I became. Before we went to bed, I halfheartedly said I was sorry, but something still wasn't right between us.

The next morning, we didn't have time to talk, as he needed to leave early to testify at a custody hearing. He called me from his car phone (ah . . . the wonders of technology) on his way to the courthouse, and we talked for a few minutes. This time, I apologized sincerely. I explained that my writing about death had stirred up my own existential anxiety: I had reacted to my own fear and sense of limitation by becoming aggressive, even arrogant. After I hung up the telephone, I read something by psychoanalyst Otto Rank that made sense to me in this context: "The death fear of the ego is lessened by the killing, the sacrifice, of the other; through the death of the other, one buys oneself free from the penalty of dying." Obviously, I didn't kill Greg literally; I did, however, come perilously close to abusing my intimate knowledge of him to wound him, something of which I'm not at all proud. This incident also reminded me tangentially of just how close the emotions of love and hate can be, and how those most close to you hold the greatest power to hurt you.

Accepting Responsibility:
A Crucial Step Toward Change

The second existential concern everyone must eventually face is that of their own freedom. You wouldn't think this would be difficult—don't we all relish freedom and independence? Here's the rub: In freedom lies responsibility, and to be responsible is to be, as philosopher Jean-Paul Sarte said, "the uncontested author of an event or a thing." In truth, you are the author of your own fate. You write not only the good story lines, but also the bad ones. If the plot of your life bores you, or your own character lacks charm, you've no one to blame but yourself. We don't mean this to sound as extreme as it might. You don't necessarily bring on each detail of what happens to you in your life. Certainly environmental and other outside factors exert their influence. We do mean, however, that you *are* responsible for the attitude or the stance you take toward what happens in your life. Like the conscious awareness of death, this notion of freedom is frightening, and people seek relief from the fear in a number of ways.

Randy and Emily are good examples of how responsibility can become displaced, in the effort to protect oneself from the fear of freedom. They'd sought counseling after Randy had experienced his second heart attack and subsequent bypass surgery. This medical emergency wreaked havoc in their relationship in many ways: Emily, not only frightened by Randy's latest brush with death, was furious because he showed no intention of making the life-style changes his doctor had ordered—for the second time around. After the first heart attack, she'd changed her cooking habits, offering the whole family a diet low in fat and cholesterol, but Randy hadn't complied. Although he'd eat "okay" at home, he frequently ate junk food while at work. He also didn't exercise as he'd been instructed, nor did he quit smoking. He frequently blamed his physician for his problems, asserting that if he'd been monitoring him more closely, none of this would've happened.

Our work with this couple focused on teaching them communication skills that would allow them to begin to talk about these issues constructively. The theme of responsibility permeated each therapy session. The crux of the problem for Randy was this: If he now committed to making the prescribed changes in his health habits, and he carried through with these commitments, wouldn't that mean that he could've done so previously? How could he reconcile himself to the fact that his lack of compliance after the first heart attack may have contributed to his second attack? Randy had to face what Yalom and others call "existential guilt." This kind of guilt isn't neurotic guilt over some imagined transgression, nor is it real guilt over some act that was, in fact, committed. Rather, existential guilt is the guilt of omission: It's the guilt that ensues when you don't live life to its fullest—when you're not true to yourself. Dr. Yalom tells the story of Hasidic rabbi Susya, who shortly before his death said, "When I get to heaven they will not ask me, 'Why were you not Moses?'

Instead, they will ask me, 'Why were you not Susya? Why did you not become what only you could become?'" As our work around the theme of responsibility progressed, Randy experienced his existential guilt, not as an enemy to be warded off (as with neurotic guilt), but as a reminder, a trigger, a call to action. Emily's anger dissipated and turned once again to support, while Randy began to feel the full weight of the responsibility he bore for his life. He gradually stopped blaming others for his problems, and began making slow-but-sure changes in his lifestyle.

This issue of responsibility frequently crops up when we give couples homework assignments to complete between sessions. These assignments are typically quite simple, designed not to take much more than 15 or 20 minutes. We learn a great deal from whether or not the individuals involved complete the homework just how much responsibility a couple is ready to assume for changing their situation. Sometimes we become frustrated when couples won't spend the short time necessary to complete the exercises. How can they come to see us for one hour a week and expect us to magically transform their marriage? Don't they realize that the majority of the effort must come from them?

Although we'll certainly discuss this issue with a couple when it arises, we also try, humbly and fairly quickly, to go back to step one and remind ourselves of the value of acceptance. We're not always so sure ourselves about where a couple needs to be at any given point in time, and we can certainly empathize with the difficulty of assuming responsibility for change.

Right after we were married, Greg helped me confront this issue of responsibility; and the experience, although difficult, changed my life. I was in therapy at the time, attempting to fully recover from being raped, as well as to deal with a number of other long-standing issues. After being in therapy with this particular counselor for some time, I felt as if we weren't getting anywhere. I developed insight after insight, but all of this marvelous understanding didn't change a thing. I kept looking to her for direction, structure, and guidance, but she offered seemingly little. I became even more frustrated when she forgot to show up for several of our sessions, and she didn't even offer good explanations for her absences.

In sharing my feelings about the entire situation with Greg, he gently confronted me about who bore the responsibility, and indeed the power, to make change occur. He wasn't excusing the counselor for missing our sessions, but he asked me to look at what I might learn from this experience. I admit that sometimes it's a pain being married to another psychologist—you can't get away with anything. After unsuccessfully attempting to work things out with the therapist, I decided to make a go of it on my own, and I believe it remains one of the best decisions I've ever made. I comprehended much more fully that I was the one who had to provide the direction, the structure, the guidance for my life—it was *my* responsibility. That summer, after I'd stopped going to counseling, I made more significant and what have proved to be lasting changes in my life than I'd ever done previously. In essence, the one insight that did lead to change was this: If no one else is going to take care of me, not even this person whom I'm paying to take care of me, then I'd better do a better job of taking care of myself.

Coping With Isolation:
Love Eases, But Can't Eradicate the Pain

The third existential concern we must struggle with is that of our fundamental isolation: Despite our relationships with others, we die alone. Why is acknowledging this fact so crucial? In recognizing our aloneness, we learn not only the rewards of relationship, but also its limits. In effect, we learn what we cannot get from others. Dr. Yalom writes, "I believe that if we are able to acknowledge our isolated situations in existence and to confront them with resoluteness, we will be able to turn lovingly toward others. If, on the other hand, we are overcome with dread before the abyss of loneliness, we will not reach out toward others but will flail at them in order not to drown in the sea of existence."

When Lane and Adam came to see us for counseling, we immediately sensed that their relationship was like the latter situation Yalom described: Lane had hurled herself at Adam, pressuring him for a commitment, before either of them was ready. Lane had been married before, in her late teens, mostly in an attempt to free herself from her parents' controlling reign. She had one daughter from that marriage. The divorce had apparently been amicable. She and her first husband had simply grown apart as they realized they'd married too young to truly know what they wanted in a relationship. Lane was dating before the divorce was even final. She felt compelled to go out every weekend, thinking it a waste of time if she spent any weekend nights at home alone. After a few brief relationships that, according to her, "didn't pan out," she met Adam. There was a mutual strong attraction between them, and they began dating.

Lane made it clear to Adam right from the start that she wasn't interested in dating "just to date": She was looking for a long-term relationship. Never married before and slightly younger than Lane, Adam was a bit wary of her attitude; but because he liked her so much, he didn't argue with her, and the relationship continued to progress. Within a few short months, Lane had brought up the topic of marriage. At this point, Adam slammed on the brakes and expressed his concern about the swift pace at which they were moving. He told Lane he wasn't ready to become not only a husband, but a stepfather, as well. Devastated, Lane sank into a deep depression, making it difficult for her to function at work or take care of her daughter. Adam still cared for her, and out of his concern, he asked whether there was anything he could do to help. When Lane suggested they seek counseling together, he agreed reluctantly.

As we mentioned at the start of this story, we fairly quickly gathered that this was a relationship constructed on panic—not the strongest of foundations.

We gave the couple our impressions, and suggested that before counseling could be of much benefit to them, Lane needed to deal with her fear of being alone. She'd never been without a man in her life, and she seemed to have no sense of identity or purpose outside of a relationship. For whatever reasons, she didn't follow through with our suggestions, and her relationship with Adam quickly ended.

In thinking about this section on isolation, Greg and I tried to generate a list of things that we, in fact, cannot provide for each other. In other words, what are the limits of a relationship—of our relationship? This is the list we came up with:

- Our relationship doesn't take away the fact that both of us will die *(although the fact that we will die can help us appreciate more fully the time we share)*.

- Our relationship doesn't protect us from bad things happening *(although the strength we draw from each other can help us face adversity and cope with the bad things that do occur)*.

- Our relationship cannot be our complete identity *(although the fact that we're loving, caring beings can be a large part in our identity)*.

- Our relationship does not obviate the need for personal responsibility *(although we can help each other bear the burden of freedom in a healthy, growth-affirming manner)*.

Writing out this list wasn't easy. It's hard to admit that there are limits to love. Going through this process, however, helped us accept on a deeper level—another one of the paradoxes of a spiritual marriage: It's from the limits of relationship that benefits are born.

Finding Meaning in Your Marriage: The Key to Fulfillment

The last of our ultimate concerns is this: How can we find a sense of meaning and purpose in a universe that often seems random and chaotic? When we first began writing this chapter, we thought this section on meaning would be the easiest to write. We're always into projects of some sort or another, forever setting new goals for ourselves (the specialness defense). We assumed that we'd first describe finding meaning in your marriage as being similar to working on a project: First, you find something to do that interests you both; then you work together on the task; and, as a result, you grow closer in the process. For example, writing this book is adding a good dose of meaning to our marriage. It's something we're working on together, something we're committed to and feel passionate about, and something we hope will touch the lives of others.

When we started doing some research for this section, however, we became confused. In talking about meaninglessness, Yalom writes, in *Existential Psychotherapy*, "The belief that life is incomplete without goal fulfillment is not so much a tragic existential fact of life as it is a Western myth, a cultural artifact. The Eastern world never assumes that there is a 'point' to life, or that it is a problem to be solved; instead, life is a mystery to be lived." This insight made us recall one of our professors in graduate school whose area of research was color perception in goldfish. His experiments typically involved goldfish swimming through different colored mazes. He'd always be hanging around the psychology building on the weekends, feeding his fish and checking on his experiments. Once, during a class, a student asked him what had prompted his interest in this area, and the professor replied, "It keeps me out of trouble." It wasn't so much that he had a burning desire to study color perception in goldfish, and he had no illusion that his research would change the face of the world. Did the goldfish simply give structure to his days?

Our thesaurus lists the following synonyms after the verb "to mean": *aim, anticipate, aspire, contemplate, design, desire, destine, direct, expect, fate, fit, make, match, plan, predestine, preordain, propose, purpose, resolve, set out, suit, want, wish.* The crux of the meaning problem, it seems to us, lies with the words "predestine" and "preordain." Is there an inherent meaning to the universe, in which case is it our job to discern and carry through with this preordained meaning? Or, does the universe consist of relatively random stimuli that bombard us from all directions, forcing us to form our own meaning—in which case it doesn't mean much anyway, because we mere mortals were the ones who created the meaning? What a mess!

Dr. Yalom helps us find our way through the maze when he points out that the ultimate concern of meaninglessness is different from death, freedom, and isolation in that you cannot confront the problem directly: Rather, he asserts, meaning must be pursued indirectly. Meaning is a byproduct of "engagement"—a spirited surge of determined action. To create meaning, you must find out what matters to you, what captivates you, what enthralls you, and then "just do it." Yalom writes, "the question of meaning in life is, as the Buddha taught, not edifying. One must immerse oneself in the river of life and let the question drift away."

So what's the answer? How do you create meaning and purpose in your marriage? The meaning in marriage lies in the quest—the answer is in the attempt. Go ahead and explore possible meanings your marriage may have—try them on for size and style. Here are a few possibilities:

- The meaning, or mission, of our marriage is to leave the world a better place to live in.

- Our marriage is dedicated to a group of political/social/spiritual causes that hold special importance for us.

- The purpose of our marriage is to create a sense of home—a safe haven—for ourselves, for the children we once were, and for our own children to carry off into the world with them.

- Our marriage is about helping each other reach our full creative potential and our full potential as conscious adults.

- Our marriage is a chance for each of us to learn the trust needed to give and receive love, to know each other and ourselves as fully as we can.

Keep in mind that the meaning of your marriage will likely change as your relationship grows and develops. For example, here's how we would briefly describe the path that meaning has taken through several stages of our marriage:

Early relationship: Healing each other's wounds; marveling at the fact that another human being could love us so unconditionally.

Birth of our child: Sharing the joy of creating a life; supporting each other through Jesse's health problems; growing in our love as we watched each other nurturing and parenting our son.

This past year: Working together as a team to make all the changes we've made; giving birth to this book.

Enjoying a sense of meaning and purpose in your marriage is accomplished by courageously wrestling with the existential givens of death, freedom, and isolation—and engaging in life fully, not in spite of, but because of, these ultimate concerns. You and your partner will find your shared meaning and purpose in the process of living and loving the questions. We'll explain this in the exercise below.

Spiritual Sharing Exercise 10: Living and Loving the Questions

The reference to living and loving the questions comes from one of our favorite quotes by Rainer Maria Rilke in *Letters to a Young Poet*:

"Be patient toward all that is unsolved in your heart and try to love the questions themselves like locked rooms and like books that are written in a foreign tongue. Do not seek the answers. . . . Live the questions now."

The benefit in doing these exercises is not in finding one right answer. In fact, you may not come up with any answers at all. If you're anything like us, you'll end up with more and more questions, and very few answers that you're absolutely certain about. Simply sharing with your partner the process of questioning is all that's needed. Take your time, and do only one or two of these exercises at a time. If you or your partner feels bogged down, be sure to take a break: Go to a park, fly a kite, take a nap. This is heavy stuff. You need to give yourself permission to take breaks, and to proceed at your own pace.

A Menu of Questions and Exercises
on the Four Ultimate Concerns

I. Death

- Close your eyes and let your mind drift back to the last argument you and your partner had. Immerse yourself in all the details. What was the setting? What was the fight about? Who did what to whom? Who said what to whom? Who was right? Who was wrong? Recall the intensity of your feelings, and all the thoughts that were running through your mind. How long did the fight last? How was it resolved? Who reached out first, signaling the end of the conflict?

   After you've remembered the incident as fully as you can, imagine the situation differently. This time, imagine you have some special knowledge that the very next day your partner will die. Picture the argument now. How would you treat your partner differently? Would the issue of who's right and who's wrong be any more or less important? Would the content of the argument be pertinent anymore? Would you choose different words? Would you resolve the argument differently? Would you let go of your negative feelings more quickly? Share your thoughts and feelings about this exercise with your spouse.

   Recall this exercise the next time you and your partner argue.

- If your spouse were to die this moment, are there things left unsaid between you? Would your partner know, really know, how much you love and cherish him or her? Make a point to tell your partner all the things you appreciate about him or her. Don't wait until it's too late.

- If you had only a year left to live, how would you spend it? How would your relationship with your partner change? Would you be working any more or less? Would you be spending more time together? Would your relationship assume a different priority level in your day-to-day activities?

- Have you and your spouse discussed and made plans for each of your deaths? Do you have a will? A living will? Have you shared your ideas for a memorial service? Have you discussed what you want done with your body after you die, such as burial versus cremation? In his book, *From Beginning to End*, Robert Fulghum includes a number of useful resources on these topics.

- Unless you've already seen it and hate it, rent the movie *Harold and Maude* and watch it together. It's a darkly humorous story of a young man obsessed with death. He meets and falls in love with an elderly woman who, as she approaches death, shows him how to live life to the fullest.

II. Freedom and Responsibility

- This exercise is based on Gestalt therapist Fritz Perls' ideas regarding assumption of responsibility. Dr. Yaloom, in *Existential Psychotherapy*, cited him as saying:

"As long as you fight a symptom, it will become worse. If you take responsibility for what you are doing to yourself, how you produce your symptoms, how you produce your illness, how you produce your existence—the very moment you get in touch with yourself—growth begins, integration begins."

Perls asked his clients to take responsibility for themselves by having them end every statement of fact about their thoughts, feelings, or behavior with "... and I take responsibility for it."

Make a list of things that bother you about your spouse. Read through the list and say, "I take responsibility for the fact that ... " For example: "I take responsibility for the fact that Greg's disorganization bothers me"; or, "I take responsibility for the fact that Barb's worrying gets to me." Notice that you don't have control *per se* over the behavior your partner engages in, but you do have control over whether or not you allow it to bother you, and how you choose to deal with it.

III. Isolation

- Practice being alone. If this is a scary idea, be sure to start in small doses. Sitting quietly with oneself without any agenda for five minutes may be enough to trigger anxiety in some. Others may be ready for more extended periods of solitude. Before I was married to Greg, I sometimes arranged special weekends for myself in which I had nothing planned other than to stay at home and write in my journal. I'd try to prepare in advance to make the time special, ensuring I had plenty of good food already in the apartment, arranging fresh flowers in a favorite vase, playing music I liked, and so on. As I'm writing this now, I remember how much I benefited from those quiet times, and I realize I need to incorporate similar solitude into my married life.

- Think about your unmet needs—needs you wish your partner would fulfill. Are these things that your partner can reasonably do for you? Or are you asking too much of the relationship? Could these be things you need to do for yourself? Are these things you need to accept as part of our human condition? Make a list, as we did earlier in the chapter, of those things you cannot reasonably expect to get from your marriage.

IV. Meaninglessness

- Discuss your thoughts and feelings with your partner about the issue of meaning. Do you believe that there's an inherent meaning and structure in the world, and that it's your job as a human being to discern this meaning? Or do you think that people create their own meaning? Or perhaps you believe that it's more of a mixture of the two scenarios: Yes, there is some fundamental meaning to the world; and as we seek this inherent meaning, we create and try out our own meaning in the process.

- Try creating a mission statement for your marriage. What do you and your partner see as the purpose(s) of your marriage? Remember—this doesn't mean that you have to accomplish some grand task together, but rather that you formulate a shared vision for your relationship. What are your long-term goals? What passions or passionate commitments do you share? Stephen Covey's book, *First Things First*, includes a "mission statement workshop" that's a good resource for this exercise. Here's a sample mission statement written by couples as a part of a marriage enrichment experience in Canada. This credo is now part of a curriculum for newlyweds sponsored by the Association for Couples in Marriage Enrichment.

Credo of an Enriched Marriage
We hereby declare and affirm:

1. That our relationship results from our choice of one another and our ongoing commitment to that choice.

2. That we are married because we are co-creators of our life and not victims of it.

3. That our marriage is created by us with God's help, here and now.

4. That we have a dream about us which constantly changes; a vision about where we are going and what we are becoming.

5. That within our natural limitation of human experience we will *act* to make our dreams come true.

6. That we will constantly feed our changing relationship with new dreams and hopes and aspirations.

7. That our marriage will never be taken for granted. We will care for, nurture, and maintain it as our most precious possession.

8. That we will live intentionally, taking responsibility for what happens to us, boldly shaping what we can of our life, never allowing ourselves to become passive or our relationship to become accidental.

9. That we will live our relationship powerfully and passionately.

10. That we offer our marriage as a sign of hope to the world of the possibility for the fulfillment of love.

Some Final Thoughts

Although all of the steps in this book are important, an awareness and a willingness to explore your fundamental, existential, human concerns is the backbone of a spiritual marriage. The information contained in this step makes the other steps matter all the more. Unfortunately, despite the importance of this chapter, it's probably the one most likely to be skipped over by all but the most dedicated and curious readers. Human nature leads people to avoid thinking about things like death and responsibility.

We remember that when we were first exposed to these ideas, we felt overwhelmed. We found these concepts daunting, yet incredibly powerful and exciting. One of our continued goals—both in our marriage, and in writing this book—is to find that delicate balance of illuminating these existential issues in such a way that we appreciate what's truly important in our lives without becoming overwhelmed by the raw truth and terror of it all.

Spotlight on the Four Ultimate Concerns

- *Death:* "Love is not only enriched by our sense of mortality but constituted by it." (*Rollo May*)

- *Freedom:* "Unless the individual is free to constitute the world in any of a number of ways, then the concept of responsibility has no meaning." (*Irvin Yalom*)

- *Isolation:* "No relationship can eliminate isolation. Each of us is alone in existence. Yet aloneness can be shared in such a way that love compensates for the pain of isolation." (*Ibid*)

- *Meaninglessness:* "When things matter, they don't need meaning to matter." (*Ibid*)

Chapter 9

Step 5: Soothe
Each Other's Soul

"Familiar acts are beautiful through love."

—Percy Bysshe Shelley

*T*ime can erode the feelings of care and concern in even the best of relationships. Within couples, men and women stop doing the nice little things they used to do for each other, because they're too tired, too stressed out, or start waiting for the other person to do something nice first. Eventually, both people feel taken for granted and horribly lonely.

Small acts of kindness—what we call soul-soothing gestures—can be any verbal or nonverbal expression of interest, concern, or affection that is offered frequently and on a regular basis. Things like taking your partner warm towels after a bath, or surprising you spouse by arranging for a baby-sitter, are both excellent examples of soul-soothing gestures. These seemingly small events are the lifeblood of a spiritual marriage, because they offer both partners frequent signs that they are valued and that the relationship is important.

Soul-Soothing at the Start of a Relationship

At the beginning of a marriage, there's much soul-soothing that happens automatically. It's usually called romance, or the honeymoon phase of a relationship—surprising your partner with flowers, leaving a love note on the table, preparing a special meal. We categorize such gestures as soul-soothing: an action taken by one partner for the purpose of comforting, supporting, nurturing, maintaining, and promoting the health, well-being, and development of the other.

Take a minute to recall all the wonderfully simple but significant gestures you used to offer your partner. Remember how much fun it was thinking about your partner and anticipating his or her needs: selecting or making the perfect card you knew he'd love; making those muffins she always raved about; giving one of your to-die-for foot-rubs; waking her up with a kiss and a cup of coffee; simply saying "I love you" and really feeling it. What leads to the decline of these soul-soothing gestures and the good feelings that go with them? We believe the answer to be surprisingly simple—it's the result of basic neglect. Over time, people who are part of a couple fail to give proper attention to their spouse, and to the relationship they share. We also believe that, in most cases, this neglect is not motivated by malice. Rather, couples stop making these soul-soothing gestures for each other, at least in part, because of mistaken assumptions about the nature of a lasting, loving, spiritually rich relationship.

Beliefs That Sabotage Soul-Soothing

Let's examine three common beliefs couples hold that prevent their understanding the true significance of soul-soothing, an understanding that keeps couples motivated to maintain these behaviors over the long (yet often lovely) haul of love.

Soul-Soothing Is Like Icing on a Cake—It Tastes Good, But It's Not Necessary for the Cake To Be a Cake

This is a common barrier to the regular practice of soul-soothing—the belief that it's somehow frivolous or nonessential in a long-term relationship. Yet what could be more important than making your partner feel cherished, important, and central in your life? All individuals need to know they are valued by their partner—not just in the beginning stages, but throughout the lifetime of the relationship. The failing in this belief is that you lose sight of the importance of courting, and you stop doing all the things you once did so naturally when forming the relationship. In order to put a halt to neglect, you must believe that the same attitudes and behaviors so characteristic of falling in love are equally important to maintaining that love.

Because These Activities Initially Come So Easily, They Should Continue To Be Easy

We hear this widely held belief over and over again in counseling sessions with couples. "If I have to work so hard at love, something must be wrong with this relationship." Or "Isn't love supposed to be spontaneous?"

We know that many people think that planning will surely take the spark out of things, but it doesn't have to. Sometimes planning can actually intensify the spark. For example, consider the conscious effort and planning that goes into a secret love affair—commonly thought of as a largely spontaneous experience. First you have to plan a time when you and your lover can meet. This must take into consideration how you'll explain your absences to the other significant parties involved. Then you have to arrange a special meeting place where you won't be spotted or disturbed by interruptions. You have to plan as carefully as a criminal how to obliterate all traces of your meeting; you're as smooth as a conman in making sure your partner notices nothing different about your mood afterwards. This is definitely not spontaneous!

While we certainly are not advocating extramarital liaisons, thinking about the logistics involved can teach you about the benefits of careful planning in a love relationship. Perhaps the major benefit is that something actually happens. If you leave love to chance, you may find that other commitments intrude, and your relationship suffers. Another benefit is that planning, in and of itself, can be an enjoyable experience. The buildup that planning engenders is another plus. The sheer anticipation of being with your partner, of doing something special for him or her, intensifies the whole experience. So while spur-of-the-moment encounters and gestures can be great, spontaneity cannot be relied on for serious soul-soothing efforts.

This belief in the merits of spontaneity—in automatically being spurred to do for and to give to your partner—is dangerous for another reason: When you first start to notice that sensations you had early in your romance are not a long-term "given" of the relationship, you're likely to panic. Something must be wrong! Maybe the relationship wasn't right to begin with—maybe you weren't really in love after all—or maybe your partner has changed. You don't stop to think that maybe the feelings are dwindling precisely because you're not doing all the little things you used to do to nurture your partner and the relationship.

You Shouldn't Have To Work at Love

Closely linked to the previous belief, many people think that love should not require any effort on their part—it should just magically happen. In truth, love requires regular refinement of basic relationship skills—skills such as listening with understanding, expressing feelings with kindness, and resolving conflict without lapsing into criticism. Couples use these relationship-enhancement skills generously in the early stages of their relationship. Over time, however, people stop using their skills and rely more and more—with increasing resentment—on the hope of getting rather than giving what they want. They stop doing what they gladly did at the begining. From outside the situation, it seems incomprehensible that someone would stop doing the relatively simple things that enhance the well-being of a relationship. Yet we can all relate to the numerous factors (lack of time, other demands, even resentment) that get in the way of our doing what we know makes our partner feel happy and loved. It's truly ironic, because the more people understand about each other, the less they tend to act on that knowledge of their partner's most intimate likes and dislikes, hopes, fears, and vunerabilities in a positive and life-enhancing way.

Soul-Soothing: It Starts With Self

In addition to the mistaken beliefs we've just described, there's another reason why couples don't continue to soothe each other's soul once they're caught up in the day-to-day activities and events that comprise a life. The reason is this: An ability to soothe and nurture your partner is intimately linked to your ability to soothe and nurture yourself. When you take proper care of yourself—not only spiritually but physically, intellectually, and emotionally—you operate from a position of abundance, and you naturally seek to empower your partner in any way possible. On the other hand, when you fail to care for yourself, you operate from a depleted, half-empty state, leaving no resources to draw from—nothing to give.

In our work, we frequently encounter people who have a difficult time caring for themselves. They're busy nurturing everyone else, but somehow feel guilty or selfish if they spend even a few minutes each day doing something they want to do. Sometimes it takes some fancy footwork to help these folks understand how crucial it is to care for themselves. One story we tell in our sessions is that of the flight attendant giving the emergency instructions prior to takeoff. The attendant stresses the fact that if oxygen masks drop from the overhead compartments, parents should put on their own masks first, and then help children with theirs. If you're so busy helping your children put on their masks that you pass out before you've accomplished the task, both you and the kids are doomed. If you put on your own mask first—even if your children were to pass out for a few seconds until you could assist with their masks—they'd likely suffer few, if any, ill effects.

When this airplane-safety analogy doesn't get our point across, or in situations where we know someone to be devoutly religious, we sometimes quote the Bible, noting that it says: "Love your neighbor *as* yourself," not "Love your neighbor *more than* yourself." Another metaphor that makes sense to some people is that of a well. You must make sure there's water in the well before you can offer others something to drink. As you finish reading this chapter, focus on what you can do to soothe your partner's soul, but also ask yourself, "What about my well? Is it empty or full or somewhere in between?" Consider the question "What can I do to fill up my well?"

Soul-Soothing Can Be Simple

Although exotic cruises and sparkling diamonds can be nice, soul-soothing doesn't have to be elaborate or expensive. In a survey, Dr. Raymond Tucker and his colleagues asked people to list and rate the things they found "romantic." The simple things in life won out. The number one romantic act was "the kiss." Most people just said "a kiss," but some were more specific and designated places they liked to be kissed, or said that an unexpected kiss was particularly romantic. All sorts of physical affection rated as highly desirable, such as a caress, holding hands, or being hugged. "Talking" was ranked number four on the list. Other simple activities that rated highly included picnics, driving to enjoy scenery, and picking apples.

Flash back to Chapter 1 when we described the process of kindling— how you can produce increasingly large effects with smaller efforts applied over time. Remember that the tiniest twigs start the fire, and the bigger sticks can only catch fire after the smaller ones. And once the fire gets going, if you put on the right kind of wood, it doesn't take a whole lot of effort to keep it going. This is exactly what happens with soul-soothing. Couples who enjoy a spiritual marriage kindle the souls of their partners and, at the same time, the spirit of the marriage. Every day these couples find ways to add freshness to their relationship. These efforts may actually be quite small and simple, but when they're on target, they produce big results. This is how soul-soothing works—it's doing the little things, the things you know work and that keep a relationship vital.

Your Soothing Voice

Some things are so simple, it's easy to lose sight of their power. I could hardly wait to get home and tell Greg about something that happened during an individual session with a client. It was my first meeting with Pam, and I had no prior knowledge of why she was seeking help. She presented as one of the most beautiful, vivacious, and engaging young women I had ever met; anyone looking at her would think she had the world by the tail. Underneath this veneer, however, she was deeply troubled, and she'd been to numerous psychologists and psychiatrists seeking help. She had the routine down pat. She knew that in the first session the goal is typically to gather a lot of background information, assess the situation, and formulate a plan. Quickly listing her symptoms without adding a lot of tangential detail, she played the role of the "good client" well. When I asked about her family background, her composure faltered, but only slightly. She seemed determined to tell her story without showing me how deep her scars were. She unfolded for me some of the most horrific stories of abuse I'd ever heard. All the training in the world didn't prepare me for such a moment, when no words could possibly convey the depth of feeling evoked. Struggling to fight back the tears, all I could say was, "I'm so sorry that happened to you."

What happened next was actually what I was so eager to tell Greg about. My simple words of sorrow, words that seemed hopelessly inadequate to me, released a myriad of emotions in her. She said that in her numerous visits to mental-health professionals in the past, not one of them had expressed anything remotely personal, such as "I'm sorry." It turned out to be a powerful session. She was able to express her anger at the doctors and therapists who, while she told of her traumatic background, kept their heads down, writing notes on their legal pads, as if she'd been talking about having a sore throat or a headache. She expressed surprise that I'd treated her not as a "patient," but a person. This was the beginning of healing for Pam. She gradually learned to treat herself with the compassion and respect she deserved.

This session reminded me of something important: It's not the techniques that matter; rather, what's important is the genuine *desire* to fully be there with another person, to want to soothe their soul. Unfortunately, genuineness can be hard to come by, for it means feeling the pain of the other as if it were your own. To share this pain, you must hold steadfast to a belief in the healing and transformative power of listening.

Think back to the exercises you did in Step 2: (Communicate With Care), and recall what sacred and holy work communication truly is. It doesn't matter if you don't say the perfect thing—there is no perfect thing to say in most cases. Just say something from the heart, and your good intentions will shine through. Here are some examples of ways you can use your voice to soothe, simply but surely:

- "I love you."

- "I miss you."

- "I can't wait to see you."

- "It looks like you've had a rough day. I want to help."

- "I admire you."

- "I appreciate you."

- "I like you."

- "I think you're great."

- "I'm here for you."

If couples said these few, short sentences to each other frequently—not in a perfunctory manner, but with unquestioned feeling—much misery in marriage could be avoided.

Your Soothing Touch

In addition to your voice, you have another soul-soothing salve literally at your fingertips—your touch. When words won't suffice, sometimes a slight touch is all that's needed to lighten your partner's load. With careful attention to your partner's needs, you'll learn to spot the signals that say, "I yearn to be touched." (Don't get too excited: We're not talking about sexual touching here.) I've learned that when Greg's in need of soul-soothing, he starts to yawn. It's not just any yawn, it's a certain kind of yawn that starts out as a strained half smile but never quite makes it. It's almost like he doesn't know that he's stressed or upset until I point it out to him. Once I notice a few of those telling yawns, I lead him over to the couch, rest his head on my lap, and rub his forehead and his temples. Five minutes of massage is often enough to help him figure out what's bothering him, and then to talk about it if he wants to. He knows my spirit is with him; I'm reaching out to him in a way that he finds soothing. Your partner may not be quite so subtle as Greg is in showing you his or her need for touch. For example, when Greg walks by me as I'm writing at the computer, and I groan while pushing the sweater off my shoulders, he doesn't have to guess that I want my neck and shoulders rubbed. Lucky is the man whose wife takes responsibility for getting her needs met! Here are some simple, soul-soothing ways to touch your partner:

- Give your partner a big hug with both arms
- Stroke your partner's cheek or hair
- Kiss your partner on the forehead
- Hold hands
- Massage your partner's hands, feet, or shoulders
- Curl up and cuddle
- Put your hand on your partner's knee
- Give your partner a great backrub

Obviously, timing is crucial, and you must know your partner's preferences: One person might love having his face caressed, while another might find it irritating. Many people love backrubs, yet a few find it tickles too much to be enjoyable, and some think it hurts. Someone may like being touched one way one time, but not another. Don't be afraid to take risks—just be sensitive and open to feedback from your partner.

Spiritual Sharing Exercise 11: Setting a Soul-Soothing Schedule

To get couples back on track with soul-soothing, we have them do this four-week exercise in which soul-soothing gestures are planned for. They're incorporated into your schedule, similar to your three-times-a-week aerobics class or that important business meeting. We'll describe in detail the instructions, and then we'll offer an example of how the exercise worked for one couple we saw in therapy.

- Independently of your partner, create a list of five soul-soothing gestures—things you could do for your partner that would be rewarding or nurturing to him or her. The items on your list should be simple and specific, such as "Take the kids outside to play after dinner so Helen has an hour to herself." Remember to think of what your partner would like, as opposed to what you would like (this is harder than it sounds). We've listed a lot of examples, sorted by category to get you started.

Examples of Soul-Soothing Gestures Catogorized by Activity

Exercise

- Walking: Take a walk with your partner and hold hands; Give your partner some time off from the family to take a walk alone

- Play some music and dance with your partner

- If your partner likes dancing, arrange an evening out dancing together (you can include a dance lesson, if appropriate)

- (Add your own ideas)

Reading

- Read a favorite story aloud to your partner at bedtime

- Surprise your partner with a book or magazine and protected time to lie in bed and read it

- Read a poem to your partner

Music

- Sing a love song to your partner (even if you don't have a great voice)

- Surprise your partner with tickets for a special concert or performance (arrange a baby-sitter if you have kids)

- Have different background music on than you usually do, something that will have special resonance for your partner

Meditation

- Help your partner spend some quiet time alone

- Arrange an outing that will allow you to meditate or spend some quiet time alone with your partner

Rest

- Let your partner sleep in 30 extra minutes while you make breakfast and get the kids up

- Encourage your partner to take a nap, or take a nap together

- Tuck your partner into bed—smooth the pillow, stroke your partner's hair, give a goodnight kiss

Crafts/Hobbies

- Support your partner in his or her pursuit of a favorite hobby

- Surprise your partner with a gift certificate for extra time to work on his or her hobby

- Arrange an outing connected with your partner's favorite craft or hobby

Movies / T.V.

- Surprise your partner and rent a favorite movie (make sure there'll be quiet time for watching it)

- Watch an old sitcom from your childhood

- Arrange a night out at the movies, selecting a movie that your spouse has particularly wanted to see

Bathtime

- Prepare a bubble bath for your partner

- Wash your partner's hair; give a good scalp massage

- Warm up the bathroom with a space heater before your partner wakes up to take his or her shower

- Put lotion on your partner's back after his or her bath or shower

- Warm up towels for your partner for after his or her bath or shower

Food

- Make your partner's favorite meal

- Pack some favorite snacks in a bag for your partner to take to work when you know he or she is going to have a long day

- Make heart-shaped food, such as pancakes or cookies

- Go on a picnic together

- Go to an old-fashioned ice cream parlor and share an ice cream soda

Nature

- Take a walk or hike through the woods

- Watch the stars together

- Go bird-watching

- Plant something together in the garden

- Go to a lake, or river; go boating

Religious/Spiritual

- Go to church or temple together
- Pray or meditate together
- Read favorite scripture or other inspirational passages to each other

Nesting

- Clean up some part of the house or finish some long-ignored house-keeping task that has hung over your partner's head (and present the fait accompli as a love gift)
- Any housecleaning activity done by her partner will likely be soul-soothing to a woman
- Fix up a special corner of the house for your partner (for example, if your partner loves to draw, create a special art nook)
- Arrange to have the whole house professionally cleaned while your wife is off somewhere enjoying herself
- Have flowers delivered

Getting Away

- Surprise your partner with a night out or a day away
- Take the children out so your partner can enjoy being at home alone
- If your partner is usually the one who does the planning, come up with your own detailed plans for a vacation or weekend getaway

Play

- Go to a park together, swing on the swings
- Fly a kite, act like a kid
- Play Monopoly or a card game
- Go to the beach
- Take a fun and physical class together—gymnastics, swimming, dance, ice skating, etc.

Touch

- Surprise your partner with a hug or a kiss, maybe in a different spot than you target—a kiss on the back of the neck, or on the forehead . . .
- Give your partner a hand massage, foot massage, neck massage, or a full-body massage using lotion or massage oil (and with no expectation of sex)
- Make love with only your partner's pleasure in mind

Scents

- Go to your local nursery during growing season and ask for a tour of all the fragrant blossoming plants, smell the flowers together, and choose something to take home and plant in your garden

- Light a scented candle

- Buy your partner one single, fragrant flower

- Go to the ocean or mountains and sniff the air together

Animals

- Take the dog (yours or someone else's) for a walk together

- Go to the zoo or a local aquarium

- Drive out to a horse farm together—pretend you're in the market for an Arabian showhorse; or go horseback riding

- Go to a pet store and look at the puppies and kittens

Don't tell each other what's on your respective lists. Each day, review your list, and make at least one of the soul-soothing gestures. Try to be low-key about it. Don't make a fanfare about the fact that you're doing something nice. Try to notice what your partner is doing for you. That's part of the fun. You can wonder to yourself, "Now, did he bring me that cup of coffee because he was doing the exercise?" In this way, you'll train yourself to pay attention to all the positive things your partner does, rather than dwelling only on the negative.

At the end of the first week, share your lists with each other. Each of you should talk about your experience. Share with your partner what felt good. Mention without blame (use your "communicating with care" skills) anything that you didn't particularly enjoy. For example, one woman we worked with made her husband a big batch of brownies, only to find out later that he had decided to cut back on sweets for a while. Did you notice the things that your partner did for you? Oftentimes, when couples are really into this exercise, they notice many more positive gestures than the daily ones prescribed. After discussing your experiences, drop any items from your list that didn't work well. Get two or three suggestions from your partner for things to add to the list.

Now continue with the program for a second week. Be sure to make time for carrying out the soul-soothing behaviors you plan. Write them on your "to do" list if you have trouble remembering. Then, after the second week, have another feedback session. Pay attention to the things your partner responded to the most. These are the "high-quality" soul-soothing behaviors that you'll want to continue—for whatever reason, they are especially nurturing to your partner. Look to see whether these items have anything in common. Do they lessen his or her workload? Do they involve physical touch? Using what you've learned, add two more items to your list, and surprise your partner with them during the next week.

By the beginning of the fourth week, you should start to notice a change in the quality of your relationship. Both of you are apt to feel more open with each other, and there may well be less conflict. The goal now is to maintain both the program and the good feelings.

Avoid These Stumbling Blocks while Doing This Exercise

- Both of you should commit to doing the soul-soothing gestures daily, regardless of whether your partner performs any. In this way, each of you accepts responsibility for your own behavior, rather than giving this control to your partner.

- You should perform these soul-soothing gestures even if they don't seem "natural" or "comfortable." Naturalness and comfort are the *consequences* of positive interactions.

- Don't expect your partner to read your mind. Each of you should take responsibility by the second week for asking for the soul-soothing gestures you would like.

Soul Soothing With a Twist

Although we frequently focus on the importance of soul-soothing in our work with couples, one couple in particular presented us with a dramatic example of how implementing simple, daily, caring behaviors can improve the quality of a marriage. A couple in their early fifties, Henry and Marjorie came to see us after experiencing serious conflict with each other for several months. The content of the conflict isn't important for our purposes, but suffice it to say that each of them was hurt and angry, neither hesitating to display their frustration in front of us. When we asked them to describe what an improved marriage might consist of, they refused to answer the question. In fact, they practically ignored us, all the while hurling accusations about what the other had done to ruin the relationship.

We intervened and introduced the idea of them performing simple soul-soothing behaviors for each other, and described the exercise we had in mind. We explained that we wanted to interrupt the cycle of blame and negativity that seemed so pervasive and destructive. Both of them expressed cynicism, doubt, and a reluctance to try anything new until the other "proved" a commitment to the marriage. Marjorie stated that the exercise would be useless, because Henry would "never" follow through with this: "He never does anything to contribute to help with running the household, much less the relationship." Henry argued that Marjorie didn't give him credit for what he did do, and he was reluctant to make himself vulnerable to more of her criticism. He feared that the suggested exercise would only lead her to complain that he didn't do things well enough, or frequently enough.

Henry and Marjorie were at an impasse. They were miserable the way they were acting, but neither felt safe enough to risk trying anything different. We decided to add a twist to the soul-soothing exercise to ease them out of their bind. We suggested that for the next week, Henry perform some very simple, thoughtful acts on a daily basis, but the acts should be so small as to be imperceptible to Marjorie. He was to keep his chosen acts of kindness a secret. We wanted Marjorie to have to recognize the change in his behavior with no prompting from him. For the first week, we suggested that they focus on only this aspect of the exercise, so Marjorie was instructed not to do extra kind things for Henry—her sole job was to try to notice what Henry was doing for her.

We were curious about what to expect at the next session, and were pleasantly surprised. The first thing we noticed was a subtle change in their attitudes. They were more lighthearted, although they still seemed quite competitive with each other. We asked Marjorie to begin the session by telling us what soul-soothing gestures she'd noticed Henry making toward her, and she appeared somewhat smug that she'd "found out" what he'd done. She began by saying that she noticed he'd put the dishes in the dishwasher on Monday. Henry smiled and said, "I usually put the dishes in the dishwasher on Monday. That's my day off, and I have time to do more things around the house." Marjorie listed a few other things she'd noticed during the week, but, in each case, she described something that Henry had already been doing.

Fortunately, Henry responded good-naturedly, rather than seizing the opportunity to be smug himself. He told Marjorie he felt good that she'd noticed some of the things he was doing to contribute to the day-to-day maintenance of the relationship, and in a low-key way he shared with her the other, new things he'd done to help out and nurture their relationship. The positive tone of the moment seemed to break the gridlock they'd been in for months, and they were able to continue the exercise in the usual manner while we began addressing some other key issues in their relationship.

Their story demonstrates that there are actually two important benefits of soothing each other's soul: You not only focus on what gestures you can offer your partner that might make his or her day go better, you also focus on the positive things your partner does for you. In this manner, this step of soothing each other's soul mitigates the tendency to keep track of transgressions. Instead, performing these not-so-random acts of kindness generates a spirit of cooperation and goodwill.

Some Final Thoughts

Many marriages die a slow, lingering death because people forget the importance of demonstrating caring and affection for each other on a daily basis.

When you make a conscientious effort to show your spouse how important he or she is to you, you greatly increase the odds of having a rewarding, spiritually alive marriage. This is a fun step: Enjoy delighting your mate and, similarly, allow yourself to be soothed by your partner. Luxuriate in the good feelings created by such mindful consideration of each other's needs.

Spotlight on Soothing Your Partner's Soul

- "A mainstay of nurturing the relationship is finding small, *frequent*, remarkable, and discriminating ways to acknowledge your sweetheart." (Jennifer Louden, *The Couple's Comfort Book*)

- Write love notes to each other; leave nice messages for each other on the answering machine. Find ways to stay connected throughout the day. Think of ideas to make your partner's day go better.

- Commit to doing simple soul-soothing gestures that demonstrate thought, caring, and appreciation. Offer these gestures even if you feel that your partner is not initially showing equal consideration to you. Try not to make this into a competition.

- Be sure to express appreciation for any caring gestures your partner makes.

Chapter 10

Step 6: Connect With Community

*"To be in community is not to be alike or to think alike.
It is to understand our often bewildering daily lives as part of the
unfolding of the larger story of life on our planet."*

—Jean Grasso Fitzpatrick

*A*merica—the land of the free and the brave. We're a culture defined by our rugged individualism; we're people who take care of ourselves and do it our own way. And yet the extreme autonomy that's so revered in our society leaves us feeling isolated and impotent, rather than supported and empowered. Problems ranging from substance abuse to violent crime have been blamed on the collapse of community. Marital dissolution is more prevalent than ever before, at least in part because community support (or perhaps pressure) helped keep couples together in days gone by.

Up until this chapter, it might have seemed that you and your partner could create a spiritual marriage from the comfort and privacy of your home—just the two of you. The truth is that a spiritual marriage starts at home, but it doesn't stay there. Spiritual marriages cannot survive, much less thrive, in a vacuum. Every relationship needs connections with community to invest it with a sense of belonging, of being part of a greater whole. In this chapter, we'll explore the meaning of community—how community is the core condition for the human species. An important part of this step is to recognize the seeds of community that already lie deep within you, and to bring these seeds forth, sowing them, and giving them context. We'll offer ideas, inspiration, and concrete suggestions for attending to this key aspect of a spiritual marriage.

What Is Community?

Some of you might be thinking, "What specifically do you mean by community?" Others may be wondering, "How can I develop community? I live in a nice neighborhood, but people keep to themselves, and my family is spread out all across the country." Still others may be worrying, "I hope they don't mean we have to join a church or something to have a spiritual marriage."

The type of community we're talking about may or may not be the kind your grandparents knew—one in which bonds were formed based on kinship, geography, or religious ideology. Although traditional communities enjoyed many strengths—including unwavering caring and commitment—they also possessed weaknesses, such as rigidity and exclusivity. In many communities of the past, if you didn't fit a particular mold, you were ostracized from the group. The type of community we advocate—the kind central to a spiritual marriage—is one that retains the care and commitment of the past, yet adds an appreciation for individual differences, and for the important role these differences can play in group process.

Carolyn Shaffer and Kristin Anundsen, authors of a comprehensive handbook on the community movement called *Creating Community Anywhere*, offer a five-point definition of community based on their extensive research. They write, "Community is a dynamic whole that emerges when a group of people:

- Participate in common practices
- Depend upon one another
- Make decisions together
- Identify themselves as part of something larger than the sum of their individual relationships
- Commit themselves for the long term to their own, one another's, and the group's well-being."

We like this definition because it's so inclusive: It can refer to more traditional types of communities, such as families, neighborhoods, and churches; and it might also refer to newer visions of community, such as groups of people who consciously choose to come together for a common purpose.

To further illuminate the concept of community, some authors have described it as the web of life, while others have depicted it as ever-widening concentric circles of friends, family, faith communities, neighborhoods, regions, the world, the universe. Martin Luther King, Jr., called this idea "the beloved community." In *The Couple's Comfort Book*, Jennifer Louden writes, "Your relationship is framed by your circle of friends and family, the community you live in, the region you inhabit, and the world condition." On page 168, we've used the image of concentric circles to diagram the various layers of community. Take a moment to reflect on the people and groups of people who make up your beloved community.

Regardless of the imagery used, an awareness and appreciation of your ties to community is vital to your well-being, both as an individual and as a couple. Results from numerous medical and psychological research studies bear this out. Psychologist Robert Ornstein and physician David Sobel conclude: "Whether we look at heart disease, cancer, depression, tuberculosis, arthritis, or problems during pregnancy, the occurrence of disease is higher in those with weakened social connectedness." In essence, the more a couple reaches out not only to each other, but to the world around them, the more energy and substance is available for that couple.

Community as Our Core Condition

If community is so important, why is our culture so steeped in the mythology of rugged individualism? To a large degree, this relates to the way in which scientists have perceived the very nature of life. Prior to the early twentieth century, the leading thinkers based their ideas on Newtonian physics, which asserted that reality existed only in isolated units of matter. People, like other forms of matter, were seen as entirely independent of one another. Only in the past few decades, with the latest discoveries of quantum mechanics and ecology, have scientists conceded that all forms of matter are connected, existing in dynamic relationships with one another. Nothing, not even an electron, can be known in isolation. We found especially intriguing a comment made in *Creating Community Anywhere*: "Systems thinker Joanna Macy likes to say that we humans have insider knowledge of community because we embody it: in the communities of bacteria in our guts and mitrochondria in our cells."

The realization that we are already community personified can ease fears we may have about giving up too much—about losing our individual identity in the process of carrying out this step of connecting with others. People often presume, perhaps based on past experiences of community that didn't work well, that they must sacrifice their uniqueness for the good of the group. Because of a phenomenon called synergy, however, it doesn't have to be this way. Stephen Covey writes that synergy is everywhere in nature: "If you plant two plants close together, the roots commingle and improve the quality of the soil so that both plants will grow better than if they were separated. If you put two pieces of wood together, they will hold much more than the total of the weight held by each separately. The whole is greater than the sum of its parts. One plus one equals three or more." Thanks to synergy, you don't have to give up "you" to enjoy the experience of "we." Community enhances and contributes to the full expression of your unique talents and gifts; it doesn't detract from it.

Creating Community: Soul Sustenance for Your Marriage

Let's get down to practicalities. How do you go about creating community when, as one woman told us, her neighbors barely associate and her family is

"The Beloved Community"

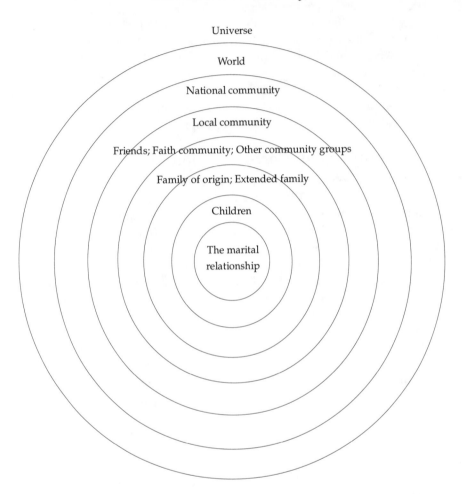

Universe

World

National community

Local community

Friends; Faith community; Other community groups

Family of origin; Extended family

Children

The marital
relationship

hundreds of miles away? In this section, we'll look at the different layers of the beloved community, showing you how to weave a richly textured tapestry to wrap around your marriage.

Marriage Is a Community of Two

The core of the beloved community is your marriage. In essence, your marriage is a long-term, committed, and caring community of two. If you've been following the steps in this book thus far, you're well on your way to being a community in every sense of the word. You're living your relationship consciously, and intentionally, making every moment count. You're communicating with care, you're soothing each other's souls, and your marriage is filled with meaning and purpose. Not that the going is always easy—that's not possible. Rather, you're transforming obstacles into opportunities, embracing inadequacies and imperfections, and, learning and growing from the mistakes you make.

One of the major challenges of a spiritual marriage is to find ways to maintain your "two-ness" while at the same time expanding the boundaries of your community to include others. When you have children, for example, your community grows, and yet you must remember that you're still a community of two. Although children certainly play a vital role in married and family life, we often find ourselves counseling couples who have become too child-focused, who are losing sight of their core connection to each other.

Andrea and Ryan are a classic example. Married for three years with a six-month-old infant, they sought couples' counseling at the suggestion of Andrea's OB/GYN; Andrea had confided in her doctor that she was feeling depressed, and believed her marriage to be a primary source of her unhappiness.

During our first session with this couple, we heard both sides of their story. Andrea shared with us that she didn't feel close to Ryan the way she had envisioned she would after they had a baby together. "I thought having a child would bring us together, make us more of a family. Instead, I feel like Ryan has backed away from me. He's always working; even when he's home, he's doing something on the computer." Ryan said to us: "Andrea had a difficult time after the delivery. Her sisters had all experienced postpartum depressions, so I thought we were somewhat prepared; but I guess it's hard to know exactly what to do. I've tried to help out. Just last Saturday, I asked my father-in-law to come over, and we spent the whole day childproofing the house. And the reason I'm on the computer so much is that I'm trying to get our finances entered into it. I want to figure out a way for Andrea not to have to work again until she's ready."

When we asked them if they'd had much time alone since the baby was born, they said they hadn't. They seemed somewhat overprotective, at least by our definition, as they didn't allow anyone to care for the baby except Andrea's mother, who lived 30 miles away and didn't like to drive. If they wanted to go out, they had to pack up the baby and all the baby gear, and drive 45 minutes to drop the baby off. Then they were in the middle of nowhere, so they'd have to drive back to the city to see a movie or go out to dinner. They said that it just seemed like too much work. They also didn't have much time for each other at home, in part because of Ryan's hectic work schedule, but also because of their difficulty in getting the baby to bed. Neither of them wanted to let the baby cry and, consequently, the baby learned to stay up later and later.

You didn't need to be a psychologist to understand why Andrea and Ryan didn't feel close. Stressed to the max with the demands of an infant, they weren't caring for even their basic needs as a couple. Sure, when you have a baby you expect that your relationship will take a backseat for a while. But after six months, unless there are special circumstances, you'd better be tending to each other, at least a bit, or you'll find the relationship on rocky ground.

Our work with Andrea and Ryan was relatively easy, as they were a caring couple, and had a basically good foundation to their relationship. Our first goal was to help them see how Ryan had channeled his insecurity about dealing with his wife's depression into trying to gain control over practical manners related to the baby. He didn't know how to fix his wife's moodiness, but he did know how to put locks on the cabinets and protective covers on the outlets. He didn't know when his wife would feel up to working, but he did know how to create a spreadsheet on the computer to analyze their finances. These were all things that needed to be done, but they didn't involve time with Andrea.

We helped Andrea appreciate that these "instrumental" tasks were Ryan's way of gaining control over the situation, as well as his way of helping; and we helped Ryan see that the more he withdrew emotionally from Andrea, the more depressed she became. We also gave them the task of asking friends for names of baby-sitters, and interviewing them to find a few with whom they might at least consider leaving the baby with for even an hour or so. We told them it was crucial to spend some regular time alone, as a couple, if their relationship was to survive. We also coached them on a behavioral plan for helping infants develop good sleep habits. What seemed to help them the most was simply developing the right mind-set: Bedtime is for parents. Couples need time alone to nurture each other and their relationship—to remember that they were husband and wife first, and parents second. This point can't be stressed enough: You must nurture and tend to your marriage, for it is the center of the rest of the community you create.

Family of Origin: First Experiences With Community

Your extended family, both your own and your partner's family of origin, forms the next layer of community. It's within your first family that you initially experienced the joys and challenges of community life. You developed methods for solving problems; you learned how to express, or not express, your feelings; you celebrated together; you grieved together; and most importantly, you developed your understanding of what it means to belong. As children grow into adolescence and then young adulthood in Western society, the goal is to separate and individuate from family. Although a few people seem to navigate their way gracefully into adulthood, forming a new identity without reactively rejecting all of their family's ways, most of us trip and fall a good deal along the path. In a marriage, how well this process of separating and individuating from one's first family was carried out holds huge implications for the health and well-being of the current family.

We worked with one couple whose problems clearly related to the problems they'd had with their families of origin. Brendan and Eve had been married for only a little over a year. During the initial counseling session, they each focused on the faults of her partner: Eve complained that Brendan was disorganized, sloppy, and emotionally distant; Brendan argued that Eve was so perfectionistic and rigid that she wasn't any fun to be with anymore. In asking about their family backgrounds, we learned that Brendan had come from a rather chaotic, alcoholic family with little structure in the home. What little routine there was revolved around his father's drinking habits. Brendan also remembered a few incidents of physical abuse in the family. Although those weren't a frequent occurrence, they were enough to lead him to become fearful of any expression of anger. Eve, on the other hand, came from a family in which anger was not expressed, period. Hers was a family that maintained a pleasant facade regardless of their true feelings. The family placed a heavy value on control and order. Eve was praised for getting good grades and accomplishing things—for being "productive." There was little room left for fun or spontaneity.

Without prompting from us, Eve and Brendan noted right away that what had initially attracted them to each other was exactly what they were complaining about now. Eve had been drawn to Brendan's "laid-back" style, which allowed her a feeling of acceptance she'd never had before. "He knew how to get me to relax—something I was never any good at," she said. She'd even found charming his unique attire of odd T-shirts and oversized jackets collected from thrift shops. Now she labeled him a "slob," and thought him lazy, and it drove her crazy how passive he seemed. Brendan, on the other hand, had been attracted to Eve's stability. "She seemed strong and secure. I didn't ever have to worry about emotions getting out of hand with her. I also liked it that she made me feel like being more responsible." Now he thought she was a "depressing control freak." Through this discussion, they learned something therapists have noticed for a long time: People usually want to get divorced for the same reasons they wanted to get married.

We worked with Brendan and Eve to understand how their first families were affecting their current marital relationship. We helped them shift from looking at all of each other's faults to recognizing that each of them had lacked something in their growing-up years. Brendan had missed out on the structure that makes a child feel secure, and he lacked appropriate models for expressing anger constructively. Eve had developed her whole identity on the basis of her accomplishments, and thus couldn't enjoy herself when she was relaxing. Although in our counseling we don't often spend a lot of time on the past, it proved quite helpful for this couple to understand the context from which they came. In effect, they learned how their first experiences in community affected their current community of two.

With their newfound insights, however, both Brendan and Eve ran into another problem. Now that they "saw the light," they had little patience for either their parents or in-laws—and they wanted to fix both sets of families. They had been in therapy for about six weeks when the Christmas holidays involved visits to both sets of families. It's not an uncommon phenomenon when people are in therapy: They get so enthusiastic that they want to convert others to their way of thinking. In *Successful Marriage*, Robert Beavers calls this the "missionary approach." Brendan and Eve didn't fare too well when they tried to convert their relatives to their way of thinking. Both families were confused, hurt, and angry: "Why are they criticizing us? This is the way we've always been." On top of their parents' displeasure, they were in conflict with each other once again.

Our goal at this point was to help Brendan and Eve regroup, and to look a little bit differently at what they'd learned. Instead of the missionary approach, we urged them to try the "anthropological approach"—to look at their families of origin with an eye toward understanding and appreciating the complexities and subtleties of the communication patterns and coping strategies that took place. Both set of parents had been married quite a long time, so there must be some strengths in the way they'd handled themselves all these years. The next time they had an opportunity to visit their families, we encouraged them to view it as a "field trip" of sorts, a chance to study different communities. When they visited each family, we had them ask themselves: What are the rules of this community? What are the values? The traditions? How is the power shared? What works and what doesn't? We wanted them to try to switch from their judgmental stance to one of simply observing and studying another culture.

This shift in attitude helped them immensely. They reported that they had enjoyed the visits with both families much more than they had previously, and that they also felt new compassion for each other when they could see where some of their behavior patterns had come from. They were able to see that both families had some strengths, and that there was no need to reject them with one fell swoop. When Brendan and Eve weren't caught up in changing their families, they were free to enjoy the good parts. We like this insight of Dr. Beavers': "Anthropologists are not prevented from loving their natives just because they study them; quite the contrary, respect for people's values and beliefs is a vital part of loving."

Extended families can be a great strength to a couple, or they can be a source of tension and conflict. Here are some tips to help you and your partner forge satisfying, nonstifling relationships with your parents and other family members.

- Don't presume without proof that your parents can't adapt to change. Some families may be a lot more flexible than you'd imagine. Acknowledge your parents' right to their opinions and ways of doing things. Many parents resist change in their children, because they feel it's a criticism of their own ways. Assert your right to do things your way, but do so nondefensively, without anger and remember to maintain emotional contact. Sometimes grown children find it so difficult to set limits with their parents that when they do so, the action comes off as punitive and rejecting. Try to maintain warmth and contact while simultaneously setting limits. When you shift your role in this manner, everyone else in the family is freer to change.

- Make it clear to your parents that just because you may not be living your life exactly as they are, it doesn't mean that you're rejecting them.

- Sometimes it can be helpful to have your parents and family over to your home. When parents or in-laws aren't on their own turf, they tend to be much more open to trying new things and doing things differently.

- Don't expect perfection from your parents. If you're a parent now yourself, you know what a difficult job it is to raise children. Your parents have done the best they could with the resources available to them. Practice acceptance.

- Please know that if you experienced physical, sexual, or emotional abuse growing up, and have chosen not to have contact with any or all of your family members, we respect your decision. Some families are so dangerously dysfunctional that there's nothing to be gained by maintaining any connection with them. Give yourself permission to grieve this loss, and to realize that you'll need to work even harder to develop a supportive community network outside your family.

The Friendship Factor

Friends can provide yet another rich source of community for a couple. Sometimes people need someone besides their spouse to turn to as a confidant, or just to have fun with. It's also wonderful to have other couples to share good times, or provide support during a rough patch. Unfortunately, some traps lurk in the friendship factor, particularly in regard to the way men and women have traditionally experienced friendship.

Michelle and Richard provide a good example of some common pitfalls found in extramarital friendships. This couple sought counseling for the vague complaint that their marriage was stagnating. They both felt there was little energy or life being brought to the relationship by either of them. They both worked full time; going to the movies by themselves was their only recreation. They enjoyed being together, but sometimes felt bored. Michelle complained that if they ever did anything socially, she was the one to arrange it. Because she tended to be a little shy, she didn't initiate things with others very often. She wished Richard would do more of the work of expanding their social life. There were a few couples she'd met and enjoyed talking with at his company

Christmas party. She'd suggested that he bring up the idea of dinner with one of the guys at work, but Richard never followed through. Richard, in contrast, felt so comfortable and content with Michelle that he wasn't as motivated to reach out to others. He didn't see it as the big deal that she did. Michelle had some women friends, but limited the time she spent with them because Richard didn't have any friendships of his own. She usually only did something with them during the workday (such as go to lunch), when it wouldn't take time away from Richard. She wished Richard had some friends of his own, so she wouldn't have to feel guilty about her own friendships.

Part of our work with this couple was to validate their experiences. In reality, it is quite difficult for men to make friends, particularly with other men. Our society is so homophobic that many men are afraid of being labeled as gay if they enjoy friendships with other men. Sometimes, men can get around this by pursuing an activity together, such as sports. While there might not be a whole lot of deep discussion that goes on while fishing or playing baseball, sometimes the relationships that develop transform into something more over time. It's also a reality that men are apt to depend on their wives for creating their social network. A problem arises when this expectation goes without discussion or questioning. Many women feel burdened by this responsibility, preferring to share it with their partners; but because the topic is rarely brought up for discussion, the opportunity is missed to work out an arrangement that feels more equitable.

Although for men the problem lies in too few friendships outside the marriage, the trap for women's friendships tends to go in the opposite direction. Women often share things with their friends that would be more appropriately discussed with their partners first. In talking with Michelle and Richard, we learned that when Michelle was upset about something in the marriage, she would avoid talking with Richard about it directly. More often she would have lunch with a girlfriend to communicate about her discontent—and her girlfriend was all too eager to complain and commiserate about the trouble with men. The gender differences displayed in Michelle and Richard's story are quite common, and certainly not insurmountable. In therapy, Richard learned to feel enough self-confidence to pursue a couple of friendships with men he liked, and Michelle learned to trust Richard enough to go to him first with their marital problems.

Later in this chapter, we offer a number of suggestions for creating community, several of which have to do with forming friendships to support your marriage. Here are some preliminary ideas to consider:

- When examining the quality of an existing friendship, or thinking about new friendships, ask yourself: "Is this person usually supportive of my marriage?" "Does he or she value marriage?" "Does he or she actively work to enrich his or her own marriage?" While certainly all your friends don't have to be alike or think alike, it can be helpful to have friends who respect your marriage, value their own marriage, and think highly of the institution of marriage.

- In general, we've found it a good balance if couples have some individual friends and also some couple-friends with whom they do things together.

- Keep in mind that the quantity of your friendships isn't nearly as important as the quality.

- Also keep in mind that individual differences play a huge role in social style. Some people are extroverts, not necessarily meaning they are always outgoing, but that they gain much of their energy from others. In contrast, introverts are not necessarily shy, but they do derive most of their energy from themselves. Everyone needs a balance of togetherness and aloneness, but this introversion-extroversion scale determines to what side the balance needs to be weighted for optimal comfort. If you and your partner are different in your social styles, this is an area that will require greater mutual understanding as well as skillful negotiation on both your parts.

Beyond Friends and Family: Other Sources for Community

So far, we've looked at the innermost layers of the beloved community: your marriage—a community of two; your families of origin (parents, in-laws, and other relatives); and friendships. In this section, we'll explore other sources for community—the ever-widening circles of your world.

Finding a Group to Enrich Your Marriage

There are a number of group activities in which you can participate to nourish your marriage. Some of these are established, formal organizations, designed solely as marriage enrichment activities. Others may be support groups, such as Alcoholics Anonymous and Al-Anon, which may hold some joint meetings with spouses. Other groups may be an informal gathering of married couples who come together to share their thoughts and feelings, their hopes and dreams, and their ideas for keeping their marriages alive.

The group we're most familiar with is called ACME, which stands for the Association of Couples in Marriage Enrichment. We've been fortunate to speak to ACME groups, to attend some of their local and national seminars, and to become acquainted with other couples who belong to the organization. We've found these couples to be some of the warmest, most welcoming people we've ever known. ACME members realize that good marriages just don't happen—and they're willing to make the effort and learn the skills to make it happen.

ACME is an international, nonprofit, nonsectarian organization uniquely dedicated to the enrichment of marriages. The organization was founded in

1973 by Dr. David and Vera Mace, the same year they celebrated their fortieth wedding anniversary. After many years of counseling married couples, they noted a lack of programs designed to strengthen marriages. Too often, couples waited until problems were completely out of control, then sought therapy and wondered why it didn't help. It wasn't simply a problem of people waiting too long to seek help; until recently, there hasn't been much talk about good marriages, or how to keep them good. In effect, the Maces' dream was to start a "marriage wellness program," which is exactly what ACME is today.

Although ACME isn't associated with any religion, and doesn't define itself as spiritual, its focus on communication—the kind of communicating we've described throughout *Illuminating the Heart*—is clearly in sync with the steps in this book. One of the key aspects of ACME is "dialoguing" (their term for the empathic listening and spiritual speaking described in Step 2) in the presence of other supportive couples. This type of public dialoguing might happen during a weekend retreat or at a monthly couples-growth group. Many people feel understandably apprehensive about sharing in front of other couples, but the participants in these groups will tell you that the gains are well worth the risks.

Rev. John Robinson and Diane Weber are one such couple. As members of ACME for eight years, they've found it a powerfully transformative experience in their marriage. They report that a major benefit is the opportunity to see other couples at various stages in their marriages. John told us, "You learn that relationships have their ups and downs, you're not alone, and you'll get beyond whatever it is you're going through." Diane added that you can also learn a lot by seeing how other couples work out certain problems. They both agree that the dialoguing process itself, whether done privately or publicly, is where the healing takes place.

John recounted the following example: "Diane and I had been arguing about what kind of vacation to take. I wanted to go to the mountains for at least six weeks. Diane felt that would be much too long. For some reason, we kept getting polarized in our arguments and couldn't reach any sort of rational compromise. Before we had resolved anything, it was time for us to participate in an ACME Advanced Leadership Workshop for five days. There was still tension between us when it was time for us to do our first dialogue within the workshop. We chose to dialogue about this vacation issue. In the course of this hour-and-a-half dialogue, which seemed like it went by in about a minute, we were able to get to the underlying issue. Diane listened to me, and by her listening in a deep and caring way, I was able to go deeper and deeper into my thoughts and feelings. What emerged came as a surprise to me, because I wasn't consciously aware of why I'd felt so compelled to spend an extended period of time in the mountains. Through dialogue, I realized that much of my intensity had to do with the fact that I was now over the 50-year mark, living in the flat Midwest, and frightened that I'd die before I got to the mountains again. I had always gained much of my spiritual nurture from nature, from the mountains, and I longed to be there again. This realization unlocked us from the power struggle we'd been in. Diane and I both now understood why I was so driven not to take her wishes into account. With the true issues exposed, we easily agreed on a solution. We went to the mountains with the understanding that it would be okay—and brought enough extra money along—for Diane to buy an airline ticket and return home whenever she wanted. As it turned out, we both had a great time, and stayed for the entire six weeks."

This kind of occurrence is not unusual in ACME. Being privileged to hear other couples share in this way can help you make your own break-throughs in understanding.

Finding a Faith Community You Can Feel Part Of

We recognize that those of you reading this may be in very different places along your spiritual path. Some of you may belong to a church, syna-gogue, or other faith community, and feel that you have a "spiritual home." Others of you may have belonged to a church in the past, but attend irregu-larly or have stopped going completely. Perhaps you and your partner come from different religious backgrounds, and one of you goes to one church, one to another. Unfortunately, some of you may have even been so traumatized by an extremely rigid religious upbringing that you feel unable to join any type of faith community again. We certainly don't believe it's a necessity for you or your partner to belong to a church, synagogue, or other religious institution. You may have found a more informal or a nonsectarian way to meet your needs for community—for example, by belonging to a marriage enrichment group such as ACME. Or, perhaps you and your partner get together with several couples on a regular basis to talk with each other about what really matters to you in your lives. All of these, alone or in any combination, are good and viable options.

For those of you who are considering looking for a faith community to nurture you and your marriage, we offer these thoughts. We're in a unique situation today. Unlike our European ancestors who went to a certain church based on what village they lived in, we're a culture that shops. We remember a *Doonesbury* cartoon in which we see a couple leaving a church and the wife says, "What did you think?" The husband replies, "I think we should check out the church down the street. I hear they have handball." We talked with John Robinson, the minister at Eliot Unitarian Chapel in Kirkwood, Missouri, about this issue. He said, "I think church shopping is basically a good thing, so long as at some point you make a commitment one way or another." He offered the following questions to ask yourself after you've visited a church, a synagogue, or any other place of worship a few times:

- Do you sense an atmosphere of openness and supportiveness?
- Do you sense a willingness to take risks?

- Are there programs that support marriages?

- "Theology is not just spoken, it's lived," John said. What is the life of the community like? Is it joyous? Somber? Just a fashion show?

Remember, too, that no church is perfect. As is the case when any human beings form relationships, there will be frustrations, disappointments, conflicts. The key lies in how these conflicts are resolved. Jean Grasso Fitzpatrick makes another important point: "Entering a house of worship does not— *should* not—mean abandoning our critical faculties. It does mean accepting the fact that a community of faith is a gathering of ordinary mortals who are 'in process,' like ourselves."

Finding Community Through Service

If the group experiences we've described so far haven't appealed to you, there are many other ways you can nurture your relationship in the context of community. We were particularly moved by one couple we knew who found meaning and fulfillment in their marriage by doing volunteer work together. Jane and Paul had struggled for years to conceive a child, but were unable to. They didn't have the financial means to pursue extensive infertility testing, nor did they have the money it now takes to adopt. Paul had his career to keep him busy, and he was active on a number of sporting teams. Jane, on the other hand, had recently lost her job, and felt there was little meaning or purpose in her life. She also felt that she and Paul had drifted apart after they realized they weren't going to have a child together. One Sunday at their church, there was an announcement that a daycare center in an inner city area was looking for volunteers. Jane was surprised when Paul suggested he take a day off during the week so they could give it a try. It turned out they enjoyed the experience so much that Paul was able to rearrange his schedule so they could volunteer regularly one day a week. Through this experience, they not only grew closer as a couple, they also met people they never would have met before (they lived in a small, rural town about an hour away). Their world, which had sometimes felt too small and stifling to Jane, suddenly expanded.

You don't have to make as great a time commitment as Jane and Paul did. There are plenty of other, smaller ways you can make a difference. Take a few minutes to look over the following menu of ideas for connecting with community. Check any that you and your partner might be interested in. Be sure to jot down your own ideas as well.

Connecting With Community: A Menu of Ideas

Make Your Marriage a True Community

☐ Follow the steps in this book

☐ Complete the Spiritual Sharing Exercises

☐ _____

Make Peace With Your Families of Origin

☐ Plan field trips to "study the natives." Remember to use the anthropological approach. What can you learn from your families' modes of behavior?

☐ Make a list of the aspects of each of your family's communities that you'd like to preserve in your current family. Are there any of these aspects you'd like to modify?

☐ Make a list of the aspects of each of your family's communities that you'd definitely like to ban from your current family. What steps, if any, do you need to take to make sure certain patterns aren't repeated?

☐ Whom in your families might you like to get to know better? How could you reach out to them?

☐ _____

Make Your Neighborhood More of a Community

☐ Get to know other families and couples in your neighborhood.

☐ Plan a couples' night out; get teenagers in your neighborhood to baby-sit.

☐ Start a neighborhood newsletter.

☐ Send out postcards inquiring about interest in a babysitting co-op.

☐ Invite your nextdoor neighbors over for dinner. Find out the story of how they met.

☐ Take a meal to a neighborhood couple who've just had a baby.

☐ _____

Find Friends Together and on Your Own

☐ Join a book group if there's one in your area—these usually meet once a month.

☐ Take a class together. A variety of classes are offered through local YMCAs or community colleges. One couple we know took ballroom dancing classes. Not only will you have fun sharing an interest with your partner, you'll also meet other couples.

☐ Encourage one another to take as much time as you need for individual interests and friendships.

☐ _____

Join Other Types of Communities

☐ You might consider joining some type of support group, either together or individually. Many women have benefited from therapy or discussion groups; more men are seeking out such experiences as well.

☐ Join a marriage enrichment group. See the listing at the back for the Association for Couples in Marriage Enrichment (ACME).

☐ The church we belonged to in St. Louis had various men's and women's groups. We liked the name of one of them, which was called SNAG (Sensitive New-Age Guys).

☐ Join a committee or a task force together to strengthen some aspect of community life, such as parks or public schools.

☐ Host a group to discuss some of the ideas in this chapter. Have a brainstorming session.

☐ _____

Find Meaning and Fun in Volunteering Together

☐ Volunteer for a local literacy program.

☐ Help out in a homeless shelter together.

☐ Do fundraising for a worthy cause; it's easier to go door-to-door with a companion than alone.

☐ Teach a Sunday School class together. Once Greg and I, along with another couple, taught a group of four-year-olds. It was truly a learning and growing experience—for the children, too.

☐ If one of you is asked to speak to a group, see if you can work it out so that you and your spouse can speak to the group together.

☐ Visit a nursing home together.

☐ Call the United Way and get a list of possible volunteer activities. Circle the ones that interest you, and then compare notes with your partner.

☐ If your church sponsors pre-marital retreats or workshops, offer to help out. What could be more rewarding than helping engaged couples get their relationships off to a good start?

☐ If you have a garage sale, donate some of the money to an organization that gives aid to needy families.

☐ _____

Spiritual Sharing Exercise 12:
Confronting the Challenges of Community

Below are some questions to help you and your partner explore the challenges you face in creating your own beloved community. As you answer the questions, you might find it helpful to look back at our diagram of community connections, and to place your ideas in the appropriate concentric circles (make photocopies of the blank model if you want to). Answer the questions on your own, and then share your answers with your spouse.

Partner 1

1. What value do I see in connecting with community? _____

   _____

   _____

2. What are my greatest fears about connecting with community? Where might these fears have originated? _____

   _____

   _____

3. What positive memories do I have involving a sense of community?

   _____

   _____

4. What negative or ambivalent memories do I have of community? ____

   _____

   _____

5. Would our marriage benefit from greater connection with community? If so, at what level? Family connections? Friendships? A faith community? Other community groups? _____

   _____

   _____

6. What are our current strengths and weaknesses in our community connections? _____

   _____

   _____

   • To whom do we reach out when we need practical assistance?

   _____

- To whom do we reach out when we're looking for advice?

  _____

- To whom do we reach out when we want to share good news?

  _____

- To whom do we reach out when we want to have fun?

  _____

- Do we have friends we can do things with as couples?

  _____

- Does each of us have our individual friends?

  _____

- What areas of community support/involvement need development for us?

  _____

- Are there situations we've experienced in which help is not readily available?

  _____

- In what areas do we feel a void or a lack of connections?

  _____

7. What prevents me/us from reaching out? _____

  _____

  _____

8. How can we deal with our barriers? How can we muster the courage to reach out? _____

  _____

  _____

9. Or, do I/we already overextend ourselves, leaving not enough time or energy for our community of two? _____

  _____

  _____

10. What can we learn from our parents' and grandparents' marriages and their sacred love stories (or from their failures)?

  _____

  _____

Partner 2

1. What value do I see in connecting with community? _____

_____

_____

2. What are my greatest fears about connecting with community?
Where might these fears have originated? _____

_____

_____

3. What positive memories do I have involving a sense of community?

_____

_____

4. What negative or ambivalent memories do I have of community? ___

_____

_____

5. Would our marriage benefit from greater connection with community? If so, at what level? Family connections? Friendships? A faith
community? Other community groups? _____

_____

_____

6. What are our current strengths and weaknesses in our community
connections? _____

_____

_____

   • To whom do we reach out when we need practical assistance?

   _____

   • To whom do we reach out when we're looking for advice?

   _____

   • To whom do we reach out when we want to share good news?

   _____

   • To whom do we reach out when we want to have fun?

   _____

- Do we have friends we can do things with as couples?

  _____ _____

- Does each of us have our individual friends?

  _____

- What areas of community support/involvement need development for us?

  _____

- Are there situations we've experienced in which help is not readily available?

  _____

- In what areas do we feel a void or a lack of connections?

  _____

7. What prevents me/us from reaching out? _____

_____

_____

8. How can we deal with our barriers? How can we muster the courage to reach out? _____

_____

_____

9. Or, do I/we already overextend ourselves, leaving not enough time or energy for our community of two? _____

_____

_____

10. What can we learn from our parents' and grandparents' marriages and their sacred love stories (or from their failures)? _____

_____

_____

Some Final Thoughts

Depending upon your personality, this step may be more or less difficult to carry out than other steps in the book. If you're like we are, tending to be on the quieter side, it may seem intimating to reach out. For others, however, connecting with community comes naturally. In either case, as you expand your awareness of who you are individually, and as as couple, you'll gain a better idea of where to begin in your efforts to connect with a broader community. You'll learn that community can be found in unexpected places; and that as a couple aren't limited to facing life's challenges alone.

Spotlight on the Community Context

- Talk with your parents and grandparents about their sacred love stories; use the questions in Chapter 1 to guide you. Do you see any connections between their stories and yours?

- "To know ourselves in community is to know our roots, to look back and learn from humanity's past mistakes, and to move forward—however haltingly—together." (*Jean Grasso Fitzpatrick*)

- "Community is a safe place precisely because no one is attempting to heal or convert you, to fix you, to change you. Instead the members accept you as you are. You are free to be you. And being so free, you are free to discard defenses, masks, disguises; free to seek your own psychological and spiritual health." (*M. Scott Peck, M.D.*)

Chapter 11

Step 7: Add Spice With Celebrations and Rituals

"Ritual behavior softens the phases of life when we are reminded how hard it is to be human. Ritual behavior enriches the phases of life when we are reminded how fine it is to be human."

—Robert Fulghum

We felt rather anxious when thinking about writing this chapter. Deeply ingrained in how we live our life together, writing about the previous steps to a spiritual marriage flowed naturally for us; but for some reason, this step seemed forced. After all, we don't walk around the house chanting prayers and lighting incense. We're just like many other busy families: We consider ourselves doing well if we sit down together for dinner on the majority of nights. When we woke up on the morning we'd planned to work on this chapter, Barb told me about a dream she'd had the previous night. In the dream, she was interviewing several people about the role of rituals in their lives, and each of them looked at her skeptically, telling her something along the lines of, "We don't have any rituals. That stuff is weird. We try to stay away from it." In the dream, Barb explained to these people that rituals didn't have to be "weird" or "way out"—they were everyday, ordinary things they probably took for granted, simply not recognizing them as ritual.

Barb's dream sparked some new ideas for us, and a new way of thinking about this topic. We decided to make a list of rituals we shared in our life, and we were astounded at what we came up with—just off the top of our heads. We had been worrying that we wouldn't have enough to say in this chapter. Yet when we made our list, it was over a page long. Part of the work of this step is simply to recognize the rituals you already have in your life. Then you can build on what's most meaningful for you.

The Role of Ritual in Your Life

Rituals abound if you only stop to notice them: the way you kiss your spouse good-bye and say, "Have a nice day"; the way you might say the same, simple grace at the dinner table each night, or wish your partner *"Bon appe'tit;"* or the way you prepare your children for bedtime. Of course, there are also the more elaborate, more easily recognized rituals of weddings, funerals, baptisms, birthdays, and anniversaries. Regardless of the event, the heart of a ritual is a sense of connection—to yourself, other people, the past or the future, to the greater mystery of life. The most profound rituals allow you to feel part of a greater whole; they somehow sanctify human existence.

In *Rituals for Our Times*, Evan Imber-Black and Janine Roberts list five purposes of rituals; the first function is *relating*. In many ways, rituals serve to shape, define, and enhance our closest interpersonal relationships. Details one might not pay much attention to—such as which family members attend what functions, or who sits by whom—all give us clues about the state of our relationships. We think of Sunday afternoons, a time we now spend visiting with family. After so many years of living considerable distances from any close relatives, we appreciate being able to get together for a meal and to catch up on family news. We value the time not only for ourselves, but for our son, who has this opportunity to feel close to his extended family. Although much of the conversation on these afternoons is of the small-talk variety, the act of getting together nonetheless affirms and validates the relationships within the family.

Another function of rituals involves *changing*—to signify the important transitions that occur in our lives. For example, in most cultures people attend weddings to witness the emergence of a new family unit, funerals to say good-bye and begin the grieving process. In our culture, we also have rituals such as bridal and baby showers, bachelor parties, and retirement dinners. Change—even an anticipated, positive one—can be frightening. Passing from one phase of life into another naturally evokes a certain degree of anxiety, for we cannot fully know what lies ahead. Rituals can ease the transition.

Rituals may also serve to promote *healing*, be it the healing of an individual, a family, or a community. In the Jewish tradition, there are various prescribed rituals to help people heal after the loss of loved one. A group of men may "sit shiva," receiving the prayers for the deceased. On the first anniversary of the person's death, the family unveils the grave monument, marking the end of the mourning period. This process serves to encourage the necessary mourning and acknowledges the deceased. As psychologists, we have worked with many people suffering from unresolved grief because there was no ritual to acknowledge their loss.

Another function of ritual involves *believing*—giving voice to what we stand for, expressing our ideas about the meaning of our lives. The ritual of eating meals together represents a belief in the importance of family time. The ritual in some marriages of having regular "dates," apart from the children, signifies a belief in the value of couple time. The fact that beliefs can change over time means that rituals, too, must not be carved in stone. One of Greg's sisters, Judy, a nun with the School Sisters of Notre Dame, explained that many of the changes in the Roman Catholic church have been difficult for those who like things to remain constant. For example, before Vatican II, mass was spoken in Latin by a priest who stood with his back to the congregation. Now most services are conducted in the congregation's native language by a priest who faces the congregation. These changes in the ritual of mass reflect Catholics' evolving beliefs about the benefits of an active rather than a passive congregation. More personally, she recounted that not so many years ago in the parochial school in which she taught, she was the first nun to wear slacks to work. For Judy, this change in "ritual behavior" announced her belief that wearing comfortable clothes was more conducive to working effectively with first-graders, allowing her to approach them more closely, both in the classroom and on the playground.

The last function of ritual, and one of the major ways in which rituals work for us, involves *celebrating*. All cultures have rituals of celebration which typically include special food, drink, clothing, music, and gifts. A major task is to make sure that rituals geared toward celebrating truly feel joyous. Too often, people go through the routine of the ritual without connecting with the underlying meaning of the event.

One couple we worked with, Nickie and Craig, marked most of their holiday rituals by giving each other expensive gifts. Over the years, both of them grew tired of trying to think of something to give the other person, something that would outdo what had already been done. Their gift-giving rituals felt more like a burden than a ritual of true celebration. Fortunately, they were able to talk with each other about their feelings, and were surprised that they were thinking along the same lines. This discussion helped them begin to clarify not only their values and beliefs about gift-giving, but also many of the other ways in which they celebrated holidays. They soon began to create new ways to acknowledge the important days in their lives.

Although we've listed the functions of rituals as though they were separate, in reality they often overlap. For example, a wedding provides a sacred time to mark change in the context of celebration. A family dinner provides a chance for relating as well as expressing beliefs. We're going to turn now to examples that illustrate some of the most important principles associated with rituals.

The Three *R*s of Rituals

Rituals Involve Remembering

Robert Fulghum, in his book on rituals, *From Beginning to End,* writes, "I see ritual when people sit together silently by an open fire. Remembering. As human beings have remembered for thousands and thousands of years." Fulghum's point about remembering brings us back full circle, to where we began in Chapter 1. There we wrote that every relationship contains its own spiritual drama, a sacred unfolding that provides a richly textured backdrop of meaning to married life. In the first Spiritual Sharing Exercise, we asked you and your partner to reminisce about how your relationship developed; about what drew you, seemingly magically, together. We wanted you to see how you formed your sacred bond through the careful caring and nurturing of each other's spirit. By completing the exercise, you retold at least the opening chapter or two of your own love story.

As a relationship progresses, the novel evolves. The plot takes twists and turns. We grow in our love for the characters as we're privileged to share in the deepest, and sometimes darkest, secrets of their souls. Like any good novel, this "book" is hard to put down. The stories demand to be told. We encourage you to deliberately take the time and make the effort to keep the narratives of your marriage alive. They will remind you of what's important, as they simultaneously point you in a productive and positive direction.

We were both passionate about journalism before deciding on psychology for our careers. Barb earned a degree in journalism, and I wrote for my college newspaper, seriously considering journalism as my life's work. We value reporting as a way of understanding our own lives as well as the world, of gaining insight and perspective on our emotional, chronological, and sensory experiences as individuals. We also believe that documenting the relationships and rituals of our lives is important. You might try creating a journal of your relationship in which you and your partner alternate writing entries during and after significant emotional events. Many people have found it meaningful to create a photo album or scrapbook documenting the special times they've shared as a couple. Barb is nearly fanatical about keeping our photo albums and scrapbooks current. She even makes sure to use only acid-free materials that won't damage photographs over time—perhaps it's a way to feel immortal. There's definitely some comfort in knowing that family members in generations to come will be able to see what we looked like, to read about our rituals and celebrations, and to know what we believed in. In *How To Write Your Life*, Frank P. Thomas says, "Members of your family want to know more about you than you think. They will treasure every word you write. To them, you are the connection between the remarkable past and the present. In fact, you are history, and history disappears if you don't record it."

Rituals Must Be Real

To be meaningful, rituals must be relevant to your present circumstances. Too often, people become rigid in their insistence on certain rituals, keeping things the same way, year after year, even if it doesn't make sense to do so anymore.

We'll never forget one Christmas when we were forced to abandon most of our traditional holiday rituals. We didn't put up a tree, wrap presents, make cookies, or take any of the usual family pictures. (Not taking the pictures is the only part we regret now.) That Christmas was Jesse's first. It was a few weeks before Christmas when Barb received a telephone call giving us the news that one of my best friends, Brian, was stricken with Guillian-Barre syndrome while he and his wife, Sue, were traveling to Bolivia to adopt a baby. When Brian and Sue finally found medical care in Bolivia, he was already becoming paralyzed, and had to be flown to a hospital in Miami. When Sue called to tell us what had happened, I knew I wanted to go see them right away. It was a tough time for everyone. While I was in Florida doing what I could to be helpful, Barb was home struggling with our own little son Jesse and his health problems. Jesse had an appointment scheduled with an ear/nose/throat specialist. Usually Barb and I went to his appointments together, but since I was out of town, Barb took Jesse alone. The doctor recommended that Jesse have tubes put in his ears right away, so he had surgery on Christmas Eve morning. Fortunately, I was able to fly home to be there during the surgery.

Everything went well with the surgery, but by Christmas Day we were wiped out. We felt somewhat guilty about not having a "real" Christmas, but tried to console ourselves with the fact that Jesse was only nine months old, so it wouldn't really matter to him. Although we didn't perform our usual rituals in the usual way, we nonetheless made it a good day. Barb and I exchanged letters we'd written to each other while I was in Florida—we hadn't managed to mail them. We had Jesse open the few presents that had been mailed to him from out-of-town relatives. We also gave thanks that Jesse had managed so well with the surgery. It was another hurdle successfully cleared, in what turned out to be a long series of hurdles. We went over to see Bill and Jerri (Barb's brother and his wife), who lived just a few blocks away; we knew they didn't have any big plans we'd be interrupting. Our intended brief visit turned into a day of nurturing and pampering. Jerri cooked us a wonderful meal, and then Bill and Jerri encouraged us to take a nap while they entertained Jesse and their daughter. Although there were fleeting moments of sadness as we remembered the festivities of Christmases past, the way we celebrated that year was "real," and we had the experience of feeling truly gratified and fed.

Evan Imbor-Black and Janine Roberts use the term "interrupted rituals" to describe what happened to us that Christmas. They note that when people are stressed or struggling through a crisis, rituals—once easily carried out—can prove impossible. If you find yourself in this situation, don't panic. The first step is to simply acknowledge the stress. If you're going through a difficult time, don't make yourself feel worse by trying to plan for and enjoy each and every one of your rituals in the same way you always have. Take steps to rally your resources, and meet your needs. It's okay to take a break from your rituals, especially if carrying them out would seem somehow false. Just remember not to make the mistake of completely abandoning your rituals in the future, even if you revise them once the crisis is over. We've known families who understandably didn't celebrate a certain holiday immediately after a close relative died, but, even years later, they denied themselves the pleasure and comfort of their rituals.

Rituals Should Be Relaxed

Although there's certainly a time and a place for elaborate and formal rituals, we prefer our own everyday rituals to be relaxed and flexible as opposed to forced and inflexible. Especially if any of your rituals involve children, it's a setup for frustration and disappointment if you insist that things go precisely a certain way. A few nights ago, Barb had prepared a special meal for Jesse and me. She suggested that we select a prayer to read from a new book she'd bought, *A Grateful Heart: Prayers for the Evening Meal From Buddha to the Beatles.* Jesse was agreeable, as long as he could hold the book himself and pick out the one he wanted. When he picked a page, Barb asked for the book back so she could read it aloud, but he resisted, saying, "No. I want to read it." In that he's only just four years old and can't yet read, we wondered how he'd solve this one. At first he only stared at the page, so Barb asked, "Would you like to hold the book while either Daddy or Mommy reads?" He said again, "No. Be quiet. I'm thinking of the words." We'd decided to keep out of a power struggle with him, and began to eat, when words started pouring out of his mouth: "Dear God, thank you for Mommy and Daddy. They are very nice to me. I love them so much. Thank you for the blueberry muffins. Thank you for the rain to help make the grass green . . ." and on and on. Once he got started, we could hardly get him to stop. Because we had let go of our preconceived ideas of how the "ritual" should go, this simple moment took on a wonderful life of its own. Jesse's prayer was much more beautiful and meaningful to us than anything we might have read from a book. If you decide to introduce some new or revised rituals involving either your spouse or your whole family, remember to start slow and keep your expectations realistic. It's better to keep the tone upbeat and relaxed, engendering positive feelings to build on the next time.

Getting Ready for Rituals

At this point, you're ready for some specifics about how to plan for and carry out your own rituals. Although there's no right or wrong way, you can increase your chances of enjoying a meaningful experience by following these general steps.

Develop a Healthy Mind-Set

To get the most out of the rituals in your life, you need to be in the right frame of mind. First of all, identify any negative statements you may be making to yourself. For example, when George decided he'd like to incorporate some customs from his family of origin into his current family life, he caught himself thinking, "Lisa's not going to like this. She's used to doing things the way her family always did them." It's important to identify anything like this that may prevent you from getting off to a good start. Negative thinking, if unchecked and unchallenged, can affect how you present your ideas to your spouse, sabotaging your efforts before you ever begin. If you see this as a potential problem, go back to Chapter Two, "Turning Obstacles into Opportunities." You can use the Thoughts and Feelings Diary in that chapter to monitor what you're saying to yourself on the subject of rituals. If, when you look over your diary, you notice some unrealistic thinking going on, you're in a position to correct the situation before it gets out of hand.

In examining your mind-set, ask yourself these questions: "What do I want to accomplish with this ritual? What is my purpose? How do I want to feel after carrying out this ritual? What do I want to have happen?" You may already have specific answers to these questions, or you may be more like George—you simply have a general feeling that you want to do something differently. If you're not yet clear about what your goals are, that's okay. You might initiate a conversation with your partner—use the communication skills outlined in Chapter 6—to explore your rituals together in an attempt to see what's working, and what's not for each of you. The Spiritual Sharing Exercise that follows this section offers a variety of ideas for rituals you might want to try.

Planning Is Helpful

After you and your partner reach a consensus about what you want to accomplish through a given ritual, take some time to plan out the details. Ask yourselves:

- Who will take part in the ritual? Do you want it to be a private ritual, involving only you and your spouse, or would it be even more meaningful to invite close friends and family? Will your children be involved?

- Where will the ritual or celebration be held? Which of you will make any necessary arrangements regarding the place, food, music, etc.?

- Will you use any special symbols? Robert Fulghum lists some common symbols used in rituals: fire or candles, which he describes as "matter becoming energy"; water—"the metaphor of life"; bread— "the staff of life"; wine, which is "the product of fermentation and time." Anything meaningful to you can become a symbol—a special photograph, mementos from another time or place, a particular piece of music.

- If any words are to be spoken, who will speak them? Who will write them?

- Will food be involved? If so, who will prepare it?

- What about gifts? Will they be made or bought? Who will take care of this?

Whether or not these questions are relevant to the ritual you have in mind, remember that it's better to make your arrangements inexpensive and simple, and to share the workload with your partner. (There's more on this in Spiritual Sharing Exercise 14.)

Evaluate the Experience Constructively

After you've carried out the ritual you've planned, you again need to watch what you say to yourself and check for negative thinking. Barb, for example, tends to be self-critical and perfectionistic; she can easily pick to pieces any ritual or celebration she's planned if she allows herself to. She must allow herself to feel good about the process, and not to worry about every detail that may not go as planned. She's getting much better at this. For example, when Jesse didn't go along with the way she'd initially envisioned reading the grace before dinner, she was flexible. She allowed the ritual to evolve in a way that turned out to be beautiful. Afterward, she gave herself a much-deserved pat on the back for the way she'd been able to switch gears—to go with the flow.

Spiritual Sharing Exercise 13:
Creating Your Own Couple Customs

Below is a list of ideas for rituals. Some of the segments also contain questions to stimulate further discussion. Read through the list with your partner, and check any ideas that appeal to either of you. Just because you check an idea, it doesn't commit you to carrying it out. This "menu" is simply a way to help you think about ideas for rituals you'd like to explore further.

After you look back over any items you've checked, decide on one idea to follow through with. Feel free to alter or expand on any of the ideas listed; or, better yet, jot down your own ideas in the blank spaces provided. You'll notice that some ideas are listed in varying forms under several of the headings. This is because many of the ideas contain common themes, and can easily be adapted to suit a number of different situations.

Creating Couple's Customs: A Menu of Ideas

Birthday Rituals

☐ Make a scrapbook celebrating each year of your partner's life. Include photos. Maybe have relatives and friends write relevant stories to include.

☐ Give a small gift to symbolize each year, or each era, of your partner's life.

☐ Read a special prayer at your partner's birthday meal. You can write your own or read one from a book. See the Resources section for some possibilities.

☐ Has your partner ever had a surprise birthday party? Unless you know with absolute certainty that this isn't a good idea for your partner, give it a try. For many people, a well-engineered and sensitively planned surprise party can be a very special honor.

☐ I did this for Barb's birthday once: Make a scavenger hunt of clues for your partner to follow and figure out in order to find his or her present. The game is as fun as the gift.

☐ Send your in-laws a card on your spouse's birthday telling them how great their son or daughter is, and how thankful you are for the fact of his or her birth.

☐ _____

Anniversary Rituals

☐ Consider celebrating not only your wedding anniversary, but the anniversary of your first date, your first whatever. Robert Fulghum devotes an entire chapter of his book on rituals to mark people's memories: "The first time I . . ." This alone could be a Spiritual Sharing Exercise—for you and your spouse to take turns asking questions and talking about "first times"("When was the first time you knew that you loved me?").

☐ Make a scrapbook celebrating each year of your life as a couple. Include photos and other mementos, such as love letters, tickets, and so on. Write about the feelings the pictures evoke. Write about what was happening then in your relationship.

☐ Look at pages in the scrapbook you've already completed. Tell the stories of your relationship—remember your sacred love story (see Spiritual Sharing Exercise 1 for examples of questions to get you started.)

☐ Read a special prayer before the meal you share on your anniversary. Again, you can write your own or read one from a book. See the Resources section for some possibilities.

☐ Reenact your first date. Wear the same clothes (if you can), go to the same places, play the same music.

☐ Go back to the same place where you celebrated your honeymoon. If you never took a honeymoon, take one now.

☐ Plan a rededication ceremony. This doesn't necessarily have to be formal or elaborate. You and your spouse might simply reread your vows as you recommit to a conscious and caring, loving relationship.

☐ _____

Other Holiday and Celebration Rituals

☐ Make a special scrapbook for holiday celebrations. Your pictures don't have to be perfect. The point is to make sure that you write a lot about who's in the pictures, and include details about your holiday rituals that you'll want to preserve through the generations.

☐ Read a special prayer at the holiday meal. You can write your own or read one from a book. See the Resources section for some possibilities.

☐ Make sure to spend some special time alone with your partner during busy holiday seasons. Don't get so caught up in the hustle and bustle that you lose your sense of connection to one another. One couple we know makes sure they spend New Year's Eve alone, as they're always so busy with children and grandchildren during Christmas. Every year, they prepare a nice meal together, which they eat on a card table, complete with a linen tablecloth, set up in front of the fireplace. They always look forward to this special time of quiet togetherness and reflection.

☐ Celebrate not only holidays, but other significant events in your lives. Celebrate the fact that you had an argument that was actually constructive. Celebrate that you're reading this book together. Celebrate new jobs, new homes, the first day of spring.

☐ _____

Healing and Loss Rituals

☐ If you've experienced some sort of painful loss or trauma, make a collage depicting what the event meant to you. You can cut words and pictures out of magazines, draw or paint your own images, or use whatever materials feel right. You might also include words or images to represent how you might have changed or grown since the loss or trauma. Share the collage with your spouse in some way. For example, Barb used to write poems about her experience of being sexually assaulted, many of which she either wrote to, or shared with, me. We included one of the poems in Chapter 1 because it was a significant part of our sacred love story. Barb also made a series of collages, which she often shared with me around the anniversary date of when she was raped depicting the effect the experience had on her, and how she had healed. You don't have to enjoy any special artistic abilities to make use of these kinds of rituals.

☐ Ask your spouse to acknowledge you in some special way on the anniversary of your loss or trauma. Perhaps you wish your partner would think of this independently but people are often unsure about what to do or say on such anniversaries, and opt for silence as the safest route. Let your partner know exactly what would help you heal.

☐ Pay a special tribute to your spouse for any of the ways in which he or she has contributed to your healing.

☐ Planting and gardening can be a healing ritual for many people. Earlier we spoke of a couple who planted a dogwood tree in remembrance of their child who died in utero. Planting a bare-root tree or shrub can hold special significance, mirroring the bleakness of grief that will eventually bloom with life and hope again. Planting bulbs can be a way to pledge your commitment to the resurgence of life in the future.

☐ Play music that evokes a certain feeling, and have your partner hold you while you listen to it. Barb used to feel better listening to Suzanne Vega's song, "Small Blue Thing" while I held her closely.

☐ Similarly, poetry can be a powerful ally in the healing process. Barb and I are avid fans of anything written by Margaret Atwood; look for the words of other writers who might lend you comfort and strength.

☐ Find ways to mark losses that many people try to keep as low-key as possible. When we had to find a new home for our dog, Chelsea, after our son was diagnosed with allergies and asthma, we had a going-away party for the dog. We each gave her special gifts to take to her new home, Frosty Paws ice cream and lots of hugs. We each told her in our own way how much we'd miss her. Other examples of losses a couple may face that have no readily established rituals include

• The loss of a baby through miscarriage

- Losses as a result of cancer (e.g., breast cancer, hysterectomy)

- Losses associated with menopause (the end of your childbearing years)

- Loss of children when they move away

- Numerous losses as a result of aging

☐ _____

Everyday Rituals

☐ Notice how you say good-bye to your partner each morning, and how you reconnect at the end of the day. These rituals are important; they help couples navigate the terrain of intimacy, learning to dance the steps of separating and joining. One couple we know announces their excitement at arriving home by honking the horn at the top of the driveway.

☐ There are rituals associated with when you talk, and when you don't. Do you try to talk while your partner is in the bathroom reading the paper, or is this sacred time, definitely not a time to be disturbed in your household? Do you talk during meals? What do you talk about? When do you make eye contact? When don't you look at each other? When do you touch? When don't you? All of these details are, in fact, rituals. You can create profound changes in a relationship by altering one of these everyday rituals even a minute bit. Try making eye contact and using your partner's full name when you speak. You may be surprised how good it can feel to have your name spoken by someone you love.

☐ Use music to create everyday rituals. Some couples have special morning music, or music they listen to while driving, music to put them in a romantic mood, or a particular piece of music they listen to on Sunday mornings.

☐ In creating everyday rituals, don't forget your other senses. Light a scented candle. Wake your partner with fresh-squeezed orange juice or a cup of tea. Incorporate the power of touch. This might be as simple as stroking your partner's cheek each morning as you say something sweet.

☐ _____

Blessing Rituals

☐ In *Prayers for the Domestic Church,* Edward Hays offers numerous prayers to bless persons or objects. Writing from a Christian perspective, he notes that the purpose of the blessing isn't to make someone or something holy, since God has already done that. "Rather, blessings call forth a special grace from God to use an object as its artistic creator intended. The blessing of a person is meant to make that person the receiver of light, love, and special affection from God . . ." You don't have to be Christian to enjoy the benefits of blessings. For example, many couples who don't believe in the theology of baptism nonetheless wish to bless their infant in some way and create their own blessing or dedication ceremony.

☐ A sampling of blessings from Ed Hays's book: Blessing Prayer for the Home; Blessing Prayer for a Garden; Blessing Prayer for Pets; Blessing Prayer When About to Leave on a Journey; Blessing Prayer for a Marriage Bed. You can say your own simple blessings. If you wish, light a candle to mark the moment. If you're blessing a garden, you might sprinkle some water as a symbol of the blessing you're offering.

☐ _____

Rituals of Gratitude

☐ Every evening before you go to sleep, thank your partner for three things that inspired your gratitude. In the morning before rising, share three other things that you are thankful for in general. Your day will be framed with a wonderful feeling of abundance and gratitude.

☐ Entertain the idea of praying with your partner. You don't have to pray to any particular deity. Simply thank some higher power for the good times. Offer thanks for the bad times, too—for the strength to persevere, and the opportunity to grow by learning.

☐ Say a prayer or blessing before each meal. In the foreword to *A Grateful Heart*, William H. Shore (executive director of Share Our Strength, an organization that fights hunger in the United States) writes: "I've always viewed mealtime as a humbling moment. The need to eat not only unites us all but underscores a basic human frailty . . . It's almost as if nature had created an infallible way to remind us, daily and nearly hourly, that we are bound to and dependent upon every other living thing in this universe, a knowledge that is surely the ultimate blessing."

☐ _____

Rituals of Reconciliation

☐ It's important to create sacred space in which to say, "I'm sorry." Ideally, this space is formed by both partners, one having the courage to come forward to seek forgiveness, and the other the humility to quickly grant it. You and your partner very well may have some sort of reconciliation ritual already. How do you know when an argument is over? Who's the first to seek a reconnection? How does the other respond? Is this pattern always the same, or does it vary?

☐   Experiment with different rituals of reconciliation. Does writing a nice note soften the rough edges between you? Maybe a quiet walk in the park? Some symbolic items you could use in your ritual might include a sponge to soak up your anger, or a piece of clay to reshape and transform your feelings.

☐   You may need a ritual to aid in forgiving yourself, especially if you've already been granted forgiveness by your partner, yet you still feel awful. Some people find water relaxing and cleansing to the spirit. Take a bath or a shower and let the negative feelings about yourself wash away. Tell yourself, "I can learn from my mistakes."

☐   _____

Spiritual Sharing Exercise 14:
Carving Out Sacred Time Together

We've found that a common denominator in couples who enjoy a rich and vibrant spiritual marriage is the faithful practice of "couple time." If you have children, this will likely involve hiring a baby-sitter or arranging regular exchanges with other parents several times a month so that you and your spouse can go out on dates. It might also mean having a relative keep your children overnight or for a weekend, so that you and your partner can enjoy some extended time away (see Chapter 13 on retreats). Sometimes you might go out with other friends or couples; at other times it may be just the two of you. Finding a balance is important. Some couples are quite active socially, yet have little quality time for each other. Other couples err in the opposite direction, spending too much time by themselves, when they actually need energy added into the system from the outside.

In *The Couple's Comfort Book,* Jennifer Louden suggests using a calendar for the sole purpose of scheduling in times you'll spend together, and noting special needs of your partner you want to tend to. It's a great idea; but if you're like us, you have so many lists and calendars going on already, it could be confusing to create yet another. We've found that what works better for us is to stick to the calendars we're already in the habit of using (our daily appointment books), and to note our sacred couple time in the book along with everything else. In this way, we see what we're committed to do each day, and we don't have to remember to pull out a special couple's calendar.

We do find it quite helpful to plan; if we don't, we're too apt to allow other things to encroach on our time together. We typically have difficulty setting limits: There's always another client in crisis who needs to be seen *now*, or someone else asking us to give a seminar or presentation. Although we like to be needed by others, it's easy to forget that we need time for each other. We have a special rule that says we can't agree to do anything outside our regular work schedules without first checking with each other (and keep notes to this effect in our appointment books). This gives us both time to think before we open our mouths and say "yes."

Set aside some time each week to plan for your time together. You might also do some longer-range planning as well, especially for weekend or longer getaways. In your planning session, decide who will take responsibility for arranging the childcare. Who will make any other necessary preparations? Make sure you discuss your feelings about the roles each of you assume. Traditionally, women have been the vacation and ritual planners in the family. We've talked to many women who resent all the work associated with taking a vacation, or collapse with exhaustion after a busy holiday time filled with elaborate rituals. Even the smaller, more personal rituals we've discussed are often planned largely by women. Consider sharing or possibly alternating the responsibility. Also, pare down your expectations if need be. Remember— what's important is not the fancy trimmings of the ritual itself, but the

---

Spotlight on Rituals and Celebrations

- Talk with your friends and family members about their rituals and celebrations. Especially take time to talk with the elder members of your family. Consider audio- or videotaping family members talking about their rituals.

- "Rituals anchor us to a center while freeing us to move on and confront the everlasting unpredictability of life. The paradox of ritual patterns and sacred habits is that they simultaneously serve as solid footing and springboard, providing a stable dynamic in our lives." (*Robert Fulghum*)

- "Rituals are not the path. They are the reminder that there is a path."(*Emmanuel and Pat Rodegast*)

- "Taking photos, making scrapbooks—surely all of this is far too serious to be considered a hobby. It's the work, after all, of posterity." (Stephen Harrigan, *Special Report Magazine*)

strengthening of relationships, the expression of meaning, and the celebration of your connections with all of life.

Some Final Thoughts

Rituals, simple and elaborate, exist within all cultures, exemplifying our basic human needs for community and meaning. You can brainstorm for ideas about new and old rituals with your partner and have fun in the process, as well as drawing closer together. Rituals you create with your partner serve to manifest the innermost meaning of your marriage. They show the importance of looking at your past and your future, of acknowledging your square in the quilt of life—and making is as rich and beautiful as possible.

PART III

Living the Light of Love

Chapter 12

Embracing the Inevitable Times of Drought

"There is no winter harsh enough to withhold the promise of spring."

—Karen Kaiser Clarke

*B*y following the previous seven steps, you should be well on your way to enjoying a spicy and spirited marriage. And yet, it's important to keep in mind that walking the spiritual path of love is a process, not a destination. There are still bound to be times when your marriage feels lifeless and dull, although these times of drought will probably be less frequent now, less intense, and of shorter duration. In this chapter, you'll see that setbacks are to be expected, and we'll show you how these times offer opportunities for growth and learning. You'll come to recognize your own early warning signs of declining spiritual closeness, and what you need to do to get back on the right track.

Spiritual Setbacks: What Are They? What Can You Do?

Maggie and Fred, a couple in their forties with three children, had seen us for marriage counseling for several months. During our sessions, we'd basically led them through the steps we've outlined in this book, and they'd made wonderful progress in a relatively short period of time. Both of them were highly motivated, completing all of the Spiritual Sharing Exercises—and they found ways to alter and expand the exercises to make them even more helpful and meaningful to them. During our last session, both spouses reported that they thought they'd made great strides in "waking up" their marriage; and we noticed how much more alive they looked in the way they interacted with each other.

One day, we received a phone call from Maggie asking whether they could come back in for a few sessions. She was worried because she felt that familiar distance and "coolness" creeping back. She didn't want to lose all the gains they'd made. We set up an appointment for early the next week. When they came for the session, both of them seemed stiffer with each other than when we'd last met. Maggie began by reporting that they were arguing about insignificant things, and she felt that Fred was criticizing her more. She also said that the easy affection that had developed between them seemed to be dwindling. She noticed that Fred had left without giving her a good-bye hug and kiss the past several mornings. She'd tried to ask Fred what was going on, but apparently she'd approached the topic in a way that only aggravated him more. Fred jumped in to tell us his side. He felt that Maggie was pressuring him recently for too much closeness. He said that she was constantly asking him what was wrong, and it was driving him crazy. He had a lot going on at work, he said, and he just needed to be left alone for a while.

We explained to Maggie and Fred that they were having a mere setback, and that this was to be expected, if not embraced. Change is not made in one fell swoop. It's often made in a step-wise fashion: several steps forward and then one or two steps back. The trick is not to panic; panicking only makes matters worse. Maggie had panicked when she sensed some distance between her and Fred, and became frightened. Her fear led her to become controlling and clingy with him, succeeding only in pushing him away. Recall in Chapter 3 that men and women typically experience intimacy differently. Men often need some emotional distance after a period of closeness to rejuvenate and find themselves again. John Gray, Ph.D., author of *Men Are From Mars, Women Are From Venus*, likens this to men needing to retreat to their caves, and he cautions women not to interfere with this natural process. In a sense, Maggie and Fred's setback occurred not so much because of the distance that emerged between them, but because of the way they handled the distance. In any relationship, even in a spiritual marriage, there is a natural ebb and flow of joining together and moving apart.

Although you don't want to panic needlessly when you sense a setback, it is helpful to notice the process—to find ways to make the dance more graceful, so you don't step on each other's toes too often. Also, you don't want a slight setback to turn into a full-blown relapse, in which you revert back to destructive old communication patterns. Every couple will dance the steps in their own unique way, but let's look at some common signs to watch for:

- Feeling more tension between you

- Not feeling "connected"

- Picking insignificant arguments

- Feeling less patient, more critical

Also look for your own idiosyncratic signs of an impending spiritual setback. For example, I notice that I begin to avoid making eye-contact with Greg when I'm feeling stressed and overwhelmed.

Setbacks occur on a continuum from slight to severe. We define a *slight* setback as one in which there's a decline in spiritual closeness (signs listed above) that lasts from a few days to a week. Signs of a *moderate* setback include

- Increasing conflict and tension
- Increasing feelings of frustration
- Increasing feelings of hopelessness
- Greater emotional distance
- Keeping things to yourself
- Isolating yourself from your spouse

We define the duration of a moderate setback to be approximately one to two weeks.

Anything longer than a few weeks, and including any of the following warning signs, is a *major* setback, if not a complete relapse:

- More arguing than anything else
- Feelings of contempt for your partner
- High levels of frustration and hopelessness
- Little or no affection or tenderness

In this case, outside intervention is probably needed, especially if the situation doesn't improve within a month or two. If you and your partner find yourself identifying with any of the signs listed above, consider seeking couples' counseling. The following suggestions and tips are geared toward the slight-to-moderate categories of setbacks.

Practice Acceptance

The work of embracing the inevitable times of drought goes straight back to the chapter on acceptance. Sometimes, you simply don't know why a certain coolness seems to settle over your relationship. You can try to figure it out, and sometimes that can be helpful. As Fred noted, he had a lot going on at work, and his mind was simply elsewhere. In this case, Maggie needed to allow Fred the space he needed, while at the same time finding ways to take care of herself. She could also look for soul-soothing gestures she could offer that would help Fred out. For example, she might encourage him to stay late at work to finish whatever he needed to finish, rather than rushing home, worrying that she'd be hurt or angry if he were late. At other times, it's impossible to pin down just what has caused the distance—and perhaps there is no cause. In such cases, you need to accept the fact that relationships are often mysterious. Sometimes there is no *why*, and you must ask instead, "What can be learned from this?" In describing the waxing and waning of love, Thomas Moore writes in *Soul Mates*, "Entering into the numbness, [couples] may find truths about their marriage and about themselves in marriage that cannot be seen from an active, enthusiastic life together. Numbness is a path, a rather perverse way toward a deeper and possibly more honest participation in life."

Stay on the Same Team

When you or your spouse sense a setback of some sort, trying to stay on the same side can be an enormous help. This is similar to the concept of "turning the problem into an it" that we discussed earlier in the book. Acknowledge the fact that the situation is awful, but that neither you nor your partner is to blame. One way that Greg and I do this is to make what we call "I wish" statements. If we're incredibly busy and don't have as much time for each other as we'd like, we both make an effort to say things like, "I wish I had more time to spend with you. I really miss you," or "I wish things were different for you and me right now." Have you ever had the flu at the same time as your partner? Last year that happened to us, and were we ever sorry sights! We both felt that we had all these incredible needs, with no one to meet them. Although at first we had our fair share of tense moments between us, we quickly got back on the right track and commiserated together. Simple statements such as, "I wish we didn't both feel so bad," and "I'm sorry I'm so sick and can't take care of you better," went a long way to soothe our souls.

Rally Your Resources

Depending on the situation, it can also help to look for outside support. When Greg and I both had the flu, we called my brother and sister-in-law to ask whether they'd let Jesse stay at their house for a few days. Look back at the chapter on connecting with community. To whom can you reach out for support? If you're in a marriage enrichment group, you'll know that other married couples go through similar phases. While such groups typically don't give direct advice, people in the group may be able to share ways in which they've handled a similar situation.

Laugh When You Can

Nurturing your sense of humor can be another great asset in learning to embrace the ups and downs of married life. Try saying something out of character to shake things up a bit. Once when Greg and I had not been getting along too well for a few days, without thinking, I borrowed a line from the television show *Roseanne* and yelled at him, "I hate you and everything you stand for." I don't watch television very much, and I'm not at all the yelling type. What possessed me to do that, I have no idea. And of course, the comment was ridiculous, because we share most of the same values and stand for the same things. Perhaps the absurdity helped the situation. We started laughing, and were then able to discuss what had been going on between us in a calmer, more productive manner. Another thing to try is to read something funny together, like Paul Reiser's book *Couplehood*. Sometimes it's important not to take yourself, or even your marriage, too seriously.

Coping With Crises and Normal Life Transitions

There are many other factors besides the natural rhythms of a relationship that can contribute to setbacks. External stresses—such as job loss, financial problems, or difficulties with children, to name just several possibilities, can put added strain on a marriage. Psychological or medical conditions affecting you and/or your spouse can also put added pressure on your relationship. Life transitions—the birth of a child, the death of a parent, a child leaving for college, a woman going through menopause—can all play a role in the quality of your marriage. These situations may vary in severity, but each of them holds the potential to create a time of crisis if effective means of coping aren't quickly adopted.

In a two-volume set of books called *Stress and the Family*, Dr. Charles Figley lists 11 characteristics he's found to differentiate between "functional" and "dysfunctional" coping strategies. We've adapted some of the items on his list to the specific needs of couples. Here are signs of effective coping:

1. An ability to identify the stressor (what's causing the problem)

2. The situation is viewed as the couple's problem, rather than being attributed to one partner only

3. The couple adopts a solution-oriented approach to the problem, rather than simply resorting to blame

4. Both members of the couple shows a tolerance for each other's reactions

5. There is a clear expression of commitment to, and affection for, each other

6. There is open and clear communication

7. There's evidence of high cohesion between the couple—you're sticking together on this

8. Each partner is comfortable with flexible roles

9. The couple utilizes resources both inside and outside the family

10. There's no physical violence or substance abuse

We've already shared a lot about events that have shaped our lives, both in the long-range past and in recent years. You know that our son Jesse has had numerous health problems since the day he was born (actually, since before he was born—Barb was restricted to bedrest during the last trimester of her pregnancy due to a condition called *placenta previa*). It was a struggle to keep up with all of Jesse's medical appointments while trying to run our own counseling practice at the same time. We both felt the strain, but for a combination of reasons. Barb's makeup was such that she fell into a deep depression. It was definitely a time of drought in our marriage. When Barb wasn't working or caring for Jesse, she was in bed sleeping, or crying. There were periods of time when she seemed completely unresponsive to me. Nothing I said or did seemed to comfort her or make a dent in her mood.

While you'd think it would be easy for us to identify the stressor (see 1 in the list of effective coping strategies) in reality, this was a difficult task for us. When Barb was at her lowest point, Jesse's health problems had actually improved. Other things were looking up, too. Our practice was growing, Barb's writing career was taking off, we had a strong marriage. I suggested that maybe she was exhausted—"falling apart" after the crisis; but she didn't think that was the complete explanation. I wondered whether I wasn't making her happy, but she assured me that wasn't the problem either. As she wrote in a previous chapter, she'd been in therapy herself, and had gained lots of insight; but she still struggled with bouts of depression. It wasn't hard to see that this problem belonged to both of us (see 2), not just Barb. We've always been a team, and her depression affected me deeply. I hated to see her in such pain, and I felt helpless most of the time. I was committed to finding an answer for her—for us (3). Even though she seemed in a world of her own sometimes, she didn't cut me off completely. She mustered enough energy to say such things as, "I do love you, even if I'm not showing it right now," or simply, "I'm sorry I'm not really here for you more." Although it wasn't in the exact same way as we'd done in the past, we somehow managed to keeping talking, and to show our love for each other (5, 6, 7).

We kept going back and forth about how to solve the problem. We worked at acceptance, trying to "flow with the depression"—in effect, giving Barb permission to be depressed. Sometimes this helped for a brief while, but it didn't seem to be the total answer. She didn't want to go into counseling again, although I was more than willing to try to find a therapist who would work with us together. Although it was an intimidating step to take for a number of reasons, Barb—I think both bravely and boldly—decided to seek a consultation from a psychiatrist (9). It wasn't an easy task to find someone to see. She didn't feel comfortable going to a doctor she knew socially or professionally for a personal problem. She also worried about whether she'd run into her own clients in the waiting rooms of doctors to whom she frequently referred her own clients. When we started calling around, most psychiatrists had a wait of well over a month to be seen for an initial evaluation. Finally, I thought of someone I'd worked with in the past who might fit Barb in sooner if I called and asked, and, sure enough, she got an appointment in two days.

To make a long story short, Barb was put on an antidepressant medication, and she's been remarkably better ever since.

There are a number of reasons why we decided to include this story. First of all, we wanted to illustrate the characteristics of effective coping which we listed above. We skipped the points about role flexibility (8), and physical violence and substance abuse (10), because those weren't issues for us (If violence or substance abuse is occurring in your marriage, please seek help from a mental-health professional). We see so many couples whose relationship is affected by depression that we felt it almost an obligation to share our experience. The statistics regarding depression are staggering. A recent issue of the *Journal of Marital and Family Therapy* reported that between 10 to 25 percent of women will experience at least one significant episode of major depression during their lives; the range for men is between 5 to 12 percent. Of those individuals who experience one episode of depression, approximately 50 percent can expect to have another episode. The *Journal* also noted that depressive episodes are more likely to occur after stressful life events; and that a close, supportive marital relationship can moderate the depressive effects of life's stresses.

Certainly, the decision about whether to take medication for depression, or any other condition, has to be made on a case-by-case basis with your physician. At first, Barb had many qualms about taking medication for depression. She thought maybe it indicated some sort of psychological or spiritual failure on her part. She sometimes labeled herself as a "fake" and said, "If I only practiced what I preached I wouldn't have to take medication." But Barb did, and does, practice what she preaches. She fills out thoughts and feelings diaries, she gets regular exercise, she reaches out to others, she practices acceptance. We finally came to the conclusion that Barb's temperament and physiology interacted with her life experiences in such a way that her brain truly needed the added neurochemical help that antidepressants can provide.

The experience of depression is only one of many examples we could've used. Perhaps your spouse has been diagnosed with a chronic physical illness. Perhaps one of you is facing unemployment or maybe you're dealing with an acting-out adolescent. Whatever your situation, in addition to following the other suggestions we've made in this chapter, keep these major points in mind:

Don't do anything drastic. Don't make any major changes or decisions if you can help it until after the crisis phase is over, and you know what you're actually dealing with. We've seen many people in our counseling work who have prematurely made decisions to separate from their spouse when they were suffering from depression or another problem not directly related to the marriage. Similarly, don't decide to quit your job or make any major purchases. People look for relief by thinking of things they can do externally, when, much of the time, that's not going to solve the problem. This again relates to the issue of acceptance. Before Barb and I could make an informed

Spiritual Marriage Relapse Prevention: Our Plan for Staying Close

Maggie's Warning Signs:

feeling insecure, watching

Fred's every move,

trying to "figure him out"

getting more irritable as time

goes on

Fred's Warning Signs:

not saying good-bye in the morning

critical of small things

being more quiet, alternating with

more frequent arguing

Length of time before some action should be taken: *I'd like*

to take action right away, but

that's usually perceived by Fred

as nagging

Length of time before some action should be taken: *I'd probably be*

comfortable going on like this for

a week or so. We'll compromise

with a few days

What Maggie finds most helpful:

I'd like Fred to acknowledge that

he's acting different, and to

reassure me it won't last.

To let me in on what's going

on so I can understand better.

What Fred finds most helpful:

Some space to figure things out

myself. For Maggie to go out with

friends and have fun so I don't

feel so guilty.

Useful Coping Statements:

Fred's distance right now probably

doesn't reflect on me or our relation-

ship. I will try to support him in

the way that he finds most helpful.

Useful Coping Statements:

If I show Maggie I care about her, she'll

be better able to give me the space

I need.

Other Actions To Be Taken/Other Things to Consider: *Probable triggers:*

work stress for Fred. If problems continue, retake the Spiritual Marriage

Inventory. Look to see what areas we might have slipped up in. If still no

improvement, schedule "booster session" with the Markways.

Spiritual Marriage Relapse Prevention:
Our Plan for Staying Close

Partner 1's Warning Signs:

_____

_____

_____

_____

_____

Partner 2's Warning Signs:

_____

_____

_____

_____

Length of time before some action should be taken:

_____

_____

_____

Length of time before some action should be taken:

_____

_____

_____

What partner 1 finds most helpful:

_____

_____

_____

_____

_____

What partner 2 finds most helpful:

_____

_____

_____

_____

_____

Useful Coping Statements:

_____

_____

_____

Useful Coping Statements:

_____

_____

_____

Other Actions To Be Taken/Other Things to Consider:

_____

_____

_____

decision about what might be helpful, we had to accept the fact that she was, indeed, depressed. For a while, I think I tried to minimize the problem, thinking that she was simply overworked and tired. If you find yourself in a time of drought in your marriage, it might be helpful to review the chapter on acceptance.

Find even small ways to stay connected. If you're going through a difficult time, feel drained, and don't have much energy to care for your relationship, at least look for some way to stay connected. It meant a lot to me when Barb made the effort to acknowledge my feelings—that she recognized the fact that she wasn't meeting my needs the way she had previously. Look back through the soul-soothing chapter for low-effort ideas. Try to make sure that when under stress you're still able to communicate with care. It might sound like an impossible task, but it's not. The trick is to make these communication skills second nature for you with lots and lots of practice. In this way, you'll have the skills at your command during even your worst moments.

Make a survival plan. Try to do this together; but if that's not possible, one of you should take charge and make a plan. Figure out what really needs to be done, and what can wait until things get more back to normal. Try to reduce both your loads in whatever ways you can. Review the chapter on connecting with community. Ask family members and friends to step in and help. You'll return the favor sometime when they're in need. Don't forget your physical needs: Make sure that both you and your partner are eating and sleeping as well as you can. And keep your expectations realistic. It might sound strange, but sometimes simply making it through the day can be a big accomplishment.

Spiritual Sharing Exercise 15:
Making a Spiritual Marriage Relapse Prevention Plan

This exercise will help you and your partner make a systematic relapse prevention plan. We want you to be prepared for the inevitable setbacks that will occur, so that they won't mushroom into anything more severe—with simple setbacks, you can at least learn and grow. We've seen too many couples in our office who let things get way out of hand before they seek help. By the time they reach us, they're so full of hatred and bitterness that it's sometimes next to impossible to turn things around. You may think that this exercise isn't necessary now, but when stress mounts, clear thinking can fly right out the window. It can be salvational to have in place a plan you've created during a calm period, a time when you and your partner still felt close and connected.

The first step is to discuss with your partner your "warning signs," the little things you notice about yourself that signal to you and your partner that there's a decline in closeness in the relationship. You can review the items we listed earlier in the chapter—such as picking petty fights, feeling less patient, and being more critical—to help you get started. Next, talk with your partner about the ways that would be most helpful to deal with a setback. Here are some questions to consider:

1. How long should we let these things go on without commenting on the process?

2. Are there any signals with which I can let my partner know that I'm once again feeling more receptive?

3. Are there any specific steps each of us should carry out?

4. Can we come up with a coping statement or two to help us deal with the setback?

Refer to Fred and Maggie's plan on page 212 as an example, and then create a plan of your own.

Spotlight on Times of Drought

- Remember—all couples go through seasons of drought. A good marriage, like a well-established tree, can survive these periods so long as the roots are strong and deep.

- "Anytime we feel something other than a sense of balance, centeredness, peace, and joy, that is an open door to the core of our feelings." (*Henry James Borys*)

- "It might be better to expect developments of all kinds, not just forward movements, but regressions and setbacks as well." (*Thomas Moore*)

Some Final Thoughts

The experience of spiritual union with another is so exquisite, so poignant, that when the feeling departs, the fullness in your heart and soul gives way to an empty ache. You may frantically seek to fill the void, but this isn't always what you need. Sometimes, you must enter the void to discern its true meaning. The biggest danger lies in presuming that a period of drought has horrible implications—that it necessarily means something bad about you, your partner, or your relationship. Sometimes a time of drought just happens, and you don't know why. Sometimes you know why, but knowing the reasons doesn't help your situation. Accept the fact that you're going through a rough time, do what you can to minimize the damage, and trust that a time of abundance is on its way.

Chapter 13

Energizing Your Relationship With Retreats and Vacations

"Vacations are not about 'getting away' but about getting 'in touch.'"

—a Chinese fortune cookie

We've offered you numerous ideas and suggestions for incorporating spirituality into your everyday married life. And yet every couple, no matter how enlightened in the everyday, needs more extended time to rejuvenate their relationship and to rekindle the spark that brought them together. This final chapter looks at the role retreats and vacations can play in sustaining and deepening a spiritually alive marriage. These getaways need not be extravagant or lengthy; you don't necessarily even need to leave your home. Spiritual couple retreats and vacations have as much to do with your attitude as they do with the particulars of where you go or what you do.

What Makes a Vacation or a Retreat Spiritual?

We've all probably either been on a vacation or heard about a vacation that didn't go as planned—that time you fought the entire way in the car, or when the weather was awful, or when one of you got sick—the vacation from hell. Although you certainly can't control things like the weather, there are measures you can to take to ensure that your vacation or retreat nurtures both you and your relationship. What makes time away spiritual is the state of mind you take with you. What's needed is a mind that's awake and alive to the newness and freshness of experience, a mind that's soft and stretchable, the mind of an enthusiastic, excited "beginner."

Can you remember the first time you went to the beach and stood with your toes at the edge of the ocean? As the waves rolled in, the sensation of water rapidly rushed up around your ankles, and then, just as quickly, the sand washed away from under your feet. As you looked out at the massive expanse of water, you felt the ground literally shift beneath you. The experience was no doubt an awesome one.

The goal of a spiritual retreat or vacation is to take this beginner's mind with you—to experience each moment as a wonderful adventure, to be fully present in the moment. For some people, getting away from the usual routine naturally inspires such an easy openness to the flow of life; for others, the lack of normal surroundings and structure evokes anxiety. You probably know which category you fall into. If you're one who vacations well, you can dive right into this chapter and find lots of new ideas to plan the ideal retreat for yourself and your partner. If you're one who gets more uptight when you try to relax, start small. Don't feel that you have to plan a complicated, extended getaway. And if you and your partner fall into the likely scenario in which one of you is an accomplished relaxer, and one of you isn't, we'll have special suggestions for you, too.

What Makes a Retreat a Retreat or a Vacation a Vacation?

We believe that time away together, just the two of you, is important for the health of your marriage. The words *retreat* and *vacation* have somewhat different meanings to different people, but for our purposes, we don't see a huge distinction, and we sometimes use the words interchangeably. Much of what we say that applies to retreats also applies to vacations. In general, retreats have more of a religious or spiritual component, typically involving a solitary time of reflection and contemplation. For our purposes, as long as you achieve some separation from your usual world, you and your partner can be solitary together. Vacations generally entail going somewhere for the purpose of fun and relaxation, but the specifics can vary greatly. While some may enjoy a vacation consisting of camping, others cannot tolerate the bugs—or the lack of indoor plumbing. Whatever your style, the important things are for you and your partner to be in sync, and to keep the idea of "beginner's mind" in the forefront.

Spiritual Sharing Exercise 16: Exploring Your Values About Vacations

You and your partner likely have very different experiences and memories of vacations past. Perhaps while you were growing up, your family took vacations to the same place year after year, yet your partner's family found it important always to travel to new destinations. Or your parents never took vacations without the kids, while your partner's parents did so on a regular basis. Perhaps vacations in your family meant visiting out-of-town relatives. Or maybe vacations didn't exist at all. As Evan Imber-Black and Janine Roberts note, in *Rituals for Our Times*, vacations tell us a lot about a family's identity.

Below are some questions to help you and your partner explore your "vacation values." Answer the questions, and then share your responses with your spouse. You can answer some of the questions both in terms of your family of origin and your current family. For example, question 1 asks, "What is your happiest vacation memory?" It may be useful to share with your partner your happiest vacation from your growing-up years, as well as the happiest vacation taken during your marriage.

Partner 1

1. What is your happiest vacation memory? What made it special for you? _____

   _____

   _____

2. What was your least favorite vacation, and why? _____

   _____

   _____

3. What do you consider the ideal length of time to get away? _____

   _____

   _____

4. What type of setting is your ideal vacation setting? A big city? The beach? The mountains? Staying in a hotel? In someone's home? Camping? With others? Only the two of you? _____

   _____

   _____

5. What are your thoughts and feelings about taking "couple vacations," in addition to "family vacations"? _____

   _____

   _____

Partner 2

1. What is your happiest vacation memory? What made it special for you? _____

   _____

   _____

2. What was your least favorite vacation, and why? _____

_____

_____

3. What do you consider the ideal length of time to get away? _____

_____

_____

4. What type of setting is your ideal vacation setting? A big city? The beach? The mountains? Staying in a hotel? In someone's home? Camping? With others? Only the two of you? _____

_____

_____

5. What are your thoughts and feelings about taking "couple vacations," in addition to "family vacations"? _____

_____

_____

Spiritual Sharing Exercise 17: Learning From Beginner's Mind

Take turns describing to your spouse a time when you felt that your mind was especially receptive and observant. Maybe you were learning to do something new, and you felt particularly excited about it. Maybe you found a novel way to do something you'd done many times before. Maybe you were outside watching the sunset, fully present in the moment. We think of our son—how enthralled he is with books right now. We find him sitting in his room, turning page after page, describing to himself each detail in the pictures he sees. Completely absorbed in the present moment, he's oblivious to everything else around him.

You don't necessarily have to be doing something new to enjoy a beginner's mind. Try doing one of your usual tasks, such as making the bed or doing the dishes, while noticing each of your motions. In other words, when you make the bed, make the bed. Often our mind strays off into a million directions when we're doing something, but you can train yourself to stay more focused in the present. One thing that can be helpful is to pay attention to your breathing as you're doing the task. Notice your breath as you pull up the sheets and the comforter; notice that it's the muscles in your arms that are making it happen.

A Spiritual Retreat for Two:
The Basic Elements To Include

Whatever type of getaway you plan, in this section we'll offer our thinking about some key elements to include. You don't have to follow all our suggestions, but at least give them some consideration.

Solitude

As we stated earlier, we believe that you can enjoy solitary time together. What's required is setting aside some sacred space to remove yourselves from your usual routine and, if possible, your usual surroundings. If going somewhere isn't feasible, you can create a retreat environment at home, although it will take extra planning on your part. You'll need to make sure to unplug the phone and let others know you won't be available. Perhaps the most difficult part is to not get caught up in household tasks or projects that beckon. If you do stay at home for your retreat, try to have your house cleaned and straightened before your designated retreat time.

In his guide on spiritual retreats, David Cooper notes that what's missing in many people's lives today is a weekly period of solitude and reflection. Even people who find ways to relax on the weekend often do so by watching television or movies, being involved in sporting activities, or going out to eat. With the popularity of home computers, many people bring work home to do on the weekends. Although nothing is wrong with any of these activities, they still entail engagement of some kind. There's typically little time dedicated to inner reflection or simple sharing.

If you don't feel that you can afford an entire week or weekend retreat, you could start with trying to keep one day of the week separate and distinct from all the others. On one day, don't do housework or any work from the office. Don't structure too much; allow the day to evolve. Many religions hold to the ideal of a sacred day, distinct from the rest. The fourth commandment says, "Remember the Sabbath day, to keep it holy." In the Jewish faith, the Sabbath is traditionally a time reserved for rest, prayer, and worship. Observant Jews take care to prepare in advance all the food they will need before sundown as the Sabbath begins, so that they can leave their everyday concerns behind them, and focus on the holiness of the day.

Simplicity

We train ourselves to think we need certain things for our comfort, when really we don't truly *need* these things. We know many homes that have televisions in nearly every room of the house. Why not take a retreat to someplace where there is no television? Or make an agreement to keep the television off. One year we took our only television to our office—we needed it to show clients some educational and training videos. We ended up leaving it there for about six months, and we noticed a remarkable difference in our home life. We read more. We talked more. The quality of our time together improved. Although we eventually brought the TV back home, we still don't watch it nearly as much as we used to.

You don't have to go to such lengths to gain benefits from simplicity. Try out a weekend together with no television, no newspapers or magazines, no radios, no connection to the outside world. Similarly, keeping your other surroundings simple can be beneficial. You don't need a fancy hotel suite, although sometimes that's certainly pleasant. Even if you don't enjoy camping, you can find cabins that have the basics, yet still offer some of the pristine quality that can enhance a spiritual retreat.

Silence

We live in a noisy world. Sometimes, it seems the day is so hectic that there's not a moment free to hear yourself think, even if you want to. We've also worked with clients who say that they can't stand silence. They believe that they must have the radio or television on as background noise, because they worry about where their thoughts will lead them.

It's important to create some silence in your life. We all need time for quiet—to be able to hear the "still, small voice" inside, to hear what life is telling us. When you take a retreat or a vacation with your partner, build in some silence. Don't feel that each moment has to be filled with conversation. One of the ways I knew my relationship with Greg was special was that even early on in our relationship, we were comfortable not talking. We could ride in the car together, not saying a word, and still feel close. On a retreat, you could try alternating periods of silence with periods of sharing.

Sharing

During your spiritual retreat, the times of silence and solitude may occur while you're alone, or you may also want to share these times with your partner. For balance, you may want to structure some time in which you're physically separate from one another, and then you can join together to share your experiences. You'll have to experiment with a schedule that suits the two of you. Some couples may be comfortable initially with mostly spending their time together, without much time alone. On the other hand, some couples may be comfortable with more separation, and less together-time. During your first experiences with taking retreats together, you'll want to stay in your comfort zone. Later, you may feel braver and want to challenge yourselves. For example, a couple who likes a lot of shared time may find benefit in pushing themselves a bit, in learning to tolerate the times of separateness.

Spiritual Practices You Can Include in Your Retreat Experience

If the idea of a retreat is new to you, you're probably still not clear on exactly what you and your partner are supposed to do during this experience. Again, there's no precise formula to follow. Below we'll list some common spiritual practices that are often included in retreats. You can pick and choose according to your interests and comfort level. Also consider retreat expert David Cooper's advice on selecting spiritual practices: "A beginning spiritual practitioner is usually best served by those practices that feel compatible. They do not have to bring 'highs,' but they certainly do not have to be unpleasant." He cautions people to reject the idea that if something hurts or is uncomfortable, it must be good for them. "It is certainly true," he writes, "that we must confront things that are not pleasant, but we should never cast aside good judgment."

Breathing

Deep breathing exercises are some of the simplest and most effective relaxation techniques that can aid in your spiritual pursuits. To practice breathing, place one hand on your chest and one hand on your abdomen. Inhale deeply in such a way that you feel your belly expanding—this indicates that you're using your diaphragm muscle in your breathing. As you exhale, notice your abdomen contracting, forcing the air out of your lungs. Once you're able to breathe in this manner, you can focus on counting to four as you inhale, and again as you exhale. This gives your breathing a steady, relaxed pace that maximizes the relaxation effects, and is an effective antidote to anxiety. Listening to soothing Baroque music, such as the Pachelbel Canon in D, can add another dimension to the experience. Once you've become comfortable with the technique, you and your partner can practice this type of relaxed breathing together.

Visualization

Visualization is the process of creatively using your imagination to achieve a desired goal. The goal may simply be to relax; or you may be trying something more specific, such as letting go of a long-standing resentment toward your partner. Creative visualization techniques can include forms of imagery, meditation, or affirmations. We often have our clients begin with a simple imagery relaxation exercise such as this one:

Imagine that you are walking along a beautiful, uncrowded beach. You can feel the warmth of the sun as it shines down on your head and shoulders. Just notice how soothing the warmth feels. You can hear the sound of the waves as they come in . . . and go out . . . in and out. With each breath you can smell the slight scent of salt in the air, and the air feels clean and refreshing. With each breath you feel more calm, more relaxed. . . .

People sometimes select for imagery relaxation scenes in the woods, lying on a raft in a lake or a swimming pool, taking a nap in a hammock, relaxing in a meadow, sitting by a stream. Concentrate on all the details, and use all your senses to complete the picture. As you look around, who's there?

Where are you in relation to other things in the image? Are you sitting or standing? What do you hear? What is the temperature of the air, the water? What do you smell? How do you feel? What else do you notice about your surroundings?

Many people worry that if they don't actually see an image while they're practicing visualization, they won't reap the benefits. In her book *Creative Visualization*, Shakti Gawain advises, "Don't get stuck on the term 'visualize.' It is not at all necessary to mentally see an image." While some people report that they actually form a visual image in their mind, others say that they experience a more general impression or feeling.

Greg and I have used creative visualization in a number of ways. If I've had a rough day, for example, Greg will help me relax by breathing with me, and then he'll talk aloud, creating a visualization as he goes. Depending on my needs at the time, he might paint a picture for me of a safe place—a place where there are no worries, no fears, where all that exists is love. Or he might help me visualize accomplishing something I've been working on or strug-gling with. If you don't want to make up your own visualizations, there are plenty of books that include actual scripts that you can use or modify. Some people tape the scripts onto a blank tape, so they can play it back, concentrat-ing on relaxing and imagining the scene.

Journaling

Take pens and two blank, spiral-bound notebooks with you on your retreat. We don't suggest using any of the fancy, blank books unless you're sure you'll use them. We have dozens of beautiful blank books that have remained blank because they seem too pretty to use. Use the notebooks to keep a record of your thoughts and feelings throughout the retreat. You could also use questions from some of the Spiritual Sharing Exercises as a place to begin.

Perhaps you and your partner would like to focus on one particular area, such as creating new rituals. You might use your separate time to write out your answers to the questions in these chapters, and then share your responses during a time of togetherness. Any of the other suggestions in the book could also be used as a springboard for activities to include in your retreat. For example, bring along photos and put together a special album honoring your relationship. Consider adding a page or two each year to your wedding al-bum, or a special anniversary album, in which you include photos and write about highlights from your life together that year.

Movement

Oftentimes on retreats, there's a lot of sitting involved, so much so that spiritual retreat books offer advice on what type of floor pillows to take along to minimize sore bottoms! We recommend that you break up long periods of sitting with movement. There's no reason why you can't engage in most of the spiritual practices mentioned here while you're walking. For example, you and your partner could take a silent walk together, matching the pace of your breathing and your footsteps. Or you could share your thoughts and feelings about something you've written in your journal earlier in the day. If you know yoga, you could practice that together. Or do simple stretching exercises. If you have access to water, go swimming. There's nothing more spiritually refreshing than the sensation of water gliding over your skin.

Massage

Be sure to pack some good massage oil; you'll want to take this opportunity to give each other the pleasure of an extended, uninterrupted massage. If you ever have the chance, take a massage class geared toward couples; we've seen half-day workshops offered through YMCAs and community colleges. We attended a one-hour massage class given at a Marriage Enrichment "festival of workshops" last year, and gained several new ideas. You can also check out a book from the library on massage, or rent an instructional video illustrating massage techniques. The best training, however, is paying attention to your partner's reactions as you touch him or her. You'll quickly learn what feels good, and what doesn't.

Prayer and Devotion

You might want to include a special time of praying together with your spouse. Don't worry if this isn't something you're used to doing. You don't have to pray in any particular way, or even to a deity. Edward Hays writes about the common embarrassment you might feel: "At first we will be ill-at-ease, but the memory of this ancient prayer-custom is rooted in our inner-selves, perhaps etched forever in our DNA code. We have only to rekindle its memory to begin to treasure with reverence the power of blessing that has been asleep for so many years and that belongs to every parent—to every person." Set aside your fear of awkwardness, and simply speak the longings of your heart. Express your gratitude for your partner and your life together. Consider planning a brief devotional service to include as a part of your retreat. Read poems or prayers that are meaningful to you, sing a song if you like, collect items from nature for your altar. Include a time of silence and reflection. Thank each other for the gift of this sacred time together.

Ideas for Theme Retreats

You can formulate your retreat using any of the ideas on the foregoing pages. If you're not already familiar with the spiritual practices we've mentioned, see the Resources section for other books that can guide you. Below are some more specific possibilities for retreats to take with your partner.

- *A Weekend in the Woods.* Couples who like the outdoors can grow closer by taking a retreat to commune with each other in nature, camping, canoeing, hiking, and so on.

- *Touching Bodies, Touching Souls.* This is a retreat for getting in touch with the spiritual dimensions of sensuality and sexuality—particularly good for busy couples who may feel spiritually connected in other ways, but have been too busy for much touching. In *Soulful Sex*, Victoria Lee gives her ideas for "A Weekend of Joy."

- *The Mission Workshop.* This is for couples who want extended time to answer such questions as, "What is the purpose and meaning of our marriage?" Activities might include making a collage together depicting what's important about the relationship, or writing a mission statement for the marriage. See Stephen Covey's *First Things First* for a comprehensive list of questions to aid you in writing a mission statement.

- *Connecting With Community.* Many couples find value in pursuing a joint community project together, and possibly with other couples, such as building homes for the homeless, planting trees in the city, and so on.

- *Marriage Encounter or Marriage Enrichment Retreats.* Couples who'd rather attend a retreat already structured for them may find a Marriage Encounter or Marriage Enrichment retreat to be just what they need. See the Resources section for phone numbers.

A Word or Two About Expectations

After the planning and the anticipation, it can be difficult to keep your expectations for a spiritual retreat realistic. You need to take a careful look at what you're hoping will happen on the retreat. If you and your spouse have been going through a difficult period, you can't expect one weekend retreat to remedy all your problems. Similarly, if you've been stressed and overworked, you're wise to allow yourself some extra time for resting and sleeping. Try to adopt the attitude that whatever happens on the retreat is okay. You're not necessarily hoping to have a peak spiritual experience. If that were to happen, fine, but it's less likely to occur if you try too hard. Also, with some practice, you'll learn how to structure your retreats in a way that gives you a time of transition. This can be difficult if you only have a short period of time, but you might come up with a ritual to mark the beginning of your retreat. A simple prayer can work nicely. There are some beautiful blessings for departing on journeys in *Prayers for the Domestic Church*. Two stanzas from a favorite one of ours read:

> *"On this trip may we take with us as part of our traveling equipment a heart wrapped in wonder with which to rejoice in all that we shall meet.*

*Along with the clothing of wonder may we have room in our luggage for
a mystic map by which we can find the invisible meanings of the events
of this journey . . ."*

Remember that in a spiritual retreat, as in a spiritual marriage, no "mistakes" are possible. Everything can be accepted and learned from.

Some Final Thoughts

It can seem such a struggle to find time in our busy lives for a retreat or a vacation, particularly a "spiritual" one. You may be asking yourself, "Who has the time for a spiritual retreat? Isn't sitting around meditating and visualizing going to be a silly waste of time?" That depends. If you remind yourself that your time on earth is limited—there may be no tomorrow—you may find yourself becoming increasingly open to new ways of looking at yourself, your partner, and the life you share. By claiming sacred time together to retreat from the outside world, you can rekindle the sparks that drew you together, and shine a light, once again, on what truly matters. In essence, you'll illuminate the heart and soul of your marriage. What better way could there be to make use of your time?

Spotlight on Spiritual Retreats and Vacations

- "Vacations often offer the most dramatic shifts for people out of regular time and locations into special protected time and space." (*Evan Imber-Black and Janine Roberts*)

- "This is what I think vacations are really for: to remind us of the importance of the *now*." (*Gregory Godek*)

- "A retreat is in itself an environment conducive to remembering." (*David Cooper*)

A Postlude of Sorts

"There are more important tragedies than the tragedy of death.
There are no more important victories than the victory of love."

—William Sloane Coffin

I've spent the last two days asking Greg, "What's wrong with me?" We've reached the deadline, we've finished the book, and here I am, overwhelmed with grief. Endings have always been painful for me. They're so much like death—so final. During one of my recent crying spells, I asked Greg, "What if I never write again? There's so much I didn't say." When my parents were in town visiting last weekend, they told us stories we'd never heard before about their marriage of 35 years, and about my grandparents' marriage of 62 years. Why hadn't I taken the time to talk with them sooner, so I could have included some of their remarkable stories? In my sadness over the end of this book, and in my obsession with death, I'm reminded once again of the whole point of this book, and maybe even of life. As I've suffered through these waves of feelings, Greg has been there, close beside me. It makes me remember some lines in a poem that I wrote for him many years ago:

I see darkness.
Dark as the inside of a coffin,
Or dark as ten feet of dirt.
You say certain things glow in the dark,
Even grow in the dark.
You see light.

I need your eyes.

I hear my words and they sound crazy.
You hear my words and say I'm sane.

I need your ears.

Since the day we met, Greg has listened to me, accepted me, and reassured me. He has loved me like I cannot love myself. And yet, because of his love, I come a little closer, day-by-day, to seeing myself the way he does, to reaching my full potential. I can only hope my love does the same for him. I truly feel that our love was, and is, a miraculous and gracious gift from God. But I also believe that we haven't taken the gift for granted. We've followed the steps we've written of in this book, not perfectly or precisely, but steadily and surely—and we'll continue to do so 'til death do us part. We thank you for allowing us the privilege and opportunity to share our vision with you of all that a spiritual marriage can be. We wish you the sweet victory of love.

Resources, References, and Recommended Reading

(This list is not exhaustive, but gives a sampling of books and other resources we've found helpful. All of the works referred to in the text can be found here.)

Community

Peck, M. S. 1987. *The Different Drum: Community Making and Peace*. New York: Simon & Schuster.

Shaffer, C. R., and D. Anundsen. 1993. *Creating Community Anywhere: Finding Support and Connection in a Fragmented World*. New York: Jeremy P. Tarcher/Putnam. (This wonderful handbook inspired many of the ideas in Chapter 10.)

See also:

A great chapter on community in the book, *Something More*, listed under "Spirituality."

For phone numbers of marriage enrichment groups, see "Organizations."

Existential Issues

Becker, E. 1973. *The Denial of Death*. New York: Free Press.

May, R. 1969. *Love and Will*. New York: Dell Publishing Co.

Tillich, P. 1952. *The Courage To Be*. New Haven and London: Yale University Press.

Yalom, I. D. 1980. *Existential Psychotherapy*. New York: Basic Books. (This brilliant book sparked much of our thinking in Chapter 8.)

Gender Issues

Gray, J. 1992. *Men Are From Mars, Women Are From Venus: A Practical Guide for Improving Communication and Getting What You Want in Your Relationships.* New York: Harper Collins.

Kingma, D. R. 1993. *The Men We Never Knew.* Berkeley, CA: Conari Press.

Tannen, D. 1990. *You Just Don't Understand: Women and Men in Conversation.* New York: Ballantine Books.

Inspiration

Breathnach, S. B. 1995. *Simple Abundance: A Daybook of Comfort and Joy.* New York: Warner Books, Inc.

Canfield, J., and M. V. Hansen. 1993. *Chicken Soup for the Soul.* Deerfield Beach, Florida: Health Communications.

Couples' Devotional Bible. 1994. Grand Rapids, Michigan: Zondervan Publishing House.

Fishel, R. *Time for Joy.* 1988. Deerfield Beach, Florida: Health Communications.

Kipfer, B. A. 1994. *Bartlett's Book of Love Quotations.* New York: Little, Brown and Company.

Rilke, R. M. 1982. *The Selected Poetry of Rainer Maria Rilke.* Ed. and trans. by Stephen Mitchell. New York: Simon and Schuster.

Setzer, C. 1994. *The Quotable Soul: Inspiring Quotations Crossing Time and Culture.* New York: John Wiley and Sons, Inc.

Organizations

The Couple's Communication Center
Barbara and Greg Markway
P.O. Box 104294
Jefferson City, MO 65109

We offer workshops, seminars, and retreats around the country. Please write to us for additional information.

The Association for Couples in Marriage Enrichment (ACME)
502 North Broad Street, P.O. Box 10596
Winston-Salem, NC 27108
(910) 724-1526 or (800) 634-8325

ACME is a nonsectarian and nonprofit organization founded in 1973. It has members in all 50 states and some 31 foreign countries. Their mission is to "promote and provide enrichment opportunities and resources that strengthen couple relationships and enhance personal growth, mutual fulfillment and family wellness."

Marriage Encounter
> (800) 795-5683

Unlike ACME, Marriage Encounter pairs itself with various Christian denominations. This phone number can put you in touch with a Marriage Encounter program associated with the denomination of your choice.

Creative Memories
> 2815 Clearwater Road
> P.O. Box 1839
> St. Cloud, MN 56302-1839
> (800) 468-9335

Creative Memories is a marketing company that provides training and supplies to help people organize, store, and display their photos and memorabilia in photo-safe, meaningful keepsake albums.

Professional Texts

Figley, C. R., and H. I. McCubbin (Eds.) 1983. *Stress and the Family*. New York: Brunner/Mazel.

Linehan, M. M. 1993. *Cognitive-Behavioral Treatment of Borderline Personality Disorder*. New York: The Guilford Press. (Although this textbook probably wouldn't interest much of the general public, Dr. Linehan's thinking about the matter of acceptance helped us immensely with Chapter 5.)

See also:

> *Existential Psychotherapy*, listed under "Existential Issues."

> *Successful Marriage*, listed under "Relationships."

Relationships

Beavers, W. 1985. *Successful Marriage: A Family Systems Approach to Couples Therapy*. New York: W. W. Norton.

Borys, H. J. 1994. *The Sacred Fire: Love as a Spiritual Path*. New York: Harper Collins.

Godek, G. 1993. *Romance 101: Lessons in Love*. Weymouth, MA: Casablanca Press.

Gottman, J. 1994. *Why Marriage Succeed or Fail: What You Can Learn From the Breakthrough Research To Make Your Marriage Last*. New York: Simon & Schuster. (Especially helpful in relation to Chapter 6, "Communicate With Care.")

Hendrix, H., and H. Hunt. 1994. *The Couples Companion: Meditations and Exercises for Getting the Love You Want*. New York: Pocket Books.

Hendrix, H. 1988. *Getting the Love You Want: A Guide for Couples.* New York: Harper Perennial.

Kingma, D. R. 1995. *Heart and Soul: Living the Joy, Truth, and Beauty of Your Intimate Relationship.* Berkeley, CA: Conari Press.

Louden, J. 1994. *The Couple's Comfort Book: A Creative Guide for Renewing Passion, Pleasure and Commitment.* New York: Harper Collins.

McKay, M., P. Fanning, and K. Paleg. 1994. *Couple Skills: Making Your Relationship Work.* Oakland, CA: New Harbinger Publications.

Miller, K., and K. Miller. 1994. *More Than You and Me: Touching Others Through the Strength of Your Marriage.* Colorado Springs, CO: Focus on the Family. (Especially helpful for couples working on the meaning of their marriage.)

Moore, T. 1994. *Soul Mates: Honoring the Mysteries of Love and Relationship.* New York: Harper Collins.

Reiser, P. 1994. *Couplehood.* New York: Bantam.

See also:

Books listed under "Gender Issues."

Rituals

Cotner, J. 1994. Graces: *Prayers and Poems for Everyday Meals and Special Occasions.* New York: Harper Collins.

Hays, E. 1979. *Prayers for the Domestic Church: A Handbook for Worship in the Home.* Easton, Kansas: Forest of Peace Books.

Fulghum, R. 1995. *From Beginning to End: The Rituals of Our Lives.* New York: Villard Books.

Imber-Black, E., and J. Roberts. 1992. *Rituals for Our Times: Celebrating, Healing, and Changing Our Lives and Our Relationships.* New York: Harper Collins. (This helpful guide inspired many of the ideas in Chapter 11.)

Ryan, M. J. 1994. *A Grateful Heart: Daily Blessings for the Evening Meal from Buddha to the Beatles.* Berkeley, CA: Conari Press.

See also:

Heart and Soul, which provides beautiful, inspirational readings about love, listed under "Relationships."

"Organizations" for phone number of Creative Memories, a company that provides acid-free, photo-safe albums and scrapbooks.

Sexuality

Gray, J. 1995. *Mars and Venus in the Bedroom.* New York: Harper Collins.

Love, P. And J. Robinson. 1994. *Hot Monogamy: Essential Steps to More Passionate, Intimate Lovemaking*. New York: Dutton.

Lee, V. 1996. *Soulful Sex: Opening Your Heart, Body and Spirit to Lifelong Passion*. Berkeley, CA: Conari Press.

Spirituality

Covey, S. R. 1989. *The Seven Habits of Highly Effective People*. New York: Simon and Schuster.

Covey, S. R., A. R. Merrill, and R. R. Merrill. 1994. *First Things First*. New York: Simon and Schuster. (Contains a very useful appendix about conducting a mission workshop.)

Fitzpatrick, J. G. 1991. *Something More: Nurturing Your Child's Spiritual Growth*. New York: Penguin Books. (For anyone with children, this is a must read.)

Gawain, S. 1978. *Creative Visualization*. San Rafael, California: New World Library.

Keen, S. 1994. *Hymns to an Unknown God: Awakening the Spirit in Everyday Life*. New York: Bantam.

Kurtz, E., and K. Ketcham. 1992. *The Spirituality of Imperfection: Storytelling and the Journey to Wholeness*. New York: Bantam.

Miller, D. P. 1995. *The Book of Practical Faith: A Path to Useful Spirituality*. New York: Henry Holt.

Moore, T. 1992. *Care of the Soul*. New York: Harper Collins.

Ochs, C. 1983. *Women and Spirituality*. Totowa, New Jersey: Rowman & Allanheld.

Peck, M. S. 1978. *The Road Less Traveled: A New Psychology of Love, Traditional Values and Spiritual Growth*. New York: Touchstone.

Spiritual Retreats and Vacations

Cooper, D. A. 1992. *Silence, Simplicity, and Solitude: A Guide for Spiritual Retreat*. New York: Bell Tower.

See also:

Chapter on vacations in *Rituals For Our Times*, listed under "Rituals."

Section on vacations in *Romance 101*, listed under "Relationships."

Marriage Encounter and Marriage Enrichment, listed under "Organizations."

Index

Barbara and Greg Markway would like to hear from you. To share your own illuminating experiences of walking the path toward a more spiritual marriage for possible inclusion in a forthcoming book, please write to them at the address below. You can also request information about future seminars, workshops, and retreats.

Barbara and Greg Markway
The Couple's Communication Center
P.O. Box 104294
Jefferson City, MO 65109

Other New Harbinger Self-Help Titles

When Anger Hurts Your Kids, $12.95
The Addiction Workbook, $17.95
The Mother's Survival Guide to Recover, $12.95
The Chronic Pain Control Workbook, Second Edition, $17.95
Fibromyalgia & Chronic Myofacial Pain Sybndrome, $19.95
Diagnosis and Treatment of Sociopaths, $44.95
Flying Without Fear, $12.95
Kid Cooperation: How to Stop Yelling, Nagging & Pleading and Get Kids to Cooperate, $12.95
The Stop Smoking Workbook: Your Guide to Healthy Quitting, $17.95
Conquering Carpal Tunnel Syndrome and Other Repetitive Strain Injuries, $17.95
The Tao of Conversation, $12.95
Wellness at Work: Building Resilience for Job Stress, $17.95
What Your Doctor Can't Tell You About Cosmetic Surgery, $13.95
An End of Panic: Breakthrough Techniques for Overcoming Panic Disorder, $17.95
On the Clients Path: A Manual for the Practice of Solution-Focused Therapy, $39.95
Living Without Procrastination: How to Stop Postponing Your Life, $12.95
Goodbye Mother, Hello Woman: Reweaving the Daughter Mother Relationship, $14.95
Letting Go of Anger: The 10 Most Common Anger Styles and What to Do About Them, $12.95
Messages: The Communication Skills Workbook, Second Edition, $13.95
Coping With Chronic Fatigue Syndrome: Nine Things You Can Do, $12.95
The Anxiety & Phobia Workbook, Second Edition, $17.95
Thueson's Guide to Over-The Counter Drugs, $13.95
Natural Women's Health: A Guide to Healthy Living for Women of Any Age, $13.95
I'd Rather Be Married: Finding Your Future Spouse, $13.95
The Relaxation & Stress Reduction Workbook, Fourth Edition, $17.95
Living Without Depression & Manic Depression: A Workbook for Maintaining Mood Stability, $17.95
Belonging: A Guide to Overcoming Loneliness, $13.95
Coping With Schizophrenia: A Guide For Families, $13.95
Visualization for Change, Second Edition, $13.95
Postpartum Survival Guide, $13.95
Angry All The Time: An Emergency Guide to Anger Control, $12.95
Couple Skills: Making Your Relationship Work, $13.95
Handbook of Clinical Psychopharmacology for Therapists, $39.95
The Warrior's Journey Home: Healing Men, Healing the Planet, $13.95
Weight Loss Through Persistence, $13.95
Post-Traumatic Stress Disorder: A Complete Treatment Guide, $39.95
Stepfamily Realities: How to Overcome Difficulties and Have a Happy Family, $13.95
Leaving the Fold: A Guide for Former Fundamentalists and Others Leaving Their Religion, $13.95
Father-Son Healing: An Adult Son's Guide, $12.95
The Chemotherapy Survival Guide, $11.95
Your Family/Your Self: How to Analyze Your Family System, $12.95
Being a Man: A Guide to the New Masculinity, $12.95
The Deadly Diet, Second Edition: Recovering from Anorexia & Bulimia, $13.95
Last Touch: Preparing for a Parent's Death, $11.95
Consuming Passions: Help for Compulsive Shoppers, $11.95
Self-Esteem, Second Edition, $13.95
I Can't Get Over It, A Handbook for Trauma Survivors, $13.95
Concerned Intervention, When Your Loved One Won't Quit Alcohol or Drugs, $11.95
Dying of Embarrassment: Help for Social Anxiety and Social Phobia, $12.95
The Depression Workbook: Living With Depression and Manic Depression, $17.95
The Marriage Bed: Renewing Love, Friendship, Trust, and Romance, $11.95
Focal Group Psychotherapy: For Mental Health Professionals, $44.95
Hot Water Therapy: Save Your Back, Neck & Shoulders in 10 Minutes a Day $11.95
Prisoners of Belief: Exposing & Changing Beliefs that Control Your Life, $12.95
Be Sick Well: A Healthy Approach to Chronic Illness, $11.95
Men & Grief: A Guide for Men Surviving the Death of a Loved One., $13.95
When the Bough Breaks: A Helping Guide for Parents of Sexually Abused Childern, $11.95
Love Addiction: A Guide to Emotional Independence, $12.95
When Once Is Not Enough: Help for Obsessive Compulsives, $13.95
The New Three Minute Meditator, $12.95
Getting to Sleep, $12.95
Beyond Grief: A Guide for Recovering from the Death of a Loved One, $13.95
Leader's Guide to the Relaxation & Stress Reduction Workbook, Fourth Edition, $19.95
The Divorce Book, $13.95
Hypnosis for Change: A Manual of Proven Techniques, 2nd Edition, $13.95
When Anger Hurts, $13.95
Free of the Shadows: Recovering from Sexual Violence, $12.95
Lifetime Weight Control, $11.95
Love and Renewal: A Couple's Guide to Commitment, $13.95

Call **toll free, 1-800-748-6273**, to order. Have your Visa or Mastercard number ready. Or send a check for the titles you want to New Harbinger Publications, Inc., 5674 Shattuck Ave., Oakland, CA 94609. Include $3.80 for the first book and 75¢ for each additional book, to cover shipping and handling. (California residents please include appropriate sales tax.) Allow four to six weeks for delivery.

Prices subject to change without notice.